POSITIVE BEHAVIOR SUPPORTS IN CLASSROOMS AND SCHOOLS

ABOUT THE AUTHORS

Keith Storey received his PhD from the University of Oregon. He is currently a Professor of Education and is the Special Education Program Chair at Touro University in Vallejo, California. He served six years as a classroom teacher working with people with a variety of disability labels. Dr. Storey is the recipient of the 1988 Alice H. Hayden Award from the Association for Persons with Severe Handicaps; the 1996 Hau-Cheng Wang Fellowship from Chapman University, which is presented for exceptional merit in scholarship; and the 2001 Robert Gaylord-Ross Memorial Scholar Award from the California Association for Persons with Severe Disabilities. He is a member of the Illinois State University College of Education Alumni Hall of Fame. He serves on the editorial boards of *Research and Practice for Persons with Severe Disabilities, Education and Treatment of Children, Career Development for Exceptional Individuals, Journal of Vocational Rehabilitation, Journal of Positive Behavior Interventions, and Education and Training in Developmental Disabilities.* He has also published the books *Systematic Instruction for Students and Adults with Disabilities, Walking Isn't Everything: An Account of the Life of Jean Denecke, The Road Ahead: Transition to Adult Life for Persons with Disabilities,* and *Functional Assessment and Program Development for Problem Behavior: A Practical Handbook.*

Michal Post is currently teaching education and special education credentialing courses for three San Francisco Bay Area universities. She has more than 30 years of experience working in the field of education, including the role of General Education Teacher, Special Education Teacher, Inclusion Specialist, Transition and Employment Specialist, and Student Teacher Supervisor for two universities. She has more than 20 years of direct experience in providing transition and employment services to adults with disabilities, and in providing trainings for teachers and support staff for including children with special needs in general education settings. For more than 13 years, she has shared her experience through annual presentations at both national and international professional conferences on topics such as self-management strategies, supported employment strategies, and behavioral supports for students with autism. She has published articles in *Teaching Exceptional Children, Journal of Vocational Rehabilitation, International Journal of Rehabilitation Research, Education and Training in Developmental Disabilities,* and *Research in Practice for Persons with Severe Disabilities.* Michal has been the project coordinator for three personnel preparation grants from the Office of Special Education and Rehabilitation Services, with two for preparing teachers and service professionals to serve students in transition planning for adult life and the other providing comprehensive training for teachers serving students on the autism spectrum.

POSITIVE BEHAVIOR SUPPORTS IN CLASSROOMS AND SCHOOLS

Effective and Practical Strategies for Teachers and Other Service Providers

By

KEITH STOREY, PH.D.

Touro University

MICHAL POST, M.A.

Touro University

CHARLES C THOMAS • PUBLISHER, LTD.
Springfield • Illinois • U.S.A.

Published and Distributed Throughout the World by

CHARLES C THOMAS • PUBLISHER, LTD.
2600 South First Street
Springfield, Illinois 62704

©2012 by CHARLES C THOMAS • PUBLISHER, LTD.

ISBN 978-0-398-08836-1 (hard)
ISBN 978-0-398-08837-8 (paper)
ISBN 978-0-398-08838-5 (ebook)

Library of Congress Catalog Card Number: 2012019944

With THOMAS BOOKS *careful attention is given to all details of manufacturing
and design. It is the Publisher's desire to present books that are satisfactory as to their
physical qualities and artistic possibilities and appropriate for their particular use.*
THOMAS BOOKS *will be true to those laws of quality that assure a good name
and good will.*

*Printed in the United States of America
CR-R-3*

Library of Congress Cataloging-in-Publication Data

Storey, Keith, 1956–
  Positive behavior supports in classrooms and schools : effective and prac-
tical strategies for teachers and other service providers / by Keith Storey,
Michal Post.
     p. cm.
  Includes bibliographical references and index.
  ISBN 978-0-398-08836-1 (hard) -- ISBN 978-0-398-08837-8 (pbk.). --
ISBN 978-0-398-08838-5 (ebook) 1. Classroom management. 2. Behavior
modification. I. Title.

LB3013.S785 2012
371.1024--dc23

                                                                    2012019944

To Jean, for her love and positive behavior supports during these many years of marriage. They are more appreciated than she will ever know.

K.S.

To my loving son, Terrence, whose love and sense of justice inspire me daily.

All love and gratitude to the following people, who, through their dedicated educational, medical, or social service to improve the welfare of children and adults, have inspired me in my career: Agnes Franzwa, Camille Campbell, David LaMay, Theresa LaMay, John La May, Marcella Leath, Miftah Leath, Richard Leath, Elizabeth Marchant, Joyce Montgomery, and, in memory, Mary Ann Campbell.

I would also like to thank the following people who helped me grow professionally by providing me with guidance and opportunities to teach: Nick Certo, John Freeman, Shirley Golightly, Haiyan Khan, Lorraine Ryor, and Keith Storey, who additionally inspires my self-determination through his ongoing mentorship.

Great appreciation to the College of Education faculty and staff at Touro University and the faculty and staff in the Department of Special Education at San Francisco State University, and to all my students.

A special remembrance with deep gratitude to Alex Krem who, in the 1950s was a pioneer in creating community-based recreational opportunities in the San Francisco Bay Area for children and adults with intellectual disabilities, and who served as my first mentor.

M.P.

FOREWORD

The development of the approach that has come to be known as positive behavioral supports (PBS) represents the integration of the empirically based principles and procedures of applied behavior analysis (ABA), and the emphasis by service recipients and their advocates on achieving valued outcomes in educational and other service settings. This development has employed effective behavior change and support technology to achieve valued outcomes in educational and other community settings (e.g., reading/literacy skills, effective social inclusion and interaction, reduction of undesirable behaviors). Another of these outcomes has been to attempt to provide alternatives to the use of more aversive, restrictive, and intrusive interventions (see Chapter 5). Caregivers, support providers, and researchers have realized that it is no longer enough to make the data line on the graph go down. Reducing the frequency and intensity of undesirable behavior only really matters if we are also making possible expanded opportunities for persons with regard to education, skill acquisition, and satisfactory social/community living.

The widespread adoption and implementation of the PBS approach in the U.S. and internationally over the last two decades represents a significant achievement in applied social/behavioral science. PBS approaches have been employed in an expanding array of service settings, including schools, adult residential and vocational programs, and juvenile justice programs and facilities. This increasing demand has created a need for effective informational and training materials for service providers. This book is a very useful resource in the area of PBS as applied in school and classroom settings. Authors Storey and Post cover a broad range of topics and strategies that sample the full range of principles and procedures that are critical components of PBS. The initial chapters provide a concise overview of the conceptual foundations of the field and delineate the critical features of PBS. The authors describe the science of ABA and how it can be applied to achieve a variety of desired outcomes in educational settings. They describe the critical importance of collecting relevant data and evaluating it to assess the impact of support strategies. As is often the case in applied settings, consumers of the book may need to engage in some "trial and error" practice to determine the data collection procedures that fit in best with their classroom or school settings and routines.

Functional behavioral assessment is a key component of PBS. Understanding the functions of problem behaviors provides the primary foundation for selecting relevant support strategies. This chapter describes the full array of current FBA strategies. It is important for practitioners to keep in mind that FBA ranges from the basics of "thinking functionally" (that is, being able to look at a situation and think about antecedents, behaviors, and consequences), to indirect methods such as questionnaires and rating scales, to direct observations in typical settings, to structured manipulations of relevant variables (functional analysis). The challenge is for practitioners to be able to select and apply the assessment strategies needed given the nature and complexity of the situations with which they are dealing. This book provides useful guidance in this regard.

A good portion of the book describes a broad array of proactive, instructional, and consequence oriented strategies to promote desired behavior and replace and reduce undesirable behavior. This fits in well with the PBS perspective of using preventative and intervention strategies in a multi-component approach. An important aspect of the book is that it provides strategies at multiple tiers, as described in Chapter 11 on school-wide PBS. This chapter describes a general approach to supporting appropriate behavior on a school-wide basis. Several of the other chapters describe both more general and more specific strategies to structure classrooms and provide support to small groups and individual students in need of more intensive interventions (e.g., peer tutoring, self-management, social skills training). There is a wealth of information for trainers and school personnel to make use of in considering preventative and intervention strategies for their schools.

This book provides a comprehensive and up-to-date menu of assessment and support strategies in the area of PBS. While interested readers may wish to pursue additional resources for more in-depth information on particular topics, this volume provides a compact overview for trainers and school personnel to the critical concepts and strategies in this important field.

ROB O'NEILL, PhD, BCBA-D
Professor and Chair
Department of Special Education
University of Utah

PREFACE

Scope

The scope of this book is to provide an overview of positive behavior supports that is written in an informational format that teachers and other service providers can immediately put to use. We have tried to write in a non-technical style that is directed toward practitioners rather than for other academics. This book is focused on positive behavior supports in school settings. It is generic across age levels, and it should be of interest to those working in the schools as teachers, classroom assistants, school psychologists, administrators, counselors, and so on.

Plan

In this book, each chapter follows the sequence of:

Key Point Questions
Window to the World Case Studies
Best Practice Recommendations
Discussion Questions
School-Based Activity Suggestions

Purpose

This book is intended to give teachers and other service providers the knowledge and skills for providing positive behavior supports in school settings, thereby improving the academic and social skills of their students. The rubber meets the road in how to teach but also in how to implement positive behavior supports so that classrooms and schools can deliver effective instruction to students. An advantage of this book is that it covers methodology that is seldom covered in detail in most texts addressing positive behavior supports and, thus, can easily be used in courses preparing teachers and others.

College instructors are likely to choose our book based on:

1. The consistent format throughout the book.
2. The "readability" of the book for students.
3. The comprehensive coverage of positive behavior supports.
4. The direct applicability to applied settings.

In addition to college instructors, we hope that others providing instruction, supervision, and training to teachers and other direct service providers will find this book useful.

K.S.
M.P.

CONTENTS

POSITIVE BEHAVIOR SUPPORTS IN CLASSROOMS AND SCHOOLS

Chapter 1

OVERVIEW OF POSITIVE BEHAVIOR SUPPORTS

Key Point Questions

1. What is Applied Behavior Analysis?
2. What are Positive Behavior Supports?
3. How are Positive Behavior Supports different than other approaches?
4. Why are Positive Behavior Supports important?
5. What are barriers to the implementation of Applied Behavior Analysis and Positive Behavior Supports?
6. How do Applied Behavior Analysis and Positive Behavior Supports relate to student learning?

Window to the World Case Study 1

Mr. Denecke is known at his high school as a model teacher. The students in his classes do well academically, are happy to be there, and are engaged in related activities outside of the classroom (homework and clubs). Parents are always pleased when their children are in his classes, and they often pester the principal to make sure that they have him as their teacher. University professors always try to place student teachers with Mr. Denecke. This semester he has Ms. Kueffner as a student teacher. The first week of her placement, the principal, Ms. Naylor, is in the classroom and notices a list that Ms. Kueffner is working on. She looks at the list and observes it is a list of what behaviors

Mr. Denecke is engaging in that are enhancing the learning of his students. It is quite an extensive list of behaviors: praising students for desirable behaviors, greeting students as they enter the classroom, going over the class rules at the start of class, having a mix of activities in the class period, not wasting a minute of instructional time, immediately correcting any student violation of classroom rules (no matter how minor) and then quickly getting back to instruction, making sure that assignments and expectations are clear to all students, and so on. This list gives Ms. Naylor an idea, and she asks for a copy of the list.

Window to the World Case Study 2

Teaching at the same school as Mr. Denecke is Mr. Walton. He is a first-year teacher and is struggling to say the least. Students in his class are disruptive, disrespectful to him, and not doing their work, and needless to say, not much learning is going on. Ms. Naylor has been quite concerned and is not sure whether he will make it as a teacher. (Mr. Walton is wondering why he gave up a career as a legal assistant to become a teacher, even though teaching was what he had always wanted to do.) After seeing Ms. Kueffner's list from Mr. Denecke's class, Ms. Naylor observes Mr. Walton's class and makes a list of what he is doing wrong (ignoring inappropriate student behavior, starting class late, being drawn into conversations that are off topic, getting into arguments with students about acceptable and unacceptable behavior, making consequences for students but not following through on them, etc.), as well as a list of what he is doing right (a very short list such as having good content knowledge and well-designed lesson plans). Ms. Naylor covers several class periods for Mr. Walton so that he can observe Mr. Denecke's class and make his list of what Mr. Denecke is doing right. She and Mr. Walton then meet and go over their lists and discuss specific behaviors that Mr. Walton can engage in to change his classroom. In addition, Mr. Walton and Mr. Denecke meet several times at lunch so that they can plan changes to Mr. Walton's class and his teaching style. Within several weeks, there is a dramatic change for the better in Mr. Walton's teaching and the academic engagement of his students. Though there are still struggles, Mr. Walton continues to improve, and by the end of the school year, both Mr. Walton and Ms. Naylor are quite satisfied with his performance, and, most importantly, his students are doing very well in learning the academic material.

Key Point Question 1. What is Applied Behavior Analysis?

The foundation of Positive Behavior Supports is Applied Behavior Analysis (ABA). ABA is derived from the work of B. F. Skinner (1953, 1971). Skinner was a psychologist who advocated that the focus of education should be on the behavior of students rather than on internal states (O'Donohue & Ferguson, 2001). Behavior may be defined as observable actions that a student does. Sitting in a seat, completing a math problem correctly, raising one's hand to answer a question, cursing, and running out of the room are all observable behaviors (verbal behaviors are classified as behaviors as well). These are all student behaviors that can be changed (for better or worse). Being motivated, trying hard, and being unruly are not observable behaviors and thus cannot be directly changed.

John Watson is often credited as being the first behavioral psychologist. In his 1913 manifesto, he wrote that, "Psychology as the behaviorist views it is a purely objective experimental branch of natural science. Its theoretical goal is the prediction and control of behavior." For Positive Behavior Supports (and education as a whole), the key words are "prediction" and "control." Good teachers are effective at predicting what will work in their classroom (such as using active responding strategies, reinforcing classroom rules, using cooperative learning strategies, etc.) and then controlling the classroom environment so that these behaviors occur. Sometimes teachers have concerns with the concept of control and view control as being a bad thing. However, not positively controlling the classroom only leads to anarchy and poor student learning. For instance, by doing things such as having set routines, classroom rules, and praising students for completing assignments the teacher is "controlling" student behavior. Having a teacher controlling a classroom environment in this way is good teaching and is not deceitful or wrong. In other words, the focus is on the cause and effect relationship between the environment and the behavior of the student (Nye, 1992). This cause and effect is not a one-way process because there is the issue of countercontrol where the behavior of the student also influences the environment (e.g., the behavior of the teacher).

As they read this, many teachers may be thinking "I do this every day." Good teachers use these types of strategies all the time. In this text, we are presenting a coherent and systematic approach to understanding the purpose of Positive Behavior Supports and how teachers can implement these strategies to arrive at the desirable results for carefully targeting the behaviors that need changing, as opposed to a "hit and miss" strategy that many teachers use.

Applied Behavior Analysis

In ABA, it is assumed that the behavior of students is lawful. This means that students do things for a reason, such as being previously reinforced for a behavior (such as turning in homework) or being punished for a behavior (such as talking out in class). In other words, students have a history of being reinforced or punished for certain behaviors, and this history influences their current behavior. For example, if a student is consistently reinforced for turning in homework (praise from teachers, positive feedback on homework, good grades, positive notes home to parents, etc.), then the student is likely to continue to turn in homework consistently. A student who does not receive this reinforcement for turning in homework is less likely to turn in homework assignments consistently.

The three basic assumptions of ABA are:

1. All behavior is learned.
2. Behavior can be changed by altering antecedents and/or consequences.
3. Factors in the environment (the classroom or school) can be changed to increase and maintain specific behaviors or to decrease specific behaviors.

Behavior analysts agree that people feel and think, but they do not consider these events (feeling and thinking) as causes of behavior. Thinking and feeling are more behaviors of the student that require explanation. For instance, a student may engage in certain "undesirable" behaviors[1] (such as talking back to the teacher or refusing to

---

[1] In this text, we use the terms "desirable" and "undesirable" in describing student behavior. A variety of terms have been used in the professional literature, such as difficult, acting out, disruptive, challenging, good/bad, appropriate/inappropriate, at-risk, target behavior, and problem behavior. Basically, these terms have been used to describe student behavior that we see as being either desirable or undesirable from the teacher's viewpoint.

complete in-class work). To analyze these behaviors as "feelings" of the student is not helpful because it is an inference as to the causes and the teacher cannot directly change the feelings of a student.

ABA focuses on the behavior of people. Behavior is not considered to be an expression of inner causes like personality, cognition, and attitude. Poor performance on exams, talking out in class, or being late to class are analyzed as problems of behavior rather than examples of a student having a "poor attitude" toward school. Interventions for these and other undesirable behaviors are directed at changing environmental events (teacher behaviors or the classroom setup) to improve behavior (e.g., to increase desirable behavior). For example, engaging in peer tutoring for exams and using a self-management strategy to eliminate talking out in class could change the student's undesirable behaviors for the better and by doing so could change the "poor attitude" of the student. But this is accomplished only by changing specific behaviors of the student (which was accomplished by changing the environment of the student through peer tutoring and teaching self-management skills).

So the focus is not only on the behaviors of students but also on understanding why students engage in certain behaviors (e.g., the function of the behavior, which is described in more detail in Chapter 3).

Kazdin (2008) succinctly summarizes this issue:

> Even today, even at our most scientifically precise,? Is there a word missing here? we can't always or even often locate the exact source of a behavior problem. . . . We know how to change behavior for the better, regardless of its exact cause, and our best bet is to just go ahead and change it. Instead of treating the child as if there's something wrong inside her that needs to be fixed, let's treat the behavior as the something wrong, and address it directly. In practice, that means locating the problem in the relationship between the child and the situation around him, in how he interacts with other people and things, (which might well include flaws in the therapy or how it's delivered). (p. 169)

Factors That Influence Behavior

There are two factors that influence behavior: antecedents (what occurs before a behavior) and consequences (what occurs after a behavior).

Antecedents become effective at producing desirable behavior only when they are a signal for a predictable consequence. For instance, if students know they get points for each time that they are at class on time and that points can be traded in for backup reinforcers (i.e., things or activities delivered at a later time, such as stickers, pizza party, etc.), then they may be more likely to be on time to school and to class.

Consequences affect behavior by strengthening the behavior (increasing its probability) or weakening the behavior (decreasing its probability). In the prior example, the on-time behavior was strengthened through positive reinforcement (the token economy). The behavior of being late could be weakened (decreased) through consequences with the use of punishment (a response cost system where students are fined points for being late).

How ABA Fits Into Today's Focus in Classrooms and Schools

Baer, Wolf, and Risley (1968, 1987) have outlined key dimensions of ABA, and here we highlight how these fit into the application of positive behavior supports.

Applied: ABA is focused on practical issues that are of importance and are socially relevant. Research in ABA occurs in "real-life" settings such as classrooms and schools rather than in laboratory settings (which is often known as Experimental Analysis of Human Behavior and is focused on basic experimental and transactional research with animal or human participants).

Behavioral: As indicated earlier in the chapter, ABA focuses on the physical/observable behavior of individuals, and references to inner states and causes are not deemed useful in that they do not serve as causes of behavior. Skinner made the distinction between overt behavior (which is observable) and covert behavior (that which occurs "within the skin").

Analytical: Applied behavior analysis looks for the condition or stimulus (what happens in the environment) that is responsible for the effect on the behavior (what the person does in response). In positive behavior supports, this is often analyzing the function of the behavior (why the student does something), the setting events (what is going on in the classroom), and the consequences (whether the behavior increases or decreases).

Technological: The intervention procedure is described in enough detail for others to do the same thing in their setting. A study on positive behavior supports should describe the intervention clearly and in enough detail so that the readers can apply the intervention in the same way in their own classroom.

Conceptual: Procedures are related to concepts of effective interventions rather than a collection of tricks. For example, functional assessment analyzes student behavior in terms of understanding whether students are engaging in a behavior to obtain or to avoid. This understanding (a student engaging in undesirable behavior in order to get teacher attention) then leads to procedures or interventions that are more likely to be effective (the teacher praising the student for desirable behavior).

Effective: The effect on student behavior and learning must be meaningful. For instance, decreasing aggressive behavior from a student from 20 to 5 times a day may be statistically significant but is not meaningful in a socially important context. There is an extensive body of research indicating that ABA procedures are effective in providing positive behavior supports for increasing desirable student behavior in classroom and school settings (Filter & Horner, 2009; Wheeler & Richey, 2010). Positive behavior support strategies are clearly scientifically based research for programs and teaching methods as defined by No Child Left Behind. The act defines this as "research that involves the application of rigorous, systematic, and objective procedures to obtain reliable and valid knowledge relevant to education activities and programs." Scientifically based research results in "replicable and applicable findings" from research that used appropriate methods to generate persuasive, empirical conclusions.

Generality: Do the effects of the intervention carry over across people, settings, behavior, and times? From the example of aggression, it would be important to eliminate the aggressive behavior of the student across people (teachers and parents), settings (school and home), behaviors (all types of aggression such as verbal and physical), and times (morning, afternoons, and evenings).

What is the Science of ABA?

In ABA, there is an emphasis on objective description with a focus on observable events. There is also a focus on absolute unit-based measurement (e.g., behaviors that have clear and limited extensions in space and time and also have easy to determine onsets and offsets) (Baer, 1986). These factors are described in more detail in Chapter 2.

ABA relies on experimental analysis to determine whether interventions are effective. This analysis often involves the use of single-case research designs (also known as single-subject designs) that involve one or a small number of participants (e.g., these may be individual students or classrooms), and the design involves data that are taken frequently over an extended time period, which allows for detailed analysis of variables that might be affecting the behavior (Kazdin, 2011). In single-case designs, the replication of the effect of the intervention is important. In other words, the experimenter demonstrates repeatedly that the intervention is causing the change in the student behavior and not something else. For example, it is the teacher increasing her rate of praise for students turning in homework rather than something that parents may be doing at home that is increasing the rate of students turning in their homework.

ABA stresses the understanding of functional relations between the student and the environment. The behavior of students is not random (although there is some variance in behavior as people are not always consistent in what they do, students can have good days and bad days due to a variety of reasons), and there are lawful relationships between what is happening in the environment (in schools, homes, and the community) and student behavior. For example, factors such as food intake (what a student has eaten in the morning or their not having had any breakfast) or sleep patterns (whether the student had a good night sleep) can influence student behavior and learning in the classroom.

By understanding the relationship between the environment and the student, it becomes possible to establish effective learning environments. For example, if a teacher understands that a student has had poor sleep the night before (from a note from the parents), then it is possible to adjust schedules, demands, and reinforcers (Durand, 1998).

It is important to emphasize that behavior is always changing. As students learn skills and antecedents and consequences change, student behavior changes. Factors such as falling into a poor peer group, doing drugs, learning positive social skills, and learning reading skills are all likely to change student behavior (some for the better, some not so). The more that teachers understand these changes, the better off they will be in developing instruction and other supports for students.

Key Point Question 2: What are Positive Behavior Supports?

The purpose of this book is to provide teachers and others with the skills to implement positive behavior interventions in classrooms as well as across the school (settings outside of the classroom, such as the hallway, cafeteria, quad, etc.). Developing and maintaining appropriate student behavior can be challenging in any classroom and school. Students may not do their work, act out, talk back to the teacher, and disrupt academic instruction. This is all too common. And, all too often, the focus of interventions in schools is on eliminating undesirable behaviors. Positive Behavior Support strategies reason that the best way to decrease undesirable behaviors is by increasing desirable behaviors and by giving students skills and supports so that they do not need to engage in undesirable behaviors. This approach is known as Positive Behavior Supports. For example, if students are being very disruptive in the lunch room line, then the behaviors to be increased would be being polite and staying in the line.

Key Point Question 3: How are Positive Behavior Supports Different Than Other Approaches?

Other approaches, while not from an ABA perspective per se (such as Outward Bound programs or the work of William Glasser), are often compatible with and can complement ABA interventions. Not all other approaches have a strong (or any) empirical basis for their effectiveness. For instance, interventions for students with Autism Spectrum Disorders such as dolphin therapy, sensory integration therapy, Auditory Integration Therapies, or electromagnetic therapy may or may not be effective interventions, but they have little, if any, empirical evidence that they are effective interventions. ABA does have an extensive empirical basis for its effectiveness in classroom and school settings.

Key Point Question 4: Why are Positive Behavior Supports Important?

Having a well-organized classroom in which students are academically and socially engaged is, in many ways, *the* key to being a successful teacher. Teachers need skills in this area and need to be able to implement positive behavior support strategies that are empirically valid. Too many teachers rely on a "bag of tricks" (and often it is a limited bag of tricks), and when those tricks do not work, they are at a loss as to what to do. Brophy (1988) presents a clear definition of why positive behavior supports are important:

Good classroom management implies not only that the teacher has elicited the cooperation of the students in minimizing misconduct and can intervene effectively when misconduct occurs, but also that worthwhile academic activities are occurring more or less continuously and that the classroom management system as a whole (which includes, but is not limited to, the teacher's disciplinary interventions) is designed to maximize student engagement in those activities, not merely to minimize misconduct. (p. 3)

Key Point Question 5: What are Barriers to the Implementation of Applied Behavior Analysis and Positive Behavior Supports?

There is often teacher resistance to ABA and Positive Behavior Support approaches. Table 1.1 outlines perceived barriers to changing behavior. This resistance may be in regard to the causes of, and procedures necessary to change, behavior in classroom settings (Tingstrom, 1989). For example, the ABA approach of functional analysis to determine why students are engaging in behavior may be in conflict with teachers who may view the internal attitudes and values of students as the primary causes of behavior. They believe that these internal characteristics must be modified in order to change behavior (Tingstrom & Edwards, 1989).

Table 1.1
Perceived Barriers to Changing Behavior

Perceived Barrier	Response
People have to want to change.	People change all the time even when they don't want to and often when they don't realize the change. These changes occur because people are constantly influenced by what people do and say to them (e.g., the environment).
Behavior is not an adequate guide to what a person is realy like	We do not know what people are thinking and feeling; the only access we have is to their behavior (e.g., what they say or do). Behavior is all we have and behavior, is all we need.
People resist change	When the immediate consequences of doing anything are negative, it is difficult to get a person to change. When the immediate consequences are positive, people want to change.
Controlling the behavior of others is controlling them	The word "control" may bring to mind restriction, repression, domination, and rule (e.g., coercion). As a teacher, it is impossible to escape controlling the behavior of others. Control is a problem only when some form of force or seduction is used to get a person to do something that is illegal, immoral, or unethical. Without some control in a person's life, there would be chaos.
A deliberate attempt to change the behavior of others is manipulation	Manipulation means to influence shrewdly or deviously. Devious manipulation is wrong, but shrewdly means having keen insight and being astute (which are good skills for teachers to have).

Continued on next page

Table 1.1 (cont.)

Perceived Barrier	Response
Change is up to the person	To change the behavior of others, you must change what you do. By changing what you do, you change the environment for those around you, which in turn changes them.
You have no right to change the behavior of others	Education is about changing the behavior of others (e.g., learning).
Only feelings cause behavior	Feelings are effects of behavior, not causes. The best way to change a feeling is to change a behavior.
The laws of behavior don't apply to everybody	Everybody is different, but the laws of behavior respect the fact that everyone is different.

Adapted from Daniels (2001).

Tingstrom and Edwards (1989) identified other reasons for teacher resistance to behavioral approaches. These involve common misconceptions about the use of behavioral approaches in schools:

1. Behavioral approaches require the use of complicated, time-consuming data-collection procedures.

Response: Not necessarily. Chapter 2 outlines data-collection procedures that are often simple and not time-consuming.

2. Behavioral approaches do not work with many students.

Response: Extensive research indicates that ABA approaches work with all types of students and for students of all ages (including adult learners).

3. It is too difficult to identify appropriate reinforcers for each student in the class.

Response: As discussed in Chapter 4, there are many ways to identify reinforcers for students, and Chapters 6, 7, 8, and 9 outline a variety of effective individual and group reinforcement strategies.

4. Behavioral interventions result in a permanent need for external reinforcement.

Response: While some students may need ongoing external reinforcement (e.g., that which is delivered by others such as a teacher or parent), other students do not because naturally occurring reinforcers often take the place of external reinforcement (e.g., being nice to and socially skilled with others may lead to friendships, which are naturally reinforcing).

5. Behavioral approaches single out problem students.

Response: Positive Behavior Supports focus on increasing positive academic and social behaviors of all students in classrooms and schools.

6. Behavioral approaches are appropriate for "behavior" problems but not for academic problems.

Response: Controlling for undesirable behavior problems allows for academic instruction. Again, there is a large body of empirical evidence that behavioral approaches are effective for academic instruction as well (Coyne, Kame'enui, & Carnine, 2011).

Key Point Question 6: How do Applied Behavior Analysis and Positive Behavior Supports relate to Student Learning?

Just as ABA is focused on observable events, so is learning. While we often talk about students "thinking" or "knowing," it is only through their observable behavior that we can tell whether they have learned skills (whether they be academic, social, etc.). For instance, a teacher may say Ngor really understands his multiplication tables. The teacher "knows" this because Ngor answers questions about multiplication tables quickly and accurately (e.g., observable behavior).

The overall purpose of Positive Behavior Supports in classrooms and schools is to create environments that are conducive to learning. For example, if a teacher is spending most of the class period getting students on task and focused (e.g., not talking to others and goofing off), then it is unlikely that much academic instruction is occurring. There is also a strong empirical base that there is an important relationship between academic achievement and positive social behavior (Algozzine, Wang, & Violette, 2011). Thus, implementing Positive Behavior Supports in classrooms and schools can increase academic performance Reid, Gonzalez, Nordness, Trout, and Epstein (2004) have summarized the issue nicely:

Nonetheless, researchers have demonstrated that academic failure is one of the most powerful predictors of problem behavior and social failure (Manguin & Loeber, 1996; Morrison & D'Incau, 1997). Con- versely, researchers have also demonstrated that academic success is associated with a decrease in problem behavior (Gottfredson, Gottfredson, & Skroban, 1996). (pp. 130–131, 141)

BEST PRACTICE RECOMMENDATIONS

1. It is important to focus on student behaviors (academic and social behaviors) rather than on thoughts or other inner states that are not observable.
2. Teachers should be focused on increasing desirable academic and social behavior.

DISCUSSION QUESTIONS

1. What is learning? How do you know when a student has learned something?
2. Can teachers only change their behavior or can they change the behavior of their students as well?
3. Can non-Positive Behavior Support approaches be effective in supporting students in school environments? What is the empirical database for these approaches?
4. Are there certain teacher behaviors that are most effective for implementing positive behavior supports?
5. What skills do students need to be effective learners?

CLASSROOM AND SCHOOL ACTIVITY SUGGESTIONS

1. Observe a teacher and list what behaviors they are engaging in that are enhancing the learning of their students. How are these behaviors related to prediction and control?
2. Observe a classroom and list feelings and thoughts that students are engaging in. Describe how you know that the feelings and thoughts are occurring.

3. Interview students about what types of classroom supports that they prefer and find effective. Put these suggestions into different categories for analyzing.

REFERENCES

Algozzine, B., Wang, C., & Violette, A. S. (2011). Reexaming the relationship between academic achievement and social behavior. *Journal of Positive Behavior Interventions, 13,* 3–16.

Baer, D. M. (1986). In application, frequence is not the only estimate of the probability of behavioral units. In T. Thompson & M. D. Zieler (Eds.), *Analysis and integration of behavioral units* (pp. 117–136). Hillsdale, NJ: Lawrence Erlbaum Associates.

Baer, D. M., Wolf, M. M., & Risley, T. R. (1968). Some current dimensions of applied behavior analysis. *Journal of Applied Behavior Analysis, 1,* 91–97.

Baer, D. M., Wolf, M. M., & Risley, T. R. (1987). Some still-current dimensions of applied behavior analysis. *Journal of Applied Behavior Analysis, 20,* 313–327.

Brophy, J. (1988). Educating teachers about managing classrooms and students. *Teaching and Teacher Education, 4,* 1–18.

Coyne, M. D., Kame'enui, E. J., & Carnine, D. W. (2011). *Effective teaching strategies that accommodate diverse learners* (4th ed.). Upper Saddle River, NJ: Pearson Education.

Daniels, A. C. (2001). *Other people's habits: How to use positive reinforcement to bring out the best in people around you.* New York: McGraw-Hill.

Durand, V. M. (1998). *Sleep better! A guide to improving sleep for children with special needs.* Baltimore, MD: Paul H. Brookes.

Filter, K. J., & Horner, R. H. (2009). Function-based academic interventions for problem behavior. *Education and Treatment of Children, 32,* 1–19.

Gottfredson, D. C., Gottfredson, G. D., & Skroban, S. (1996). A multimodel school-based prevention demonstration. *Journal of Adolescent Research, 11,* 97–115.

Kazdin, A. E. (2008). *The Kazdin method for parenting the defiant child.* Boston, MA: Houghton Mifflin.

Kazdin, A. E. (2011). *Single-case research designs: Methods for clinical and applied settings* (2nd ed.). New York: Oxford University Press.

Maguin, E., & Loeber, R. (1996). Academic performance and delinquency. In M. Tonry (Ed.), *Crime and justice: An annual review of research* (Vol. 20, pp. 145–264). Chicago, IL: University of Chicago Press.

Morrison, G. M., & D'Incau, B. (1997). The web of zero-tolerance: Characteristics of students who are recommened for expulsion from school. *Education and Treatment of Children, 20,* 316–335.

Nye, R. D. (1992). *The legacy of B. F. Skinner: Concepts and perspectives, controversies and misunderstandings.* Belmont, CA: Wadsworth.

O'Donohue, W., & Ferguson, K. E. (2001). *The psychology of B. F. Skinner.* Thousand Oaks, CA: Sage Publications.

Reid, R., Gonzalez, J. E., Nordness, P. D., Trout, A., & Epstein, M. H. (2004). A meta-analysis of the academic status of students with emotional/behavioral disturbance. *Journal of Special Education, 38,* 130–143.

Skinner, B. F. (1953). *Science and human behavior.* New York: Macmillan.

Skinner, B. F. (1971). *Beyond freedom and dignity.* New York: Knopf.

Tingstrom, D. H. (1989). Increasing acceptability of alternative behavioral interventions through education. *Psychology in the Schools, 26,* 194–201.

Tingstrom, D. H., & Edwards, R. (1989). Eliminating common misconceptions about behavior psychology: One step toward increased academic productivity. *Psychology in the Schools, 26,* 194–202.

Watson, J. B. (1913). Psychology as the behaviorist views it. *Psychological Review, 20,* 158–177.

Wheeler, J. J., & Richey, D. D. (2010). *Behavior management: Principles and practices of positive behavior supports* (2nd ed.). Upper Saddle River, NJ: Prentice-Hall.

Chapter 2

MEASURING BEHAVIOR

Key Point Questions

1. Why is it important to collect data?
2. How do you operationally define behavior and why is it important to do so?
3. What are dimensions of behavior for measurement purposes?
4. What are good ways to collect data?
5. How do you know whether student behavior has changed?
6. How do you best present data for analysis?
7. How can you use technology in data collection?

Window to the World Case Study 1

Ms. Yathay is a vice principal at a middle school. She has been tasked by the principal to determine whether the new School Wide Positive Behavior Support program is working. She was not sure about what "unit of analysis" viewpoint to take, either macro (looking big) or micro (looking small). After reading some articles on School Wide Positive Behavior Supports in the *Journal of Positive Behavior Interventions,* she decided to use one macro- and one micromeasure as she felt that this would give her one measure on a large number of students and one measure on the behavior of individual students. So, she chose to use student office referrals as her macroanalysis. For the micro-analysis, she decided to measure how many students had a formal positive behavior support plan in place.

The principal and teachers were pleased with these choices as they were easy to use and would provide them with frequent feedback on how well their School Wide Positive Behavior Support program was working, as well as indicate specific areas in which changes were needed (e.g., areas in which referrals were being made such as in the quad and the lunchroom).

Window to the World Case Study 2

Mr. Oberhelman was wondering what behaviors he should assess in his ninth grade classroom. When looking around the classroom, he noticed his "classroom rules" poster displayed over the classroom door. This seemed to be a logical place to start as it told his students what behaviors were expected.

He decided to measure one rule: "Be to class on time and be ready to work when the bell rings." He decided to measure the number of students who were ready when the bell rang (momentary time sampling). This involved a quick scan of the room when the bell rang and writing down on a slip of paper the number of students ready to work (he also listed the class period and the number of students in that period). At the end of the day, he entered the data onto a spreadsheet, which graphed the data and showed the percentage of students ready at the beginning of the class period (the behavior he desired to see). This data collection and analysis took only a few minutes each day. At the end of the week, he was quite surprised and also discouraged to find that less than half of his students were ready to work at the beginning of the class period in each of his classes.

Key Point Question 1: Why Is It Important To Collect Data?

The only trustworthy way to know whether the behavior of a student has changed is if you use a reliable measurement (data-collection) system. With appropriate data collection, you can determine the extent to which the skill or behavior of concern is performed prior to instruction. Then the data collection can reflect change in the behavior after the instruction is begun. This change in behavior can be described in words (Kevin had a mean of 5.2 occurrences of non-compliance per class period before the intervention and a mean of 0.3 occurrences per class period following the intervention), graphs (see Figure 2.1), or both.

Student: George

Behavior: Talking Out

Operational Definition: Any statement made by a student that interrupted or interfered with instruction or disrupted other students' attention to task (academic engagement), or any verbal utterance made without being called on or asked a question directly (Carter & Horner, 2007).

Time Period	Occurrences	Activity	Data Collector
8:00 - 9:00	/ / / /	Science class	Keith
9:00 - 10:00	/ / / / / / / /	English class	Keith
10:00 - 11:00	0 occurrences	PE	Keith
11:00 - 12:00	/ / /	Art class	Michal
12:00 - 1:00	no data collection	Lunch	n/a
1:00 - 2:00	/	History class	Michal

Figure 2.1. Event Data Sheet.

Measurement is the process used to assign values to variables. For example, "Most of the time" becomes 80% of the time or 8 out of 10, and "Hardly ever" becomes 10% of the time or 1 out of 10 opportunities. These measurements are specific and allow for deciding whether the behavior has changed. If the behavior has changed, a decision can be made as to whether it has changed for the better or for the worse.

While it is tempting to rely on human judgment or general impressions to evaluate the extent to which behavior is performed or whether change has occurred, human judgments may distort the relative amount of behavioral concern. For example, a young student may have tantrums so intense that teachers may recall them as occurring very often even when they are relatively infrequent. In contrast, some students may have tantrums so frequently that teachers may become accustomed to a high rate and perceive them as being less frequent than they really are.

Key Point Question 2: How Do You Operationally Define Behavior and Why Is It Important To Do So?

Measurement should be:

1. **Valid:** An accurate gauging of a dimensional quality (accuracy). The measurement system should measure what it is supposed to measure. For example, in measuring aggressive behavior, you could record the number of hits, which would be an accurate measure, whereas recording the number of noncompliant behaviors would not be an accurate measure of aggression.
2. **Reliable:** The capacity of the assessment method to yield the same measurement value when repeated measurement is made of the behavior (stability). For example, if five different teachers and staff are collecting data on Carmen's aggressive behavior but they are all defining aggression differently, then their data will not be reliable and will not provide an accurate representation of Carmen's behavior. The data collection then becomes a waste of everyone's time and an example of "garbage in, garbage out."

Issues in Measurement

1. Defining the unit of measure.
   For measurement purposes, constructs may be thought of as concepts that cannot be directly measured. For example, "being good" is a construct. Direct measures of behavior that represents being good could include following teacher directions, speaking appropriately to authority figures, or turning in homework on time. These measures could be used to represent "being good."

Units of measure relate to the level of measurement. Analysis may take place regarding: (a) an individual student (does the student ask questions appropriately?), (b) at a classroom level (how frequently are students making it to class on time?), and (c) at the school level (do students walk through the halls appropriately). The unit of measure to be used depends on the information that is needed. It is possible to combine these units of measures to provide a more comprehensive picture of what is happening in a school, such as whether a School Wide Positive Behavior Support approach is having a positive impact on academic performance at the individual or classroom level.

Table 2.1
Examples of Observable and Nonobservable Behaviors

Examples of Observable Behaviors	Examples of Nonobservable Behaviors
Jenny will complete her assignments during math class.	Jenny will be a good girl during math class.
Bruce will use his fork to eat his food during lunch time.	Bruce will be polite during lunch time.
Salomea will talk to other children on the playground.	Salomea will be cooperative on the playground.
Evan will ask for a break when he is angry.	Evan will think before he acts when he is angry.
Jeff will wait for his turn during group work at school.	Jeff will get along with others during group work.
Matthew will complete all school assignments before going home.	Matthew will remember to do his schoolwork.

One of the problems with many definitions of the behavior to be assessed is the ambiguity of the wording. Definitions of behavior are often written so that few, if any, can read them and "know" what behavior they should actually be measuring. Precisely defined behaviors are stated in terms that are observable and measurable.

Observable: You can see the behavior occur (e.g., "thinking" is not observable, whereas complying to a teacher's direction is observable). Table 2.1 presents examples of observable and non-observable behaviors.

Measurable: You can quantify the frequency, duration, or other measures of the behavior (e.g., counting the number of times a student talks out in class can easily be quantified).

EX: Increasing Gertrude's "desired" behavior and decreasing Gertrude's "undesired" behavior are not target behaviors that are stated in observable and measurable terms; the behaviors are not directly observable because the observer does not have a precise behavior (what is "desired" or "undesired" behavior) to observe.

EX: Increasing Gertrude's on-time attendance in English class is precise and may be easily observed and measured.

A definition should meet three criteria:

Objectivity

This refers to observable characteristics of behavior or environmental events. The behavior and the environment are described in terms that do not require a person collecting data to infer, or guess, what is meant. A definition should not refer to inner states of the individual such as aggressiveness or emotional disturbances. Covert feelings or states are not objective. For example, "hitting other students" is overt and can be observed and measured. "Feeling angry at other students" is a state that is difficult to define, observe, and accurately measure.

Clear

The definition of the behavior should be so unambiguous that it can be read, repeated, and paraphrased by observers. For example, stating that a student "will behave" during group activities is not a clearly defined target behavior and may be interpreted quite differently by different observers, or it may change across time for an observer. Stating that the student "will stay seated during group activities" is clear and unambiguous.

Complete

The definition must delineate the boundary conditions so that the responses to be included and excluded can be enumerated. The definition tells both what is included and excluded from the definition. This clarity is very important in order for observers to know what to record as occurrences of the behavior (throwing a chair at someone counts as aggression toward others) as well as what not to record (throwing a chair out the window does not count as aggression toward others). This means that the definition of the behavior includes both positive examples (also known as occurrences) of what the behavior is and negative examples (nonoccurrences) of what the behavior is not. These examples and nonexamples help to ensure that all people collecting data are consistent in measuring behaviors as there are often

Table 2.2
Examples of Definitions of Behavior

Bickering: Verbal arguments louder than the normal speaking voice between any two children or among all three children (Christophersen, Arnold, Hill, & Quilitch, 1972).

Talking to Oneself: Any vocalization not directed at another person but excluding physiological functions such as coughing (Wong, Terranova, Bowen, Zarate, Massel, & Liberman, 1987).

Active Student Responding: Engaging in the behavior that was expected during the specific opportunities to respond condition and included (a) independent hand raising for the individual responding, and (b) responding in unison with the group for choral responding (Godfrey, Grisham-Brown, Schuster, & Hemmeter, 2003).

Compliance: Engaging in requested behavior within 10 seconds of a given request (Ellingson, Miltenberger, Stricker, Galensky, & Garlinghouse, 2000).

Leaving seat: Leaving seat when other students are sitting, except when verbal permission is given by the teacher in advance (Ryan, Halsey, & Matthews, 2003).

Disruption: Talking out to peers and teacher without teacher permission, using profanity or sexually related language, leaving desk during instruction, making distracting facial expressions or obscene hand gestures to others in the classroom, and making repeated audible noises with tangible items (e.g., tapping pencil or paper clip repetitiously on desk) (Wright-Gallo et al., 2006).

Talk out: Any statement made by a student that interrupted or interfered with instruction or disrupted other students' attention to task (academic engagement), or any verbal utterance made without being called on or asked a question directly (Carter & Horner, 2007).

Academic engagement: Orienting toward the board, overhead, or teacher; engaging physically or verbally with materials, objects, or tasks; writing or reading the assigned task during independent work time; contributing to assigned cooperative activities; or engaging in appropriate activities approved by the teacher if independent work was completed early (Carter & Horner, 2007).

Disruptive Behavior: Behavior that (a) had the potential to disrupt learning even if unnoticed, (b) was inappropriate for the current activity, and (c) was not in line with classroom expectations (e.g., shouting out, talking to peers, throwing an object, or making noises) (Myers, Simonsen, & Sugai, 2011).

"gray areas" in deciding whether a behavior is a positive (occurrence) example. For instance, when recording aggressive behavior by a student, it may be decided that only physical acts toward another person are "aggression." Physical acts toward oneself (hitting oneself in the head) or threatening another person ("I'm going to punch you") may be defined as negative (nonoccurrence) examples of the behavior for this student. The student may engage in a behavior that has not occurred before (e.g., squirting another student with a water pistol), and the team of data collectors can then decide whether that counts as aggression for future recording. Without this agreement, you may have some staff members counting verbal threats as aggression while

Table 2.3
Behavioral Definition of Aggression with Positive and Negative Examples

Global Definition:
  Aggression is verbal or physical behavior toward another person that results in or has the potential to result in harm to that person.

Positive (occurrence) examples:
  Poking eye of other person.
  Slapping other person.
  Hitting other person with object.
  Pulling ear of other person.
  Banging heads of other people together.
Negative (nonoccurrence) examples:
  Saying thank you.
  Hugging.
  Smashing objects.
  Removing glasses and breaking them.
  Laughing.

others are not. Thus, you would be getting unreliable data that do not accurately represent the student's behavior. Table 2.2 presents examples of operational definitions of behavior taken from professional journal articles. Table 2.3 presents an operational definition of aggression along with positive and negative examples.

Key Point Question 3: What Are Dimensions of Behavior for Measurement Purposes?

There are three approaches to measurement: Observational, Standardized Tests, and Survey (Questionnaire/Interview). This chapter and book focus on observational methods as they are most relevant and most frequently used in positive behavior supports. Dimension of behavior represent the construct that you are trying to measure. For instance, "desirable student behavior" is a construct, whereas specific student behaviors could be following directions, interacting with teachers and peers appropriately, completing homework, and so on. Each one of these behaviors represents possible measures of the construct of "desirable student behavior," although of course no one measure completely represents the construct as a whole. Then, specific measurement systems (discussed after this section) can be used to collect data on student behaviors.

Measurement Via Observational Procedures

Type (Goal for Target Behavior). First you need to define the purpose and the process of measurement. You need to consider this *before* you begin your data collection. What is the overall goal you are trying to accomplish considering target skills and behavioral concerns? There are seven types of goals:

1. **Description.** Are you wanting to describe the current state of the behavior?
2. **Increase.** Are you wanting to see whether the behavior increases?
3. **Decrease.** Are you wanting to see whether the behavior decreases?
4. **Acquisition.** Are you wanting to see whether a student learns a new skill?
5. **Maintenance.** Are you wanting to see whether a student continues to perform a behavior over time?
6. **Generality.** Are you wanting to see whether a student can generalize what he or she has learned (across time, settings, people, and/or behaviors)?
7. **Fluency.** Are you wanting to know how proficient a student is (such as being able to easily read and understand text)?

The purpose of your data collection will determine what method of data collection best meets your needs. For instance, using frequency counts would probably be helpful in determining whether a behavior has increased or decreased, but it might not be good in determining fluency.

Dimensions of Behavior

There are a variety of dimensions of behavior and these then relate to the specific observational method that may be chosen to record the behavior of students.

1. Frequency

Frequency is the number of occurrences for a specified period of time. This may also be expressed as the rate of behavior, which is the mean number of occurrences per minute or other standard of time such as an hour or a class period.

Examples of Frequency:
Number of words read correctly per minute.
Number of times a student attends a school club.
Number of objects thrown by a student.
Number of times homework is turned in on time by a student.

Advantages in Using Frequency Data

1. Extremely sensitive to behavior changes.
2. Convert behavior counts to a standard or constant scale (responses per minute).
3. Relatively simple to score and evaluate.

Disadvantages in Using Frequency Data

1. Ongoing behaviors such as smiling, sitting in one's seat, lying down, and talking are difficult to record simply by counting because each response may occur for a different amount of time (talking to a peer for 15 seconds and to another peer for 30 minutes would each be scored as one instance of talking).
2. Very rapid behaviors may be difficult to count (a student who is tapping their pencil on their desk).

2. Percent
Percent is the number of occurrences of the behavior divided by opportunity. Percent can be used for skills or behaviors having differing opportunities across days or observation times.

Examples of Percent:
Percent of addition problems performed correctly.
Percent of times a student arrives to class on time.
Percent of times that a student greets other students appropriately.

Advantages in Using Percent Recording

1. Percent converts unequal opportunities to respond across sessions or days to a common scale, thereby "equalizing" the number of

opportunities to respond for purposes of data summation and evaluation.
2. They are an efficient means of summarizing large numbers of responses.
3. They are a simple way to summarizing overall performance on a graph or chart.
4. They are often more familiar to people than other measures and therefore facilitate communication of performance.

Disadvantages in Using Percent Recording

1. They make no reference to the time over which a behavior was observed, thus limiting what can be said about response proficiency.
2. Percents place upper and lower limits (i.e., 100% and 0%) on reporting data and do not refer to the actual number of responses or opportunities to respond.
3. Percents can mask trends in the data by not revealing when a response occurs during a particular observation period.
4. Percents should not be used when the total number of opportunities to respond is less than 20, in which case one change in the numerator will produce greater than a 5% change.

3. Latency

Latency is from the beginning of a discriminative stimulus (such as a teacher direction to line up for recess) to the initiation of the response or behavior (time from cue to onset of behavior, how long does it take the student to start lining up for recess).

Examples of Latency:
Number of seconds it takes a student to return to desk after being instructed to by teacher.
Number of minutes it takes a student to get ready once the bell rings.

Advantages in Using Latency Recording

1. Appropriate measure with compliance problems.
2. Appropriate for assessing student delays in responding to discriminative stimuli.

Disadvantages in Using Latency Recording

1. Can be difficult to accurately measure.

4. Duration

Duration is the time of responding (time from the onset of the behavior to the termination of the behavior).

Examples of Duration Recording:
Number of seconds it takes a student to complete a division problem.
Number of minutes spent talking out in class.
Number of minutes engaged in conversation with peers.
Number of minutes of "on-task" behavior by a student.
Duration may involve the total time of a behavior across occurrences (how many minutes a student was on-task during a 50-minute class period) or maybe per occurrence (how long a student was on task before going "off task"). Using duration data per occurrence can also allow for the collection of frequency of behavior as well as duration.

Advantages in Using Duration Recording

1. Good for determining whether behavior that requires a time period or length of interaction (such as interacting appropriately with peers) has occurred or changed.

Disadvantages in Using Duration Recording

1. Data collector needs to be in constant observation of the student being observed.
2. Need a device for determining start and stop times.

5. Lasting Effect of Behavior

This represents a permanent physical product (or artifact) that the student produces.

Examples of Lasting Effects of Behavior:
Written samples of academic work.
Videotapes of student performance.

Advantages

1. Efficient.
2. Easy to go back to product to evaluate.

Disadvantages

1. Prone to problems if product produced via an alternative behavior (such as someone else doing the assignment).

6. Intensity

This represents the forcefulness or severity of a behavior. It usually requires some automated-quantitative apparatus (such as noise level) or a subjective rating of the behavior.

Examples of Intensity:
Classroom noise level.
How hard the student hit his hand against the wall.

Advantages

1. Can add an important dimension of assessment when combined with other types.

Disadvantages

1. Can be too subjective, and differences in scoring can occur across time or across observers.

7. Subjective Measures

These often use Likert-type rating scales (e.g., rate from 1–10) to add subjective data to objective data (Storey & Horner, 1991; Wolf, 1978).

Examples of Subjective Measures:
Rating from 1 to 10 of how loud a student yelled (with 1 being *lowest* and 10 being *loudest*).
Rating from 1 to 10 of how effective the social skills program was on increasing a student's positive social interactions with peers (with 1 being *not effective at all* and 10 being *very effective*).

8. Multiple Measures

Multiple measures involve using more than one of the measures above in order to obtain a more complete measurement of student performance. This can be important because often the measurement needs to describe a complex situation or construct.

Examples of Multiple Measures:
Social integration (might include frequency and duration of interactions and a subjective rating of the quality of the interactions).
Academic competence (might include percent of problems correct and duration of how long it took the student to complete problems).

Key Point Question 4. What Are Good Ways to Collect Data?

Training Observers
An often overlooked component of data collection is that you can't necessarily expect a staff member to go and collect reliable and valid data without any training. With any data collection system, you should:

1. Discuss the purpose of the data collection as well as any logistical issues related to data collection (e.g., where to observe the student from, what if the student asks what you are doing, etc.).
2. Discuss the operational definition and positive and negative examples of the behavior.
3. Practice using the data-collection system through role playing and/or videotapes of the student. Discuss individual occurrences of the behavior during the videotape and come to agreement across observers.
4. Have observers independently score from role playing/videotapes and then compare with other observers (this is known as interobserver agreement). Try to get at 80% agreement or higher.
5. Conduct data collection on the student in the situation in which data will be collected. Compare data across observers.
6. Retrain as necessary as new examples of the behavior may occur, and there is often "observer drift," where observers may intentionally or unintentionally change their interpretation of the operational definition of the behavior or the examples and nonexamples.

1. Event Recording

Event recording involves continuous observation. The number of "events" or occurrences of the behavior are counted. This is the total number of times the behavior occurred during a predetermined observation period. It is important to have a clear start and a clear stop time of the behavior (e.g., hand flapping).

Figure 2.1 presents an event recording data form. In this example, George has had four occurrences of "talking out" behavior during Science class, eight during English class, 0 during PE, three during Art class, and one during History class.

Advantages

1. Most common.
2. Good when event is obvious or produces a permanent product.
3. Good when event is low to moderate frequency.

Disadvantages

1. Less effective when event has several different behaviors.
2. Problem if behavior occurs too frequently.
3. No time information.
4. The observer must be continuously monitoring the student during the observation period.

2. Duration Recording

This is the length of time for each occurrence of the target behavior within a predefined observation period (may be either total duration or duration per occurrence). Usually a stopwatch, computer, or an automatic recording device is needed.

Figure 2.2 presents an example of Paul's academic engagement during Circle Time across three days. Over the 40-minute time period, his academic engagement was 9 minutes, 24 minutes, and 30 minutes.

Advantages

1. Easy to score.

Disadvantages

2. Very intense as data collector must be constantly focused on student.
3. May be difficult to measure behaviors of very short duration.

Student: Paul

Behavior: Academic Engagement

Operational Definition: Orienting toward the board, overhead, or teacher, engaging physically or verbally with materials, objects, or tasks; writing or reading the assigned task during independent work time; contributing to assigned cooperative activities; or engaging in appropriate activities approved by the teacher if independent work was completed early (Carter & Horner, 2007).

Date	Start Time	Stop Time	Total Time	Activity	Data Collector
9/6	8:14	8:19	5 min	Circle Time	Michal
9/6	8:22	8:23	1 min	Circle Time	Michal
9/6	8:31	8:35	4 min	Circle Time	Michal
9/7	8:10	8:21	11 min	Circle Time	Michal
9/7	8:23	8:36	13 min	Circle Time	Michal
9/8	8:11	8:32	21 min	Circle Time	Keith
9/8	8:35	8:44	9 min	Circle Time	Keith

Figure 2.2. Duration Data Sheet.

3. Latency Recording

Latency recording can be used to measure the time it takes a student to comply with teacher directions or other discriminative stimuli in the environment.

Figure 2.3 provides an example of latency recording for compliance to directions. In this example, Valerie had a mean of 88 seconds (range 30–200 seconds) in responding to the cue (Sd) from the teacher for completing her math work.

Student: Valerie

Behavior: Compliance

Operational Definition: Engaging in requested behavior within 10 seconds of a given request.

(Ellingson, Miltenberger, Stricker, Galensky, & Garlinghouse, 2000).

Date	Cue (Sd)	Time to Response	Activity	Data Collector
2/29	Go to group	45 sec	Math/group work	Keith
2/29	Get work out	33 sec	English	Keith
2/29	Write word to look up	68 sec	English	Keith
2/29	Put materials away	30 sec	English	Keith
3/1	Put cell phone away	200 sec	History/group work	Michal
3/1	Get materials out	150 sec	History	Michal

Figure 2.3. Latency Data Sheet.

4. Interval Recording

This is also known as time sampling. This type of recording procedure is often used when the behavior of concern or skill can (or does) occur throughout the day. The observation period is divided into intervals (such as every minute or every five minutes), and it is recorded whether the behavior occurred within the interval. It is best to choose an interval that allows the behavior to occur at least once during that interval. For example, you could observe for 10 seconds and then record for 5 seconds. The behavior is scored as having occurred or not occurred during that interval. Generally, several occurrences of the behavior within an interval are not counted separately (although it is possible to combine event recording with interval recording). You then end up with a percentage of intervals in which the behavior occurred.

Advantages

1. Good for high rate of behavior.
2. Good for complex codes (such as recording three different types of aggressive behavior and four different types of noncompliance on the same data sheet).
3. Good for behaviors that are of long duration.
4. Easily converted into percentages for when observations occur across different periods of time (such as when one class period may be 50 minutes and then on a different day 120 minutes due to block scheduling).

Disadvantages

1. May artificially truncate behavior (because you do not have information on the duration of the behavior). .
2. Need to select interval small enough or could lose information.
3. Coding is intermittent so sequential information is usually lost.

Partial Interval Recording:
This is when a behavior is recorded as having occurred if it occurs at any point during the recording interval. For instance, if the interval is one minute and the behavior occurs at 25 seconds into that interval then it is scored as having occurred.

Whole Interval Recording:

This is when a behavior must occur during the complete interval time period in order to be counted as an occurrence of the behavior. For example, if the interval is one minute, then the behavior must occur for that complete minute in order to be scored as an occurrence of the behavior.

Momentary Interval Recording:

With momentary interval recording, the student is observed and the behavior is scored as having occurred or not occurred only at a set point in time, such as every minute. At that minute, there is a cue for the observer (minute hand on a watch or a beep on a recording device) that cues the observer to look at the student and record whether the behavior is occurring or not occurring at that specific point in time. Figure 2.4 presents the example of time sampling of Graham's verbal arguments. He had a verbal argument in 8 of the 70 intervals (11% of the intervals).

Key Point Question 5: How Do You Know Whether Student Behavior Has Changed?

In order to know whether student behavior has changed, some sort of summarization or analysis of the data is necessary. This may be a table, a narrative, or a graph, see Figure 2.5. Without this summarization, it is only possible to guess whether the behavior has changed as well as to what extent it has changed. This guessing is not a strong way to gauge change and is unlikely to impress colleagues, supervisors, family members, legislators, attorneys, or other relevant people. The analysis should include a description of the behavior before the intervention and then during the intervention (Kennedy, 2005).

Key Point Question 6: How Do You Best Present Data For Analysis?

Visual representation of data in a graph is an efficient method for presenting information. It can easily be looked at and understood, and it can be quickly analyzed to see whether change in behavior has occurred. Figure 2.6 provides an example of the frequency of socially desirable remarks by a student to peers using an A-B Single Case Research Design (Kennedy, 2005). In the figure, the Baseline Assessment (also known as the "A" phase or before the intervention has

Student: Graham

Behavior: Bickering

Operational Definition: Verbal arguments louder than the normal speaking voice between any two children or among all three children (Christophersen, Arnold, Hill, & Quilitch, 1972).

Time	1	2	3	4	5	6	7	8	9	10
9:00	0	+	0	0	0	0	0	0	0	0
9:10	+	0	+	0	0	0	0	0	0	0
9:20	0	+	+	+	0	0	0	0	0	0
9:30	+	0	0	0	0	0	0	0	0	0
9:40	0	0	0	0	0	0	0	+	0	0
9:50	0	0	0	0	0	0	0	0	0	0
10:00	0	0	0	0	0	0	0	0	0	0

Record a + of the behavior occurred. Record a 0 of the behavior did not occur.

Type 1: Whole Interval: + = behavior occurred during the whole interval time period.

Type 2: Partial Interval: + = behavior occurred at some point during the interval time period.

Type 3: Momentary Interval: + = behavior occurred at beginning of the interval time period.

Figure 2.4. Interval Data Sheet.

occurred) data show that socially desirable remarks occurred with a mean of 38.6 times per week (range 30–46). The intervention (also known as the "B" phase) consisted of Video Modeling and Social Skills instruction. During the intervention, the student made socially desirable remarks with a mean of 70.1 times per week (range 52–86). In addition, it is easy to look at the graph and determine that the student's behavior is improving over time with the intervention.

Student: Haing

Behavior: Correct computation of math problems.

Operational Definition: Correct computation of the math problem.

Date	# opportunities	# behavior	Percentage	Activity	Data Collector
9/9	20	10	50%	Division	Keith
9/10	20	12	60%	Division	Keith
9/11	20	15	75%	Division	Keith
9/12	20	18	90%	Division	Keith

Figure 2.5. Percent Data Sheet.

A table consists of rows and columns that present numbers for analysis. Table 2.4 presents the same data as in Figure 2.5 and is one example of how data might be presented in table format. Even though Table 2.4 contains the same data, it is not as easy to analyze the behavior change as in Figure 2.6.

Key Point Question 7: How Can You Use Technology in Data Collection?

Technology in data collection may be "low" tech (such as a sheet of paper) or "high tech" (such as a laptop with software specifically designed for data collection). What is necessary is that the system of data

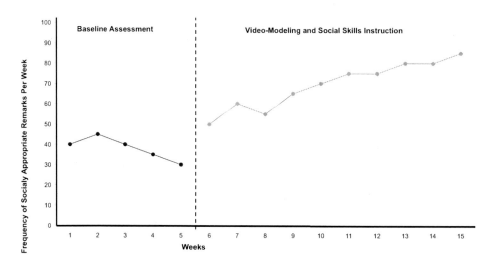

Figure 2.6. Frequency of Socially Desired Remarks by Student to Peers.

collection works for the specific situation and for the people using the system. Some issues to consider in selecting the data collection system are:

1. The system is user friendly and collects reliable data.
2. It is easy and not time-consuming to summarize data from the system.
3. The more people collecting data, the more simple that you want the system to be.
4. Data collection can be done covertly, if necessary. (For example, preschool students may not understand that, when a teacher writes something down on a clipboard, the data are being collected on their behavior. High school students, however, will understand, and thus the teacher may reach into a pocket and push a button on a smart phone, with the students unaware that data have been collected.)

Equipment/procedures such as a smart phone or laptop with observation software, a notebook, wrist counters, a clipboard, a small pad of paper, or moving coins from one pocket to another may be used for collecting data. These systems can be preset for the appropriate data-collection methodology, such as a data sheet being shrunk in size so that it fits into a day planner. There are a variety of software programs and "apps" available for data collection.

Table 2.4
Frequency of Socially Desired Remarks by Student to Peers

Week	Frequency	Phase
1	41	Baseline
2	46	Baseline
3	41	Baseline
4	35	Baseline
5	30	Baseline
6	52	Intervention
7	59	Intervention
8	57	Intervention
9	65	Intervention
10	70	Intervention
11	75	Intervention
12	75	Intervention
13	81	Intervention
14	81	Intervention
15	86	Intervention

No matter what system is being used, certain elements should be present for data collection. These are:

1. The student or student's name.
2. Date.
3. Condition (baseline or intervention).
4. Skill or behavior being recorded with operational definition.
5. Observer collecting data (this is important if different people are collecting data on the same student).

6. The representation of the system for data collection (how the format is set for actual collection of the data).
7. Summarization of the data. This may be for a specific class, or on a daily, weekly, etc. basis.

BEST PRACTICE RECOMMENDATIONS

1. Only collect data on important behaviors.
2. Collect data on desirable as well as undesirable behaviors.
3. Analyze your data and use it for decision making, otherwise don't bother to waste your time collecting data you do not use.
4. Collect data on Individual Education Plan goals.
5. Use data-collection systems that are described in the Method section of professional journal articles. Professional journals are a good source for illustration of valid and well-tested methods (see suggested journals in the Appendix).

DISCUSSION QUESTIONS

1. What is the best way to determine whether student behavior has changed?
2. How often should data be collected and analyzed?
3. Who should collect data (e.g., teachers, aides, students, volunteers, etc.)?
4. What are good ways to share data analysis with other teachers, administrators, family members, students, and so on?
5. What are important and meaningful behaviors to take data on?

CLASSROOM AND SCHOOL ACTIVITY SUGGESTIONS

1. Choose a student behavior and write an operational definition with positive and negative examples.
2. Compare your operational definition with similar ones in the Method section of professional journals articles.
3. Choose a positive teacher skill (such as praising students or providing feedback) and collect data on how often you engage in that behavior.

4. Have multiple people collect data on a student at the same time. Compare the results to see how reliable they are across the observers (Kennedy, 2005).

REFERENCES

Carter, D. R., & Horner, R. H. (2007). Adding functional behavioral assessment to first step to success: A case study. *Journal of Positive Behavior Interventions, 9*, 229–238.

Christophersen, E. R., Arnold, C. M., Hill, D. W., & Quilitch, H. R. (1972). The home point system: Token reinforcement procedures for application by parents of children with behavior problems. *Journal of Applied Behavior Analysis, 5*, 485–497.

Ellingson, S. A., Miltenberger, R. G., Stricker, J., Galensky, T. L., & Garlinghouse, M. (2000). Functional assessment and intervention for challenging behaviors in the classroom by general classroom teachers. *Journal of Positive Behavior Interventions, 2*, 85–97.

Godfrey, S. A., Grisham-Brown, J., Schuster, J. W., & Hemmeter, M. L. (2003). The effects of three techniques on student participation with preschool children with attending problems. *Education and Treatment of Children, 26*, 255–272.

Kennedy, C. (2005). *Single-case designs for educational research.* Boston, MA: Allyn & Bacon.

Myers, D. M., Simonsen, B., & Sugai, G. (2011). Increasing teachers' use of praise with a response-to-intervention approach. *Education and Treatment of Children, 34*, 35–59.

Ryan, A. L., Halsey, H. N., & Matthews, W. J. (2003). Using functional assessment to promote desirable student behavior in school. *Teaching Exceptional Children, 35*, 8–15.

Storey, K., & Horner, R. H. (1991). An evaluative review of social validation research involving persons with handicaps. *Journal of Special Education, 25*, 352–401.

Wolf, M. M. (1978). Social validity: The case for subjective measurement or how applied behavior analysis is finding its heart. *Journal of Applied Behavior Analysis, 11*, 203–214.

Wong, S. E., Terranova, M. D., Bowen, L., Zarate, R., Massel, H. K., & Liberman, R. P. (1987). Providing independent recreational activities to reduce stereotypic vocalizations in chronic schizophrenics. *Journal of Applied Behavior Analysis, 20*, 77–81.

Wright-Gallo, G. L., Higbee, T. S., Reagon, K., & Davey, B. J. (2006). Classroom-based functional analysis and intervention for students with emotional/behavioral disorders. *Education and Treatment of Children, 29*, 421–436,

Chapter 3

FUNCTIONAL ASSESSMENT AND ANALYSIS

Key Point Questions

1. What is the function of behavior?
2. What role do antecedents and consequences play in the understanding of behavior?
3. What is ABC analysis?
4. How should interviews be used in determining the function of the behavior?
5. How should direct observations be used in determining the function of the behavior?
6. How should systematic manipulations be used in determining the function of the behavior?
7. How do you determine replacement behaviors that serve the same function as the undesirable behaviors?

WINDOW OF THE WORLD CASE STUDY 1

Corbitant is an eight-year-old who is known to be off task for much of his academic day. These off-task behaviors include talking and yelling out during class (an average of 10 times per hour), getting out of his seat (an average of five times per hour), and getting under his desk and playing with objects (approximately twice per hour). Corbitant also frequently touches others' property and makes negative comments to his peers. A functional assessment revealed that these behaviors occur across academic subjects and tend to happen when Corbitant is presented with academic work to do. Direct observation has also revealed that following Corbitant's behavior, teachers frequently send him to the office. In fact, Corbitant is spending more and more time in the office and less and less time on academic tasks.

After performing a comprehensive functional assessment, the behavior specialist hypothesized that Corbitant was acting out in order to escape academic tasks, especially those that involved reading. After consulting with a reading specialist, the behavior specialist was then able to choose from a menu of interventions and write them into a positive behavior plan. In terms of ecological manipulations, teachers provided Corbitant with extra reading instruction that focused on decoding skills, arranged for an older peer from the fifth grade to provide reading instruction through an after school program, and provided him with an "out" where he could use an escape card once per period. The escape card could be used to provide him with an alternative task (such as taking a note to the office) and avoid being publically embarrassed during oral reading times. Finally, teachers no longer sent him to the office for any acting out behaviors. When he did act out, the teachers knew that he was engaging in escape behavior due to difficult readings and realized that other students may find the readings difficult. To address this, the teachers would stop the work, go over words that they thought might be difficult, and then go back to the task at hand. Teachers also frequently reinforced Corbitant for his successful reading behavior (and that of other students as well). In addition, his parents asked what they could do to help and were provided with a list of supplemental books for home reading. Corbitant and his parents planned to stop at the public library on their way home from school, and they established a special reading time after dinner where he and one parent spent time reading to each other. Because of these multiple interventions, Corbitant's acting out behaviors decreased to almost zero, and, not surprisingly, his reading ability increased dramatically.

WINDOW OF THE WORLD CASE STUDY 2

Eduardo, age six, was identified by his kindergarten teacher as displaying disruptive behaviors. He had been referred by his kindergarten teacher for special education services. In the kindergarten class, the daily routine was organized into different activities. Two of these activities, whole-group instruction and independent seat work, made up the academic portion of the day. During whole-group instruction, students were seated on the floor facing the whiteboard while the teacher modeled correct completion of a reading or math worksheet displayed on the board. Students were expected to sit quietly and raise their hands in order to be called on to participate. This was followed by another academic activity and then independent seat work. Students were seated at tables and given a copy of the same worksheet taught in the whole-group lesson.

Initial discussions with Eduardo's teacher indicated that his disruptive behaviors were interfering with his learning. A functional analysis interview with the teacher indicated that Eduardo displayed excessive movement, talking out during instructional times, touching others inappropriately, throwing objects across the classroom, and taunting classmates. Based on the information from the teacher interview, a functional analysis observation was conducted to determine the frequency and function(s) of Eduardo's disruptive behaviors. Observations were made over a three-day period during the entire time Eduardo was in the kindergarten classroom. The following were recorded: (a) target behaviors, (b) setting events/discriminative stimuli, (c) perceived functions (get/obtain or escape/avoid), and (d) actual consequences.

The two most frequently occurring disruptive behaviors (talking out and excessive movement) during instruction time were targeted for intervention. Because the interview and direct observation assessments indicated that Eduardo was engaging in the disruptive behaviors in order to obtain attention, a self-management program was designed to provide reinforcement from the teacher for appropriate behavior. The following materials were used to implement the self-management program:

(a) a poster exemplifying "acceptable" versus "unacceptable" behaviors;
(b) reinforcers such as coloring books, toy cars, play flashlights, and stickers;
(c) a desk chart (3 x 5 index card) containing 20 squares, which Eduardo scored with a plus (if he was engaging in acceptable

behaviors) or a zero (if he was engaging in unacceptable behaviors) when a timer sounded; and

(d) a timer that sounded at two-minute intervals.

Prior to each session, the teacher attached the chart to Eduardo's desk, briefly reviewed the posters, and allowed him to select a reinforcer. In addition, two other students in the class were included in the intervention and received reinforcers for the same behavior, which strengthened the desirable behaviors for all of the students in the class. This intervention was quite successful, and Eduardo's unacceptable behaviors decreased from 70% of the intervals during baseline to 5% of the intervals by the end of the first week of the intervention.

Key Point Question 1: What Is the Function of Behavior?

Research has increasingly shown that many behaviors, traditionally viewed as undesirable, are used to convey social intent or, in other words, serve a function for the student (Cipani & Schock, 2011; Filter & Horner, 2009; Waller, 2009). For example, students may tease one another in an attempt to gain attention from their peers. Other students may "mouth off" to a teacher in order to escape or avoid academic tasks or other classroom demands. Undesirable behaviors are frequently misinterpreted by school personnel as nonfunctional and in need of immediate suppression. However, once these students are taught alternatives to undesirable behaviors that are more adaptive (that build skills for the student) and serve the same function, undesirable behaviors often rapidly disappear (Chandler & Dahlquist, 2010).

Determining the function of an undesirable behavior is critically important to understanding and developing an intervention (whether formal or informal) for any undesirable behavior. Functional assessment is *the key* to effective behavioral support. Functional assessment should lead to a focus on preventing undesirable behaviors from occurring rather than waiting for the behavior to occur and then punishing it. Because the focus of assessment is on determining the function of the behavior, intervention is more likely to be successful because the focus is on replacing disruptive behavior with appropriate behaviors that serve the same function (O'Neill, Horner, Albin, Sprague, Storey, & Newton, 1997).

Table 3.1
Examples of Hypothesis Statements

1. Basil puts his head down on his desk in order to avoid academic tasks that are difficult for him.
2. Olga is likely to leave her seat during reading tasks but not during math work.
3. When Winston is not receiving teacher or peer attention, he will loudly make an inappropriate comment during class time.
4. When there are transitions (from setting to setting or task to task), Tuol will refuse to move to the new setting or to leave the task that he is working on.
5. When the teacher or other staff stand too close (within two feet) of Bernal, he will push them away with his hands.

A functional assessment is a process whereby informed hypothesis statements are developed about relationships between events in the environment and the occurrence of a student's undesirable behaviors (Larson & Maag, 1998). Table 3.1 provides examples of hypothesis statements. These relationships have been characterized as involving either: (a) the operations of a reinforcement contingency, including both positive and negative reinforcement; or (b) controlling antecedent stimulus in the environment (Foster Johnson & Dunlap, 1993).

Current perspectives on disruptive behaviors call for identifying the specific functions served by undesirable behavior. The two major functions that behaviors may serve are: (a) to obtain something desirable, and (b) to escape or avoid something undesirable. A functional analysis is an assessment method of identifying the relationship between behaviors and the setting, antecedent, and consequent events that maintain the behaviors. The difference between functional assessment and functional analysis is that a functional assessment includes interviews and/or direct observations, whereas a functional analysis involves systematic manipulations of environmental events.

A complete functional analysis involves three strategies: (a) interview, (b) direct observation, and (c) systematic manipulations. It is often possible to understand the function of a behavior with interviews and simple observations, and there is then no need for a complete functional analysis. For instance, seeing a young child lying on the floor in a grocery store kicking and screaming out "Daddy, Daddy, I want the candy," the function of the behavior is clearly understood to obtain the candy. There would be no need to conduct a formal functional analysis.

The purposes of the functional analysis are to understand the function served by behavior and to plan interventions based on those functions. For example, Burke, Hagan-Burke, and Sugai (2003) conducted a functional analysis of the undesirable behaviors of a third grade student. First, the student and two of his teachers were interviewed using the format from O'Neill et al. (1997). From this initial information, a curriculum-based measurement was used to assess the student's reading skills. Then interval recording procedures were used to collect information on the types of undesirable behaviors, the instructional context, antecedents, and consequences observed. Third, systematic manipulations were conducted, where different variables were manipulated during reading times as well as out-of-class times. A hypothesis statement was developed from this information ("When presented with reading tasks that require comprehension, Mario displays problem behaviors to escape these tasks"). The intervention developed was to preteach vocabulary concepts to the student that occurred the day before the student was likely to encounter them in his reading class. In addition, the student was provided with a set of vocabulary cards, and he reviewed these cards the next morning in his homeroom class before going to reading class. With this intervention, the student's on-task behavior increased as did his reading ability.

A functional analysis is complete when five main outcomes are accomplished:

1. A clear description of the undesirable behavior(s), including classes (classes of behavior are groups of behavior that are of the same topography and serve the same function; e.g., hitting, kicking, and biting may be classed as "aggressive behaviors") or sequences of behaviors that frequently occur together.

2. Identification of the events, times, and situations that predict when the undesirable behavior(s) *will* and *will not* occur across the full range of typical daily routines (knowing when undesirable behavior does not occur, such as small-group instruction, can provide information that is as important as knowing when undesirable behavior does occur).

3. Identification of the consequences that maintain the undesirable behaviors (i.e., what function(s) the behavior appears to serve for the student).

4. Development of one or more summary statements or hypotheses that describe specific behaviors, a specific type of situation in

which they occur, and the outcomes or reinforcers maintaining them in that situation.

5. Collection of direct observation data that support the summary statements that have been developed.

In addition, the functional assessment:

1. Provides practical academic and social skills that enable the student to succeed in the schools.
2. Contains an ecological emphasis that looks at the student functioning in his or her school environment.
3. Examines the process of learning and performance.
4. Suggests intervention techniques that may be successful.
5. Specifies ongoing assessment procedures (see Chapter 2) that can evaluate intervention progress.
6. Avoids stressing deficits of the student in isolation from what is happening in the classroom and school.
7. Avoids reporting scores or labels.
8. Assessment is not episodic, it is formative as it interacts with ongoing instruction and evaluation.

The objective of the previous procedures is that results of a functional assessment can be translated into effective intervention strategies. Because the process is based on some "value-laden" assumptions, it is important that these be made clear (see Table 3.2 for a summary of these values). Foster Johnson and Dunlap (1993) and O'Neill et al. (1997) have reported that functional assessment procedures are based on the following basic assumptions.

First, students do not engage in undesirable behaviors on a random basis. There is logic to their behavior, and functional assessment is an attempt to understand that logic. Undesirable behaviors are not abnormalities, but are reasonable adaptations necessitated by the abilities of students and the limitations of their environment to support them. For example, students who act verbally aggressive toward their peers (with the function being to get peer attention) may not have the necessary social skills to initiate interactions in a more appropriate fashion (Gresham, 1997).

A second assumption of functional assessment is that the objective is not to define and eliminate undesirable behavior, but to understand

Table 3.2
Values of Functional Analysis

1. Behavioral support must be conducted with the dignity of the student as a primary regard.
    A. Functional analysis is appropriate because it acknowledges that a student's undesirable behavior is reasonable from that student's perspective.
    B. Students do not engage in undesirable behavior because they have a disability label such as Down syndrome or emotional disturbance or are regarded as obnoxious, bad students, etc.
    C. There is logic to student behavior, and functional analysis is an attempt to understand that logic.
2. The objective of functional analysis is not to define and eliminate an undesirable behavior but to understand the structure and function of that behavior in order to teach the student how to develop positive skills and to therefore not need to engage in the undesirable behavior.
3. Functional analysis is a process for looking at relationships between behavior and the environment.
    A. It is as much an analysis of the environment (schedules, teacher and staff behavior, curriculum, physical settings) as it is of the behavior of the student.
    B. Functional analysis is not a process that "blames" the student for behaving in undesirable ways.

the structure and function of that behavior in order to teach and develop effective alternative behaviors that are desirable. According to O'Neill et al. (1997), functional assessment will identify: (a) unnecessary situations that prompt the undesirable behavior, (b) new skills one can teach that will make undesirable behaviors unnecessary, and (c) effective staff responses to the both desirable and undesirable behaviors. This focus is more likely to be effective than interventions that simply attempt to reduce undesirable behavior. This focus also promotes greater awareness of and therefore better manipulation of ecological components of the student's environment.

A third assumption is that undesirable behavior is related to the "context" in which it occurs. Undesirable behaviors occur in response to some stimulus or situation that can be identified. Therefore, changes in the circumstances can be important in changing the behavior. Context refers to all the events and sensations that might affect a student, including: environmental events, instructions, staff behavior, peer interactions, assigned activities, curricular expectations, seating arrangements, and physiological and emotional conditions (e.g., anxiety, fatigue, pain, hunger). By assuming that behavior is related to context, the focus of responsibility remains on those who work with the student. Service providers must examine the environment in which the student functions and not, as is too often the case, use circular definitions to explain away undesirable behavior. Behavior difficulties cannot be attributed to broad personality characteristics or states or be blamed on other factors such as a poor home life or biological factors.

It is important to understand that individual behaviors may serve multiple functions for a student. For example, talking back to a teacher may allow the student to gain social attention in one situation (the function being to get) and in another situation to escape an academically difficult task (the function being to avoid). This understanding helps to facilitate the process of intervention in classroom and school settings for students. Thus, an intervention such as sending the student to the office for talking back to the teacher when trying to get peer attention would be appropriate (it would be punishing the behavior), but it would not be successful when the student is talking back in order to escape the difficult academic task (the student would be negatively reinforced and the behavior would be likely to occur more frequently when the student is presented with a difficult task).

Key Point Question 2: What Role do Antecedents and Consequences Play in the Understanding of the Function of Behavior?

As noted in Chapter 1, antecedents are what occur before a behavior, and consequences are what occur after a behavior. The purpose of functional assessment is to understand how the antecedents and consequences are influencing the occurrence of the behavior of concern.

Antecedents evaluate classroom (group vs. individual instruction), health (allergies), home (did the student have breakfast before school), and school factors (what happened on the playground before school) that predict the occurrence as well as the nonoccurrence of the undesirable behaviors (and also the prediction of desirable behavior).

Consequences increase, maintain, or decrease behavior. Understanding the consequences that occur after the undesirable behavior can be very important in functional assessment and in developing effective interventions. For example, if a student talks back to a teacher when given a direction and is sent out of the room, then the student has been reinforced for this talking back (escape behavior) and in the future is more likely to engage in this undesirable behavior when given a teacher direction.

Key Point Question 3: What is ABC Analysis?

In the ABC analysis, the A stands for antecedent, the B for behavior, and the C for consequence. The collection of data in this easy-to-use process can be helpful in analyzing the function of the behavior when there is one undesirable behavior and it occurs consistently. Figure 3.1 provides an ABC data sheet where escape is the undesirable behavior. The potential problem with an ABC analysis is the large amount of data collected, making it difficult to summarize and evaluate. For instance, in Figure 3.1, while there are nine instances of behavior, it is hard to look at the information on the data sheet and tell what the function of the behavior is or to determine a pattern to the behavior. And these are data for only one day. Similar data over a 10-day period would be even more difficult to evaluate.

Key Point Question 4: How Should Interviews be Used in Determining the Function of the Behavior?

The first step in performing a functional assessment is to conduct an in-depth interview with teachers and other staff as well as parents and other direct caregivers. Interviewing the student may also be appropriate in many instances. There are a number of structured interview formats available (Dunlap, Kern Dunlap, Clarke, & Robbins, 1991; Kern, Dunlap, Clarke, & Childs, 1995; O'Neill et al., 1997), which assist in identifying target and available alternative replacement behaviors, setting events commonly associated with incidences of undesirable behavior, and observed social and environmental consequences of behaviors. The primary purpose of interview data is to begin to develop hypotheses about behavioral functions of undesirable behavior being exhibited by the student. Taking the time to carefully interview will also assist teachers and others in examining their own actions as they relate to undesirable student behaviors. It is with the interview that the intervention and training process actually begins. Table 3.3 lists important questions for a functional assessment interview. At this point in the functional assessment process, it is also

Student: Hubert

Behavior: Escape Behavior

Operational Definition: Any behavior that involves leaving the table such as pushing away from the table with arms or legs, sliding out of the chair, standing up and turning away from the workstation, and crawling or climbing under or over the table (Bennett, Reichow, & Wolery, 2011).

Date	Antecedent	Behavior	Consequence
2/1	Teacher cue	Left table	Physical prompt to return
2/1	No attention	Crawled under table	Verbal prompt to return
2/1	Given work	Slide out of chair	Physical prompt to return
2/1	Teacher cue	Pushed away from table	Teacher ignored behavior
2/1	Given work	Turned away from table	Verbal prompt to return
2/1	No attention	Climbed over table	Teacher ignored behavior
2/1	Teacher cue	Pushed away from table	Verbal prompt to return
2/1	Teacher cue	Crawled under table	Teacher ignored behavior
2/1	Given work	Climbed over table	Verbal prompt to return to seat

Figure 3.1. ABC Data Sheet.

Table 3.3
Questions for a Functional Assessment Interview

---

1. List, describe, and prioritize behavior(s) of concern.
2. What do you think causes the behavior (e.g., what are the antecedents)?
3. What do you think is the function of the behavior?
4. How often do these behaviors occur?
5. Is there any circumstance under which the behavior does not occur?
6. Is there any circumstance under which the behavior always occurs?
7. Does the behavior occur more often during certain times of the day?
8. Does the behavior occur in response to the number of people present?
9. Does the behavior occur only with certain people?
10. Does the behavior occur only during certain subjects?
11. Could the behavior be related to any skills deficit?
12. What observable events signal that the behavior is about to occur?
13. What one thing could you do that would likely make the undesirable behavior occur?
14. What are the consequences of the behavior?

Adapted from Dunlap, Kern Dunlap, Clarke, and Robbins, (1991); and O'Neill et al. (1997).

important for the interventionist to think about potential medical issues that may be contributing to undesirable behavior. If medical conditions are present (e.g., sleep disorders, allergies, dietary, etc.), educators and parents will need to work closely with medical practitioners in addressing the problems. The interview should also attempt to identify other ecological and historical variables that commonly contribute to the undesirable behavior of students, such as the teacher's behavioral history with the student, academic difficulties, inconsistent past use of behavioral interventions, and significant family variables such as history of domestic violence, abuse, or neglect.

Key Point Question 5: How Should Direct Observations be Used in Determining the Function of the Behavior?

Following the interview, systematic observation should be conducted using systems designed to contribute to hypothesis formation and validation. These systems may include a variety of direct observation methods including ABC data-collection sheets (Cipani, 1993) scatter plots (Touchette, MacDonald, & Langer, 1985), and functional assessment observations systems (O'Neill et al., 1997).

Functional Assessment Observation Form

Name: Joe

Starting Date: 3-16   Ending Date: 3-17

Behaviors: Slap Others, Spit (on desk), Scream, Demand/Request, Difficult Task, Transitions, Interruption, Alone (no attention)

Predictors: Marsha, Bill, John

Perceived Functions

Get/Obtain: Attention, Desired Item/Activity, Self-Stimulation

Escape/Avoid: Demand/Request, Activity ( ), Person

Other/Don't Know, Ignore

Actual Conseq.: Block/Redirect, Comment (if nothing happened in period, write initials)

Time	Slap Others	Spit (on desk)	Scream	Demand/Request	Interruption	Alone (no attention)	Marsha	Bill	John	Attention	Demand/Request	Other/Don't Know	Ignore	Block/Redirect
8:50–9:35 Reading	1 11	2 10	1 11	1 11	1 11	2 10	1 11	1 11		2 10	1 11	2 10	1 11	2-read on own. 1-read on own
9:40–10:25 Lang Arts	3 4 5 12 13		12	3 4 5 12 13	3 4 5 12 13		3 4 5 12 13				3 4 5 12 13		3 4 5 12 13	
10:30–11:15 Choir		14												MJ.
11:20–12:05 Math	6 7		6 7	6 7	14	6 7	6 7			14	6 7	14	6 7	14-seat work
12:05–12:50 Lunch														
12:55–1:40 Social Studies	8 15		8 8 15	8 15		8 15	8 15				8 15		8 15	B.W.
1:45–2:30 Science	17	9	16 17	17	16	9		16 17		9	17 16	9 16	17	J.S.
2:35–3:20 P.E.														
Totals	13	4	9											

Events: 1 2 3 4 5 6 7 8 9 10 11 12 13 14 15 16 17 18 19 20 21 22 23 24 25

Date: 3/16   3/17

Figure 3.2. Example of a Completed Functional Assessment Observation Form.

The Functional Assessment Observation (FAO) form (O'Neill et al., 1997) is useful for collecting direct observation data. Figure 3.2 provides an example of the FAO form from O'Neill et al. (1997) for a student named Joe. In this example, data have been collected over two days (3-16 and 3-17). The first section of the form lists the time frames for data collection (in this example, it is class sessions). The second section lists undesirable behaviors (slapping others, spitting, and screaming). The third section lists predictors (e.g., antecedents) for the behavior. The fourth section has the perceived function of the behavior (get/obtain or escape/avoid). The fifth section lists the consequences. Then there is a section for comments. At the bottom of the form, there is a section for scoring frequency per day. The first time an undesirable behavior occurs, the appropriate boxes are marked with a number 1. For the occurrence, a number 1 is marked in each of the behavior, predictor, perceived function, and consequence sections of the form. In this example, the first occurrence was screaming, which happened during reading class. The predictor was a demand/request, and the staff person was Marsha. The perceived function was to escape the demand/request. The consequence was that Joe was redirected. Then the number 1 in the events section was crossed off. Then each occurrence of the undesirable behavior was marked with a 2, then a 3, and so on. In this example, there were nine occurrences of undesirable behavior during the first day. During the second day, the first occurrence in this example was scored as a 10. This allowed an overlay of data on the observation form so that patterns of behavior could more easily be analyzed.

In Figure 3.2, clear patterns for the undesirable behavior are evident. First, the slapping and screaming behaviors often occurred together, which suggests that they are members of the same response class and serve the same function (escape from demand/requests). The consequence was that staff would block the behavior and redirect the student. The spitting behavior occurred when Joe was alone or not receiving attention, and the perceived function was to get attention. The consequence was that staff would ignore the behavior. Another clear pattern was that no incidents of undesirable behavior occurred during choir, PE classes, or lunch times. This information is just as important as knowing when undesirable behavior is occurring because it allows analysis of what is happening during these times so that Joe does not have to engage in undesirable behaviors. This understanding can help lead to positive and proactive interventions in other classes.

Key Point Question 6: How Should Systematic Manipulations be Used in Determining the Function of the Behavior?

One way to develop and/or verify hypothesized functions of behavior is to engage in functional analysis, also referred to as systematic manipulations (O'Neill et al., 1997). Functional analysis has been differentiated from functional assessment as a process in which the identified variables are directly manipulated in order to verify or clarify hypothesized relationships. The direct manipulations are conducted in the context of reversal or alternating treatment designs and have been referred to as experimental analysis or hypothesis testing (Dunlap et al., 1993). For instance, it could be hypothesized that when a teacher stands within one foot of Immanuel and gives him a directive, he becomes aggressive. In order to test this hypothesis, the teacher could alternate standing within one foot of Immanuel and then farther away while giving him directives. By doing this, the teacher can evaluate whether he does become aggressive when she is within one foot but does not when she is farther away. Table 3.4 provides guidelines for conducting a systematic manipulation in a functional analysis.

Table 3.4
Guidelines for Conducting Functional Analysis Manipulations

A: Identify specific variables to be assessed during manipulations.
B: Determine the level of risk that may be involved.
C: Ensure that relevant variables can be controlled and manipulated.
D: Obtain appropriate reviews and approvals.
E: Have enough staff available to maintain safety during sessions.
F: Determine specific criteria for terminating sessions if needed.
G: Consider the use of protective equipment for individuals and/or teaching/support staff.
H: Consider using precursor behaviors as signals for terminating sessions.
I: Employ appropriate data collection and design procedures

Key Point Question 7: How Do You Determine Replacement Behaviors That Serve the Same Function as the Undesirable Behaviors?

The primary goal of functional assessment is to identify the function of undesirable behavior. Once the function of the behavior is understood, it is possible to effectively develop strategies that replace undesirable behaviors, with more adaptive alternative behaviors (also known as skill-building or replacement behaviors). When the intervention is based on the function of the undesirable behavior the general strategy is to both weaken the maintaining consequence and strengthen a positive skill building behavior that services the same function (Mace, Yankanich, & West, 1989). For example, if Freda is engaging in the behavior of disrupting a class in order to get teacher attention, a replacement behavior could be teaching Freda appropriate methods of getting teacher attention, such as asking a relevant question. The teacher could also give Freda attention at times when she is engaged in her work, which would make it less necessary for Freda to engage in undesirable behaviors to get attention and would also reinforce Freda's on-task behavior.

All too often the intervention chosen is based on the topography of the behavior rather than the function of the behavior. For example, a teacher may send any student who curses (the topography) to the office. While this may be an effective intervention for some students, for students who are engaging in the behavior in order to escape from a difficult academic task, the intervention is ineffective due to the teacher inadvertently reinforcing the escape behavior. In this situation, the student will be more likely to curse in the future when presented with a difficult academic task.

The focus on teaching replacement behavior is proactive. In other words, the intervention takes place when the undesirable behavior is not occurring and is focused on making desirable behaviors more probable. This is in contrast to nonfunctional interventions, which are mainly focused on decreasing undesirable behavior (Carr, Robinson, & Palumbo, 1990). The problem with a focus on nonfunctional interventions is that while an undesirable behavior may be decreased, if the student does not have a desirable behavior to replace it with, then the student may engage in a different undesirable behavior that services the same function. For instance, if Mausolus hits his head in order to get staff attention and this undesirable behavior is eliminated through the use of punishment, then Mausolus still has no desirable way of getting staff attention. So he may then pound his head in order to get staff attention. Table 3.5 provides examples of replacement behaviors that serve the same function as the undesirable behaviors.

Table 3.5
Examples of Matching Interventions with Replacement Behaviors That Serve
the Same Function

Function of Behavior	Potential Interventions
Dawn becomes aggressive toward others when she doesn't understand teacher directions (escape behavior).	Teach how to ask for help when directions are not clear.
Kristin likes to receive attention from peers (get behavior) but greets them inappropriately, which evokes a negative response from her peers.	Teach appropriate greeting skills.
Johann excessively asks questions during class (get behavior, teacher attention).	Teach a self-management strategy for limited question asking and then self-recruited feedback for teacher attention and reinforcement.
Roald gets very anxious during tests and will cause commotion in the hallway before a test in class so that he is sent to the office (escape behavior).	Teach relaxation techniques in addition to test-taking skills.

In developing replacement behaviors, it is important that the replacement behavior is functionally equivalent to the undesirable behavior (it services the same function). The replacement behavior should:

1. Be as efficient for the student as the undesirable behavior (Horner, Sprague, O'Brien, & Tuesday Heathfield, 1990).
2. Is something that the student chooses or wants to do.
3. Is skill building for the student.

BEST PRACTICE RECOMMENDATIONS

1. The function of the undesirable behavior should be understood before developing an intervention.
2. Interventions should teach positive (or replacement) behaviors that serve the same function as the undesirable behavior so that

students have positive skills that they can use and do not have to rely on undesirable behaviors.

DISCUSSION QUESTIONS

1. Are their other functions of behavior other than to get or to avoid?
2. Do interventions have to be based on the function of the behavior to be successful?
3. How do you set up classroom rules when different students may be engaging in the same undesirable behavior but for different functions?
4. What is wrong with reducing undesirable behaviors?

CLASSROOM AND SCHOOL ACTIVITY

1. Observe different undesirable behaviors in a classroom and classify each behavior according to what you think its function is (to get or to avoid).
2. Ask the teacher and/or students in the class as to what they perceive the function of their undesirable behavior to be. See if their perceived function matches with yours.

REFERENCES

Bennett, K., Reichow, B., & Wolery, M. (2011). Effects of structured teaching on the behavior of young children with disabilities. *Focus on Autism and Other Developmental Disabilities, 26,* 143–152.

Burke, M. D., Hagan-Burke, S., & Sugai, G. (2003). The efficacy of function-based interventions for students with learning disabilities who exhibit escape-maintained problem behaviors: Preliminary results from a single-case experiment. *Learning Disability Quarterly, 26,* 15–25.

Carr, E. G., Robinson, S., & Palumbo, L. W. (1990). The wrong issue: Aversive versus nonaversive treatment. The right issue: Functional versus nonfunctional treatment. In A. C. Repp & N. N. Singh (Eds.), *Perspectives on the use of nonaversive and aversive interventions for persons with developmental disabilities* (pp. 361–379). Sycamore, IL: Sycamore Publishing Company.

Chandler, L. K., & Dahlquist, C. M. (2010). *Functional assessment: Strategies to prevent and remediate challenging behavior in school settings* (3rd ed.). Upper Saddle River, NJ: Merrill/Pearson.

Cipani, E. (1993). *The Cipani behavioral assessment and diagnostic system.* Bellevue, WA: Edmark Publishers.

Cipani, E., & Schock, K. M. (2011). *Functional behavioral assessment, diagnosis, and treatment: A complete system for education and mental health settings* (2nd ed.). New York: Springer Publishing.

Dunlap, G., Kern Dunlap, L., Clarke, S., & Robbins, F. R. (1991). Functional assessment, curricular revision, and severe behavior problems. *Journal of Applied Behavior Analysis, 24*, 387–397.

Dunlap, G., Kern, L., dePerczel, M., Clarke, S., Wilson, D., Childs, K. E., White R., & Falk, G. D. (1993). Functional analysis of classroom variables for students with emotional and behavioral disorders. *Behavioral Disorders, 18*, 275–291.

Filter, K. J., & Horner, R. H. (2009). Function-based academic interventions for problem behavior. *Education and Treatment of Children, 32*, 1–19.

Foster Johnson, L., & Dunlap, G. (1993). Using functional assessment to develop effective, individualized interventions for challenging behaviors. *Teaching Exceptional Children, 25*, 44–50.

Gresham, F. M. (1997). Social competence and students with behavioral disorders: Where we've been, where we are, and where we should go. *Education and Treatment of Children, 20*, 233–249.

Horner, R. H., Sprague, J. R., O'Brien, M., & Tuesday Heathfield, L. (1990). The role of response efficiency in the reduction of problem behaviors through functional equivalence training: A case study. *Journal of the Association for Persons with Severe Handicaps, 15*, 91–97.

Kern, L., Dunlap, G., Clarke, S., & Childs, K. E. (1995). Student-assisted functional assessment interview. *Diagnostique, 19*, 29–39.

Larson, P. K., & Maag, J. W. (1998). Applying functional assessment in general education classrooms: Issues and recommendations. *Remedial and Special Education, 19*, 338–349.

Mace, F. C., Yankovich, M. A., & West, B. (1989). Toward a methodology of experimental analysis and treatment of aberrant classroom behaviors. *Special Services in the Schools, 4*, 71–88.

O'Neill, R. E., Horner, R. H., Albin, R. W., Sprague, J. R., Storey, K., & Newton, S. J. (1997). *Functional assessment and program development for problem behavior: A practical handbook* (2nd ed.). Pacific Grove, CA: Brooks/Cole Publishing Company.

Touchette, P. E., MacDonald, R. F., & Langer, S. N. (1985). A scatter plot for identifying stimulus control of problem behavior. *Journal of Applied Behavior Analysis, 18*, 343–351.

Waller, R. J. (2009). *The teacher's concise guide to functional behavioral assessment.* Thousand Oaks, CA: Corwin Press.

Chapter 4

REINFORCEMENT

Key Point Questions

1. What is positive reinforcement?
2. What is negative reinforcement?
3. What are criticisms of using reinforcement?
4. What are applications of reinforcement?
5. What are guidelines for using reinforcement?
6. What are different types of reinforcement?
7. How do you use reinforcement to increase behaviors?
8. How do you use reinforcement to decrease behaviors?

WINDOW OF THE WORLD CASE STUDY 1

Hobbes is only in second grade and already is known as the terror of the school. He is defiant, a bully, and verbally and physically aggressive toward peers and staff. His academic work is poor as he generally refuses to do assignments and doesn't turn in homework at all. Needless to say, most of the teachers and staff, as well as many parents, want him out of the school and believe that he would be best served in a school for students with emotional disabilities. Stepping into this morass is Ms. Yathay, the no-nonsense inclusion specialist. She immediately conducted a functional assessment of the situation and chaired a student study team regarding Hobbes. From the functional assessment and student study report, it was clear that Hobbes engaged in the defiant and aggressive behaviors in order to escape from academic work, especially when he was expected to sit in his seat for more than 15 minutes. Both the bullying and the aggressive behaviors (multiple functions) serve to get peer and staff attention.

Based on these findings, Ms. Yathay implemented a multipronged intervention. First, a reading specialist implemented a direct instruction reading program (Carnine, Silbert, Kame'enui, & Tarver, 2006, 2010) for Hobbes and several other students who were having trouble with decoding skills. Second, every 10 minutes during his academic periods, the teacher used a variety of methods to give Hobbes (as well as other students) a chance to move about a bit. These included a quick stretch break, a short stand and answer academic question session where the teacher would ask students content questions for a minute or two, and a chance for Hobbes and other students to engage in activities such as passing out papers or getting materials ready.

Due to Hobbes's difficulty getting peer and staff attention appropriately, a variety of strategies were used to teach him appropriate social skills. First, a Skillstreaming (McGinnis & Goldstein, 1997) curriculum was implemented for the whole class (Hobbes was not the only student having difficulties in social interactions). Second, at the start of recess periods, the teacher provided Hobbes and two other students a role-playing session for specific social interactions most difficult for Hobbes (students in the class were rotated through this group).

As a result of these combined interventions, there was a remarkable change in Hobbes's behavior. Hobbes no longer engaged in escape behaviors during academic times, and, with the social skills instruction, he got along much better with his peers (and they with him and each other). Owing to these interventions, he started making friends both within and outside of school. There was no longer any discussion of sending Hobbes to a different setting or of him having an "emotional disability." In fact, his future now looks quite bright.

WINDOW OF THE WORLD CASE STUDY 2

Ferron is a middle-school student who is often off task and engaging in disruptive behaviors, such as making inappropriate comments about the academic content, making noises, and dropping things. Her teachers have tried a variety of interventions such as giving reprimands, sending her to the office, relaying notes to her parents, and asking her to behave. None of these things has worked, and at a teacher meeting, it is agreed that her behaviors are increasing rather than decreasing.

The teachers set up a meeting with the vice principal, who has the district school psychologist, Ms. Flannery, sit in on the meeting. The teachers say that they have tried everything they can think of and nothing has worked. The vice principal turns to Ms. Flannery and asks what she suggests that they do. Ms. Flannery asks the teachers what the function of the behaviors appears to be. After some discussion, they come to an agreement that it is to get teacher attention. Then she asks the teachers how often it occurs. After more discussion, the consensus is about four to five times in a 50-minute period.

Based on this information, Ms. Flannery suggests that the teachers have their smart phones set to vibrate every eight minutes in their pocket during class times with Ferron. When the phone vibrates, they are to praise or make a positive comment to Ferron about her work. Concurrently, they are to do the same for one or two other students. This allows for positive teacher attention to be delivered more frequently and also makes the class climate more positive for all of the students. As a result of this intervention, Ferron no longer has to engage in the disruptive behaviors to get teacher attention, and her academic work is increasing as she is being specifically reinforced for that work.

Key Point Question 1: What is Positive Reinforcement?

Positive reinforcement is an event or stimulus presented after a response has been performed that increased the frequency of the behavior it follows (Kazdin, 2001). In other words, positive reinforcement is a process. You can only see that reinforcement has happened when an individual's behavior increases following the delivery of the reinforcer. If the behavior doesn't increase, it isn't a reinforcer. For instance, if Humera lines up appropriately for recess and the teacher praises her ("Humera, I like the way you lined up right away for recess") and if the teacher's praise is reinforcing for Humera, then she will be more likely to line up appropriately in the future (an increase in her behavior).

Another way to analyze reinforcement is by arranging conditions under which a student gets things rather than is being given things. Though reward and reinforcement are sometimes used interchangeably, an important distinction to recognize is that students are rewarded, but behavior is reinforced. In other words, you can say something nice to a student and they may appreciate it, but that does not necessarily mean that a student's specific behavior will increase.

It is important to note that not all items or events are reinforcers for everyone. One student may like teacher praise, another not. One student may like choosing the order in which to do tasks, another may prefer that the teacher set the schedule. Once again, unless the behavior increases following the presentation of the stimulus or event, the stimulus or event is not a reinforcer.

It is important to understand that it is as easy to inadvertently reinforce undesirable as desirable behaviors. This is tied to the function of the student behavior. For instance, if Georgi is talking to a peer during a lecture and the function is to obtain teacher attention and the teacher says, "Georgi, you need to pay attention and not talk to others," then the teacher may be unwittingly reinforcing the talking behavior.

The determination to use positive reinforcement to change student behavior is both a philosophical and pragmatic decision. This determination stems from not only knowing reinforcement is effective, but also making a philosophical decision that reinforcement is a more desirable and humane way to change student behavior than the absence of any reinforcement or through the use of punishment.

Key Point Question 2: What is Negative Reinforcement?

Negative reinforcement is the contingent removal of an aversive stimulus immediately following a response that increases the future rate and/or probability of the response (Alberto & Troutman, 2009). The key words in this definition are **"increases"** and **"removal."** Both positive and negative reinforcement increase behavior. Negative reinforcement refers to the increase in the frequency of a response by removing an aversive event immediately after the response has been performed.

With positive reinforcement, when a student performs a behavior, the teacher gives the student something he or she likes to increase the behavior. With negative reinforcement, when a student performs a behavior, the teacher removes something that the student dislikes. For example, students work at a faster pace after their teacher states that she will relieve them of homework if they complete a certain amount of academic work in class (20 math problems correct). The homework is the negative reinforcer which is then removed following the desired behavior (completion of academic work). Table 4.1 provides more examples of negative reinforcement.

Table 4.1
Examples of Negative Reinforcement

1. Taking medicine to relieve a headache may be negatively reinforced by the termination of pain.
2. Nagging by parent may increase room cleaning by a child. The aversive event (parental nagging) is terminated by performing the behavior.
3. Leaving the house to escape from an argument from one's significant other.
4. Turning off an alarm to escape from a loud noise.
5. A student may have frequent outbursts during an assignment that he dislikes. The teacher may attempt to reduce outbursts by placing the student in a corner of the room. The student however, prefers isolation to doing the assignment.
6. Closing a window to shut off a draft.
7. Responding to a child to escape from the crying.
8. Turn on the heat to escape from the cold.
9. Putting on a seat belt in the car to end buzzer noise.
10. Student frequently complains that assignments are too difficult. Teacher responds to the complaints by consistently reducing the difficulty of the assignments. Complaints are negatively reinforced (by making the task easier), and teacher should expect complaints to increase.
11. Leaving the room when someone is rude or critical because this behavior has ended other aversive conversations.
12. Teacher informs a class that those scoring 85% or better on assignments will not have to take the final exam. If the procedure is effective, the desired goal of improved performance on assignments will be achieved.

The use of the term "negative" often confuses people into misunderstanding that it means decreasing or punishing behavior (punishment is discussed in Chapter 5). However, both positive and negative reinforcement result in increases in behavior. An event is a negative reinforcer only if its removal after a response increases performance of that response. Negative reinforcement is not a judgment of something being good or bad. It is important to remember that negative reinforcement can produce desirable behavior. Negative reinforcement works because the student performs the behavior to escape the aversive stimulus.

Contrary to popular belief, many off-task and disruptive behaviors in classrooms are probably not maintained by teacher attention. Instead, students often use these behaviors to escape or avoid an instructional task (negative reinforcement). There are three questions to ask in order to determine whether negative reinforcement contingencies are controlling undesirable behaviors:

1. Does the behavior result in the termination or postponement of specific teacher requests, instructional demands, or instructional tasks, activities, or materials? For example, the teacher tells Kristin to get her reading book out, and Kristin makes an obscene remark to the teacher. The teacher then sends Kristin to the office for cursing. The specific teacher request (to get the reading book out) has been terminated.

2. Is the student not competent with regard to the specific instructions, tasks, teacher requests, or materials, identified in 1 above? For instance, Humera is a kindergarten student, and on the first day of school (which is also Humera's first day in any school), the teacher instructs her to line up for recess. Humera does not understand what it means to "line up for recess," so she does not respond and continues to sit at her desk.

3. Does the problem behavior occur more frequently under those specific content areas, tasks, materials, or teacher requests identified in 1 and 2 above (in contrast to other content areas or tasks where the student is more capable academically)? For example, Betsy has trouble with math, and during math class, if she is called to the board to complete a problem, she will often engage in undesirable behavior. In contrast, Betsy is very good in reading and language arts, and in this class, when she is called to the board to diagram sentences, she is very enthusiastic and never displays any undesirable behavior.

Key Point Question 3: What are Criticisms of Using Reinforcement?

The use of reinforcement has not been without its criticism. Common concerns are:

Reinforcement is just bribery. They should just do it because it is good for them. Why should that student get something special when other students don't?

First, are reinforcement and bribery the same thing? No! They do have similarity in that you are trying to encourage a student to behave in a certain manner by offering a reward. The difference is that with bribery, the student is being influenced to perform a dishonest or an illegal act. Helping a student to learn academic and other skills they need to be successful in school, and in other environments, is certainly not dishonest or illegal; indeed, it is the main role of teachers.

It is a common belief that students should do something because it is good for them. However, we all work under some system of reinforcement. Not everyone is "intrinsically" motivated for everything that they do. How many people would continue to work on the job if they weren't paid? However, reinforcement can be used to develop intrinsic and desirable behaviors in students, which is a good thing (Cameron & Pierce, 1994; Eisenberger & Cameron, 1996).

Third, why should one student get something special when others don't? This brings us to the issue of developing supports and instruction specifically for the needs of an individual student. One student may need some additional reinforcement to do something while another student doesn't. This doesn't mean that you can't fade the reinforcement later, but if the student needs reinforcement to acquire a skill, it is better for the student to learn the skill using positive reinforcement rather than not learning it. In addition, the reinforcement systems discussed in later chapters (such as the good behavior game) can be used to increase the desirable behaviors of all students.

Key Point Question 4: What Are Applications of Reinforcement?

The systematic use of reinforcement involves different reinforcement schedules. Just because a student does a behavior (whether desirable or undesirable), it doesn't mean that he or she is going to be reinforced every time.

Continuous reinforcement. On this schedule, every instance of the behavior is reinforced. For instance, if a student is on a continuous reinforcement, every time that he or she engages in a specific behavior, such as turning in homework on time, he or she would receive a reinforcer for each occurrence. Continuous reinforcement schedules are not necessarily bad. In fact, they may be appropriate at times such as for initial skill acquisition. When a student is first learning how to do something, he or she may be unsure of him or herself or may not understand the reinforcement contingencies associated with what he or she is doing. Remember that continuous reinforcement generates a high rate of behavior. When a student is first learning how to do something, you usually want him or her to do it repeatedly so you can determine whether he or she knows how to perform the behavior; therefore, delivering continuous reinforcement may be necessary for the behavior you want to increase.

Once a student has learned how to do something, he or she probably doesn't need to be reinforced all the time for it. You can then go to intermittent reinforcement schedules for skill proficiency and maintenance. A good way to fade teacher-provided reinforcers is by pairing those reinforcers with naturally occurring reinforcers. For example, a young student may not initially understand the connection between a behavior (putting dishes away after snack) and the reinforcer (a star on his or her chart, which can be turned in for a tangible reinforcer). In this case, the teacher could pair praise for putting dishes away with giving the star, then immediately exchange the star for the tangible reinforcer.

Fixed ratio. A fixed ratio reinforcement schedule refers to reinforcement being delivered based on some frequency of responses. For example, a student might be reinforced every third time that he or she turns in homework (FR3). There are several advantages to using a fixed ratio schedule, such as (a) you often get a fast response from the student, (b) the schedule is highly predictable to the student, and (c) because it is based on frequency, there is no limit to receiving reinforcers. Sometimes, though, a student pauses after reinforcement is delivered as he or she knows that a certain number of responses have to occur before he or she gets reinforced again.

Variable ratio. In a variable ratio reinforcement schedule, the frequency of responses necessary to get a reinforcer changes. From our example above, the student may get reinforced after one time of turning in homework, then after five times, then three times, then four times, and so on. A variable ratio schedule can be powerful because the student doesn't know when he or she will be reinforced and thus is likely to continue to work hard in order to obtain the reinforcer. Some considerations in using a variable ratio schedule include: (a) you must always indicate the range of responses necessary to get a reinforcer (from the homework example, you probably don't want the student to have to turn in homework 50 times before getting reinforced; it would be better to keep the range small, such as one to five times), (b) you need to make sure that there is a change in predictability (with a variable ratio schedule, you don't want the student to know when he or she is going to get reinforced), (c) you don't get pauses as with fixed ratio, and (d) behavior under control of a variable ratio schedule is extinguished more slowly than a fixed ratio schedule.

Fixed interval. A fixed interval schedule refers to delivering a reinforcer after same time period, such as every two minutes or every 30 seconds. An advantage to fixed interval schedules is that they are easy to use. You can easily set a timer to go off every 10 minutes and deliver reinforcement then.

Variable interval. A variable interval schedule is also time based. However, instead of reinforcement being delivered after the same interval period each time, the interval varies. For instance, reinforcement for on-task behavior could be delivered after 2 minutes, then after 10 minutes, then 6 minutes, then 11 minutes, and so on. Resistance to extinction is greater with intermittent reinforcement than with a fixed interval schedule.

Key Point Question 5: What Are Guidelines for Using Reinforcement?

This section provides general guidelines that make the use of reinforcement more effective. Some common mistakes made in the use of reinforcement are outlined in Table 4.2.

1. *Only reinforce correct responses.* Recognize that reinforcement strengthens the behavior that it follows; don't want to inadvertently reinforce undesirable behaviors instead of desirable ones.
2. *If you provide instruction or assistance, also provide reinforcement.* Reinforcement strengthens the behavior, so make sure that you deliver the reinforcement after the student performs the response correctly. Since you are delivering instruction on some-

Table 4.2
Common Errors in Delivering Reinforcement:

---

1. The perception error: "Everybody likes. . . ." To use reinforcement effectively, you must know what reinforces a student's behavior. The perception error occurs when you perceive that something will reinforce a student's behavior when in fact it won't.
2. No one reinforcer works for all students. Different students may have different reinforcers.
3. Not making reinforcement contingent on behavior.
4. Delaying reinforcement.
5. A "reward" may not be a reinforcer. Reinforcement is in the eye of the beholder.
6. Expecting too much behavior change before delivering reinforcement. It is much better to reinforce small changes than big changes (shaping).
7. Combining reinforcement and corrective feedback at the same time. "You did good, but. . . . " The student will remember only what came after the "but."

---

thing that is difficult for a student, you want to be sure and increase that behavior. Make sure that the reinforcement comes after the instruction and after the correct performance. Some general rules concerning the use of reinforcement for correct performance are presented in Table 4.3.

3. *Use a positive tone.* Vary your tone from warm and pleasant to strong and enthusiastic. The degree of reinforcement should match the importance of the response.

4. *Be brief.* You want to be brief because you do not want to interrupt the student and take them off task or to take time out of instruction.

5. *Vary what you say.* You don't always have to say "good job." It is easy to get in a rut of saying the same word or phrase over and over and over and over, so be sure to vary your praise.

6. *Make sure that you are reinforcing.* You want to be pleasant and positive so that the student you are working with will want to interact with you and receive instruction from you. This will make the praise reinforcing and other reinforcers less necessary. So be nice!

7. *Do not reinforce simply attending to the task.* You want to reinforce correct performance (i.e., outcome). You want to reinforce. If you only reinforce attending to the task (i.e., process), the correct performance may not increase. If you reinforce correct performance, attending to the task behavior will improve. Of course, it is easier to reinforce on-task student behavior, and this is okay, though on-task behavior does not necessarily lead to outcomes.

Table 4.3
General Rules Concerning the Use of Reinforcement for Correct Performance.

1. Select a reinforcing event on the basis of initial evaluation of the student and apparent function of events used in previous instructional trials.
2. Pair all reinforcers for step completion with the naturally occurring consequences for correct performance.
   A) Delivery the reinforcer immediately on completion of the task.
   B) Deliver reinforcement only when the student is attending to the task.
   C) Deliver reinforcement at the same time as assistance on the next step so that the student continues through the task without interruption (i.e., make it short and sweet).
3. Do not establish any cues other than the task and setting that signal an increased probability of reinforcement.

Adapted from Bellamy, Horner, and Inman (1979).

8. Fade external reinforcement as soon as possible. As a general rule, you want to eliminate external reinforcement. This isn't always possible or desirable, but it is a good goal.

Key Point Question 6: What Are Different Types of Reinforcement?

Reinforcers may be activities (being first in line, having lunch with teacher, being the flag raiser), social (phone call to parents, student of the day), or a tangible item (food, sticker, book). Reinforcers may be delivered to individual students, groups of students, or a whole class.

Participation and instruction in school settings is often activity based. Activity based means that a chain or sequence of behaviors are performed, which produce an outcome that is functional for the individual (e.g., the sequence of getting ready for PE class includes going to the locker room, getting dressed in PE clothes, going to the gym, participating in the class activities, going back to locker room, showering, putting clothes on, and going to the next class). Thus, it is possible to reinforce at different points in the sequence and/or at the end of the chain of behaviors. The activities can also often serve as reinforcers for students.

There are a variety of ways to select reinforcers for students. One simple way to find out what a student likes is to ask them! When students have a choice for their reinforcer, they are more likely to "buy in" to the intervention. However, for some students, you may need a more structured interview to help the student think through the different reinforcers available (Raschke, 1981; Schanding, Tingstrom, & Sterling Turner, 2009). If the student is not able to easily tell you what he or she likes (as with younger students or students with severe disabilities), someone else who knows them well might be able to. Family members and friends can be good resources. Besides interviews, direct observations may be useful in assessing reinforcement preference. These observations may involve recording foods the student prefers at mealtimes, the type of activities they prefer to engage in, or with whom they prefer to interact.

Key Point Question 7: How Do You Use Reinforcement to Increase Behaviors?

Externally Delivered Reinforcement

Timing. The timing of reinforcement delivery is important. Generally, reinforcement must be immediate if it is to be successful. The longer the delay between the behavior and the delivery of reinforcement, the more likely the student will not understand the connection. With a long delay, it is also possible that something else may happen in the meantime; consequently, the teacher will inadvertently reinforce an undesirable behavior instead of the intended desirable behavior.

Contingency. This is probably the most important consideration for delivering reinforcement. Is the reinforcement contingent on what the student does? Contingency means that when the student does a certain behavior (such as lining up quickly and correctly at the end of recess), he or she gets a specific reinforcer (i.e., a token from the playground supervisor). If he or she is not ready on time and lined up correctly, then he or she doesn't get the token.

One way to help make the connection between the reinforcement and the behavior is to label the reinforcement contingencies. In other words, tell the student why he or she is being reinforced. For example, if a student lines up quickly and correctly after recess, the supervisor could say, "That was a great job of lining up. Way to go! Here is a token for each student who did so."

The reinforcer should only be given when the specific behavior occurs. In the prior example, if a student doesn't line up quickly and correctly (say he or she was late or did not stand in the line), then he or she needs corrective feedback ("In order to get a token, you need to have lined up on time and be standing in the line") rather than reinforcement.

Predictability. Can the student you are working with predict when he or she is going to get reinforced? Usually you want the reinforcement to be predictable rather than unpredictable. This relates to the point above concerning contingency. If the student cannot predict when he or she is going to get reinforced, he or she may not consider it contingent on his or her behavior, and he or she may miss the connection.

Density of reinforcement. When a student is learning a new skill (learning long division) or engaging in a new behavior (turning in homework), it is best to favor dense reinforcement (a lot of praise and the use of activity or other reinforcers) versus thin reinforcement (only praising and using other reinforcers occasionally). Though the teacher may eventually want to fade the reinforcement (not eliminate it), it is important to initially make sure that the student is getting enough reinforcement so that the desirable behavior is increased.

Satiation. A reinforcer may lose its power over time. For instance, a student may like salted peanuts a lot but after a few handfuls not want anymore. This is known as satiation. At this point, something to drink would probably be more reinforcing than another handful of peanuts. It is important that different reinforcers be used and that they are mixed so that the person doesn't satiate on one reinforcer. Some ways to prevent satiation are: (a) have different reinforcers available for different tasks, (b) alternate reinforcers during instructional sessions, (c) gradually decrease the size or amount of the reinforcer, (d) be sure that the reinforcer being used is not something the student has easy access to at other times, and (e) change the pool of reinforcers to choose from;you don't want the student to always pick the same reinforcer and possibly become satiated.

Premack Principle. The Premack Principle is based on using higher probability behaviors to reinforce lower probability behaviors. For instance, completion of a task such as finishing math work (lower probability behavior) can be increased by following it with a snack in the break area (higher probability behavior). This is also known as the "Grandmother Rule," as in, "You have to eat your vegetables before you get any dessert."

General comment. Remember that you **want** the student to be reinforced for desirable behaviors. A common mistake is when the instructor thinks that the student should have to work harder or do something extra to get reinforced. In this case, the teacher tries to make it as difficult as possible for the student to get the reinforcer by continuously raising the ante. What usually happens, in this case, is that the student becomes frustrated or angry because he or she is not receiving the expected reinforcement. This results in the student not doing what the instructor expects of him or her, creating a "Catch-22" situation. Therefore, be sure that instructors are delivering reinforcement often enough.

Self-Delivered Reinforcement

Probably the most efficient way to deliver reinforcement is to have the students do it themselves! Then an instructor doesn't have to stop instruction to deliver the reinforcer, and the student is more in control of his or her own behavior. Chapter 9 provides information on self-management strategies that are effective for self-delivery of reinforcement.

Key Point Question 7: How Do You Use Reinforcement to Decrease Behaviors?

Besides increasing desirable behaviors, reinforcement can be used to decrease undesirable behaviors. For instance, if a student talks out during class (with the function being to get teacher attention), the teacher could praise the student when he or she raises his or her hand to ask a question, thus reinforcing the desirable behavior which could make the undesirable behavior less likely to occur. The following three methods use reinforcement to decrease behaviors.

Differential Reinforcement of Incompatible Behavior (DRI)

One way to decrease undesirable behaviors is to reinforce a behavior that is desirable **and** incompatible with the undesirable behavior. For example, if students are out of their seats, then reinforcing in-seat behavior would make the undesirable behavior less likely to occur.

Considerations in using DRI procedures include:

1. Make sure that the behavior reinforced is incompatible with the undesirable behavior. For instance, it is not possible to be out of a seat and in a seat at the same time.
2. The behavior selected for reinforcement is functional for the student. For example, the student is reinforced by getting to go to a computer and work on a fun program for vocabulary words.
3. The student knows how to perform the behavior.
4. In addition, the reinforcer chosen is stronger or more powerful than the reinforcement that the student gets for performing the undesirable behavior.

Differential Reinforcement of Other Behavior (DRO)

With DRO, the student gets reinforced when the undesirable behavior does not occur. For instance, if a student is not out of his or her seat when the timer goes off, then he or she would receive a reinforcer. When using DRO, it is important that the reinforcement interval selected corresponds to the student behavior so that he or she gets frequent reinforcement. For eliminating talking out behavior, a teacher might employ a DRO 10 (minute) schedule of reinforcement. If the student does not talk out during the 10 minutes, then he or she would get reinforced, and a new 10-minute cycle is started. When using DRO, it is important that the teacher select a reinforcement interval that corresponds to the student's undesirable behavior so that he or she gets frequent reinforcement. For instance, if a student talks out every 45 seconds, using an interval of one minute to reinforce him or her would not be effective because he or she would always talk out before the one-minute interval and never get reinforced. So, the teacher would want to choose an interval of less than 45 seconds so the student gets reinforced for not talking out. Once the student is consistently being reinforced, it would be possible to gradually increase the interval length.

A problem with DRO procedures is that, though the student may not engage in the undesirable behavior, such as talking out, he or she may engage in a different behavior, which is also undesirable (such as dropping a pencil onto the floor). Inadvertently, the teacher may end up reinforcing a different undesirable behavior. So DRO procedures don't really teach the student a specific skill to replace the undesirable behavior.

Differential Reinforcement of Low Rates of Behavior (DRL)

Another way to decrease behavior, but not eliminate it, is to reinforce low rates of the undesirable behavior. DRL is for when you want to decrease a behavior but not eliminate it completely (e.g., a student who is constantly asking questions during a class period). Asking questions per se is not a bad thing. Asking 15 questions a class period would be too much, though. A teacher could set a limit of three questions per period for that student and then reinforce the student each period he or she asked three questions or fewer.

BEST PRACTICE RECOMMENDATIONS

1. Reinforcement can be used to teach new behaviors or strengthen behaviors the student already has.
2. Reinforcement is the key to any intervention procedure and should always be included.
3. Negative reinforcement plays an important role (often unrecognized) in student/teacher interactions.
4. Don't assume that your "reinforcer" is in fact reinforcing behavior.
5. Reinforcement is the most effective way to change any behavior.

DISCUSSION QUESTIONS

1. Do teachers have a positive effect on students because their motives and intentions are positive? Is having a positive attitude and using positive reinforcement the same thing?
2. Should students be expected to engage in desirable behavior without the use of reinforcers?
3. Are strategies besides the use of reinforcement as effective or even more effective for changing student behavior?

CLASSROOM AND SCHOOL ACTIVITY SUGGESTIONS

1. Visit a classroom and use frequency counts for scoring the number and type of reinforcers occurring in the classroom.
2. As a teacher, record the number of times you deliver praise or other reinforcers to students.

REFERENCES

Alberto, P. A., & Troutman, A. C. (2009). *Applied behavior analysis for teachers* (8th ed.). Englewood Cliffs, NJ: Prentice-Hall.

Bellamy, G. T., Horner, R. H., & Inman, D. P. (1979). *Vocational habilitation of severely retarded adults: A direct service technology.* Baltimore, MD: University Park Press.

Cameron, J., & Pierce, W. D. (1994). Reinforcement, reward, and intrinsic motivation: A meta-analysis. *Review of Educational Research, 64,* 363–423.

Carnine, D. W., Silbert, J., Kame'enui, E. J., & Tarver, S. G. (2006). *Teaching struggling and at-risk readers: A direct instruction approach.* Upper Saddle River, NJ: Merrill Prentice-Hall.

Carnine, D. W., Silbert, J., Kame'enui, E. J., & Tarver, S. G. (2010). *Direct instruction reading* (5th ed.). Upper Saddle River, NJ: Merrill Prentice-Hall.

Eisenberger, R., & Cameron, J. (1996). Detrimental effects of reward: Reality or myth? *American Psychologist, 51,* 1153–1166.

Kazdin, A. E. (2001). *Behavior modification in applied settings* (6th ed.). Belmont, CA: Wadsworth/Thomson Learning.

McGinnis, E., & Goldstein, A. P. (1997). *Skillstreaming the elementary school child: New strategies and perspectives for teaching prosocial skills.* Champaign, IL: Research Press.

Raschke, D. (1981). Designing reinforcement surveys: Let the student choose the reward. *Teaching Exceptional Children, 14,* 92–96.

Schanding, G. T., Tingstrom, D., & Sterling Turner, H. (2009). Evaluation of stimulus preference assessment methods with general education students. *Psychology in the Schools, 46,* 89–99.

Chapter 5

PUNISHMENT

Key Point Questions

1. What is Type 1 punishment?
2. What is Type 2 punishment?
3. What are criticisms of using punishment?
4. What are applications of punishment?
5. What are guidelines for using punishment?
6. What are different types of punishment?

WINDOW OF THE WORLD CASE STUDY 1

Thurisind is a kindergarten student who has limited English skills and is new to a school environment. Transitions (from task to task or setting to setting) are difficult for him, and he often becomes aggressive toward staff during these times. In addition, he will often grab toys or other objects away from his peers and run to another part of the classroom to play with them.

His kindergarten teacher, Ms. Epictetus, decides on several different interventions to help Thurisind. For transition times, an antecedent cue procedure is introduced where a picture is shown to Thurisind shortly before the transition is to occur (one drawing depicting him moving from task to task and another one for setting to setting). A token is then placed next to the picture, and he is told that when he moves or changes, he will receive the token. These situations are practiced with him at the beginning of the day and at other times through-out the day so that he understands the contingencies and has multiple opportunities to practice and be reinforced. Tokens can be immedi-ately turned in for a small snack (such as a few raisins or nuts) or can be saved for other items such as a sticker, special tasks (helping the teacher), or materials (using crayons). If he does become aggressive during transition times, he is told "no hitting" in a calm voice, his hands are held in his lap by the teacher, and the teacher turns away from him until he is calm for 15 seconds. At that point, he is redirect-ed to the transition.

When Thurisind grabs toys or objects from his peers, he is immedi-ately blocked from leaving the area, he is told "no taking things from others" in a calm voice, a token is removed from his holder, he is directed to return the object, and he is not allowed to move from the area until he returns the object. Once he returns the object, he is redi-rected to other objects that are not currently being used. In addition, because this is sometimes a problem for other students as well, there is a brief lesson on appropriately asking others for sharing objects dur-ing circle time three times a week (McGinnis & Goldstein, 2003).

WINDOW OF THE WORLD CASE STUDY 2

Mr. Fogg wants to be a popular teacher with his students. He and they often joke around with each other during class time, and the dis-cussion often gets off topic from world cultures to recent movies, base-ball, and music videos. His last evaluation by the principal was not very positive, leading Mr. Fogg to consult with his mentor teacher, Mr. Palin, who is known as a respected but "tough" teacher by his students. Mr. Palin observed Mr. Fogg's class several times and came up with a series of recommendations.

First, it is obvious that Mr. Fogg is being taken off task with the stu-dent joking and off-topic discussions. Mr. Palin recommends that Mr. Fogg ignore all jokes and off-topic discussions (extinction) and that he continue with his instruction. Second, Mr. Palin suggests that Mr. Fogg implement a token economy for students completing work. This involves individual as well as group work using the good behavior game (see Chapter 7) for reinforcing group work that students have often failed to complete. When a group gets a certain amount of points, it can choose from a menu of reinforcers (free time during the class period, bonus points for grades, complementary emails from Mr. Fogg to parents, etc.). Finally, Mr. Palin advises a response cost procedure with the token economy, where students are fined for not completing individual work as well as for not completing group work. This uses peer pressure for all students to complete group work both for the reinforcement as well as for avoiding the response cost.

These combined procedures have an immediate positive impact as now there is direct reinforcement for desirable behaviors (on-task behavior and task completion) as well as punishment for the occurrence of undesirable behaviors (non-task completion). The principal is impressed with the turnaround as both the social atmosphere and the academic performance has improved in Mr. Fogg's classroom.

Key Point Question 1: What is Type One Punishment?

Type 1 punishment is the presentation of a stimulus or an event after a behavior that decreases the frequency of the behavior (Kazdin, 2001). Punishment can be said to have occurred only if the student's rate of emitting the behavior has been reduced. Punishment, like reinforcement, is defined solely by its effect on behavior (that it decreases the behavior). If the behavior doesn't decrease, it isn't a punisher. For instance, Carlos, a kindergarten student, is aggressive toward peers when they get too close to his work materials. When aggressive, his teacher, Ms. Muraviov, blocks his hits, puts his hands on his desk, and tells him, "Carlos, there is no hitting in school." This serves as a punisher as Carlos's hitting behavior decreases.

Just like with reinforcement, it is important to note that not all items or events are punishing for all students. One student may find a teacher reprimand punishing while another student may not. Once again, unless the behavior decreases following the presentation of the stimulus or event, the stimulus or event is not a punisher.

Also like reinforcement, it is as easy to inadvertently punish desirable as undesirable behaviors. This is tied to the function of the student behavior. For example, if Colin blurts out an answer during math group because of this enthusiasm for the topic and his teacher says, "Colin, it is not okay to talk unless I call on you," she may be punishing his enthusiasm for math and his wanting to answer questions in the future.

Punishment per se is not necessarily either a "good" or a "bad" thing. When combined with reinforcement and other positive interventions, the use of punishment can be an effective strategy in implementing positive behavior supports. The more effective the positive interventions are, the more effective and enhanced the mild and brief punishment procedures will be. As Horner (2002) has pointed out:

> It is important to acknowledge that punishment is a natural and ongoing part of life, and we need to better understand the role of punishment if we are to be successful in our efforts to engineer environments in which children and adults with deviant behavior are successful. Teachers, parents, employers, and friends in all parts of our society regularly deliver contingent punishers that result in reduction of specific responses. (p. 465).

Key Point Question 2: What is Type 2 Punishment?

Type 2 punishment is the removal of a stimulus or an event after a behavior that decreases the frequency of the behavior (Kazdin, 2001). With Type 2 punishment, when a student performs a behavior, the teacher removes something that the student likes. For example, if Molly is constantly raising her hand to ask questions (and she knows the answer) and the teacher decides that the function is to get teacher attention, the teacher could then ignore the hand raising. If Molly's hand raising then decreases (as the ignoring is punishing), then Molly's behavior was decreased by the removal of the stimulus (teacher attention) after the behavior.

Key Point Questions 3: What Are Criticisms of Using Punishment?

Perhaps the most important criticism is that punishment may not be the most effective way of changing student behavior for the better. Just eliminating an undesirable behavior does not necessarily mean that there will be an increase in desirable behavior. At best punishment just stops a behavior. Just stopping a behavior doesn't solve problems. As noted in Chapter 3, the function of the behavior must be addressed. Stopping one undesirable behavior, without providing the student

Table 5.1
Punishment Procedures Should be Accountable for Eight Basic Criteria:

1. The punishment should result in a durable reduction of undesirable behavior.
2. The reduction of undesirable behavior should generalize across the full range of people, places, times, and materials that the student will encounter as part of his or her normal daily routine.
3. The punishment should not involve the use of procedures that result in physical pain or tissue damage.
4. The procedures should be appropriate for use in regular school settings.
5. The procedures should always include systematic reinforcement and instruction of adaptive alternative behaviors.
6. The procedures used to reduce undesirable behavior should be adequately safeguarded against abuse by unskilled staff implementing procedures.
7. The technology should always include continuous monitoring, external observation, and review by a knowledgeable review panel.
8. The procedures to reduce undesirable behavior should be the least intrusive needed to be effective and in no case exceed normal community standards of appropriateness.

Adapted from Horner et al. (1990).

with a desirable behavior that serves the same function, will probably only replace the previous undesirable behavior with another undesirable behavior. By punishing undesirable behaviors without reinforcing or teaching a constructive alternative behavior, it will be easier for the student to engage in another undesirable behavior that serves the same function. Horner et al. (1990) provided eight basic criteria in which punishment procedures should be accountable (see Table 5.1).

With schools being educational institutions, it seems contradictory that students who engage in undesirable behaviors would be punished rather than receive instruction in how to behavior more productively (Jones & Jones, 2007). In other words, the use of punishment can inhibit learning. For example, the use of extra homework or academic activities (writing something over and over) as punishment may decrease student interest in these activities.

Punishment leads to narrow stimulus control, where the student will only refrain from engaging in the undesirable behavior when someone who could punish them is present. In this case, a student might do the undesirable behavior of bullying on the quad if a teacher is not present. In other words, generalization is poor when punishment alone is used. The student is unlikely to eliminate the undesirable behavior across settings, people, times, and/or behaviors.

Students who are punished often engage in escape or avoidance behaviors. Teachers often punish students and expect the student to stop the undesirable behavior when, in fact, it leads to escape behavior. For instance, most people do not want to be around a person who is punishing them, no matter what the situation is. Students may skip class or school in order to avoid being around that teacher, or they may engage in undesirable behaviors in order to be sent out of the presence of the teacher (a negative reinforcement paradigm). In other words, the teacher has become an aversive stimulus for the student.

With the use of punishment, the student is more likely to then follow the punishment with an aggressive or inappropriate response than with positive reinforcement. This means that the teacher must then deal with an additional undesirable behavior. The aggressive behavior may then serve as a negative reinforcer for the student being punished in that they are likely to be removed (escape) from the situation.

Maintenance is often poor with the use of punishment procedures. Often undesirable behaviors return when the punishment procedures are withdrawn, as the student may not engage in a desirable behavior that serves the same function.

With punishment there is often an emotional or a physiological arousal and side effects. For example, if Carmen hits Isabelle and the teacher holds Carmen's hands to her side, tells her "no hitting," and turns her head away from Carmen for one minute, Carmen's heart rate is likely to increase as well as her receiving an endorphin release, which can then inhibit Carmen's ability to learn for a time period afterward. These effects are then counterproductive to learning and the establishment of positive relations between the teacher and that student (and likely between other students as well who are observing the punishment).

There may be side effects to the punishment, such as emotional reactions (nervousness, crying, anger, etc.). The cues for punishment (teacher presence) may produce similar reactions in the absence of punishment. For instance, Mr. Legree is a stern, sour, unsmiling teacher who makes sarcastic comments to students when they answer a question wrong (often even when they get one right, such as, "I'm surprised that you answered that one correctly"). Students in his class are nervous that they will be called on, and when they are called on, they sweat, they become tense, and their thinking freezes. Even if students are not called on, they have these emotional and physical reactions going on during the class period.

Punishment may interfere with new learning. The student may be unresponsive to the social environment and less willing to engage in desirable academic and social behavior (why should I try when all I get is punishment). Furthermore, the use of punishment can serve as a modeling response, resulting in the punished students being more likely to use punishment themselves. Apart from this, the teacher who uses punishment is negatively reinforced for using punishment. For instance, when Luanna talks back to the teacher and is sent to the office, from the teacher's perspective, it is negative reinforcement (Luanna, the negative stimulus, is removed). Thus, there is the perpetuation of punishment, and the teacher is likely to repeatedly use punishment. In addition, from Luanna's perspective, it may also be a negative reinforcement paradigm (she is removed from the situation), so that in the future, she is more likely to engage in the talking back behavior.

Many types of aversive punishment procedures used with students, especially those with disabilities, have often been used with political prisoners and condemned by Human Rights groups. Examples of some of these aversive procedures are electric shock, plunged into ice water, verbal abuse, enforced standing, ammonia held under the nose, and hair pulling (Farmer & Stinson, 2009/2010; Repp & Singh, 1990). The use of these aversive punishment procedures is inappropriate to use with any student.

Key Point Questions 4: What Are Applications of Punishment?

A plethora of variables influence whether a punishment procedure will be effective:

1. Whether the punishment is implemented immediately after the undesirable behavior. The longer the delay between the undesirable behavior and the punishment, the less effective the punishment will be. For example, if a student engages in an undesirable behavior such as pushing another student right before school starts but then is sent to detention after school, then the delay will weaken the effect of the punishment.
2. The intensity of the punishment. The stronger or more aversive the punishment, the more effective it will be.
3. The schedule of the punishment. Punishment may be delivered on schedules just like with reinforcement (fixed or variable ratio and fixed or variable intervals).

4. Whether a desirable (e.g., an alternative or skill-building behavior) that serves the same function has been taught and reinforced. This is of critical importance.

Key Point Questions 5: What Are Guidelines for Using Punishment?

1. Punishment should be only short term. By definition, punishment should reduce the occurrence of the undesirable behavior. If this reduction is not occurring, then the stimulus or event is not actually a punisher, and its use should be immediately discontinued.
2. Punishment should only be used so that adaptive behavior can be taught to the student.
3. The punishment should be compatible with school and community norms.
4. Academic activities such as writing sentences and assigning additional homework should not be as punishment as these decrease the behaviors that you want to increase, while creating a negative attitude toward academic work.
5. The student cannot avoid or escape from the punishment (by hiding, cheating, being aggressive, etc.).
6. If punishment is threatened and the behavior occurs, then the punishment must be carried out.
7. Teachers should never make a threat of punishment that they cannot follow through on or back up.
8. Punishment should be carried out in a calm manner.
9. Positive desirable behaviors should be reinforced in conjunction with use of punishment.

The following are four questions to ask before using behavior-reduction procedures such as punishment:

A. Is the behavior change important for the student? In other words, is it socially important that this undesirable behavior be eliminated?
B. Have regulations regarding behavior-reduction procedures been reviewed by those who will implement them?
C. Is the undesirable behavior being replaced with a functional alternative behavior in addition to the punishment?

D. Has it been assessed whether a medical problem is causing the undesirable behavior? (Lee & Axelrod, 2005)

Key Point Questions 6: What are Different Types of Punishment?

Extinction

Extinction is the withholding of reinforcement from a previously reinforced response. Extinction discontinues the reinforcement that follows the behavior.

Extinction has most often been used with teacher attention. For example, a preschooler has temper tantrums, and the teacher pays attention to the student. The student is getting reinforced for the temper tantrums. If the teacher stops paying attention to the student when he tantrums, then the student's tantrum behavior is on extinction. Extinction is best used in conjunction with reinforcing other more appropriate behaviors.

There are six considerations before making a decision to use extinction (Benoit and Mayer (1974):

1. Can the undesirable behavior be tolerated temporarily based on its topography (e.g., aggression) and on its current rate of occurrence?
2. Can an increase in the undesirable behavior be tolerated?
3. Is the undesirable behavior likely to be imitated by other students?
4. Are the reinforcers controlling the undesirable behavior known?
5. Can reinforcement be withheld? For instance, if the student is the "class clown" and the function of the undesirable behavior is to get peer attention, then the teacher would be unable to withhold the reinforcement (peer attention) through the use of extinction.
6. Have alternative desirable behaviors that serve the same function been identified for reinforcement?

Characteristics of the extinction process are:

1. A behavior undergoing extinction usually decreases slowly in rate. Thus, extinction should not be used unless the teacher can afford to tolerate a gradual reduction in the undesirable behavior.

2. When reinforcement no longer follows a behavior, the undesirable behavior first occurs at a greater rate before it diminishes. This is known as an extinction burst.
3. The longer a student has been reinforced for a behavior, the longer it will probably take for the extinction process to work.
4. The more effort it takes the student to engage in the undesirable behavior, the more likely it is that the student will stop the undesirable behavior when extinction is used.
5. Spontaneous recovery may occur. This is a process in which a behavior that has apparently disappeared through extinction suddenly reappears. For instance, a student may "check" to see how a teacher will respond when he or she engages in a behavior (cursing in class) after it has been put on extinction. This does not mean that the use of extinction has been unsuccessful and the undesirable behavior can continue to be ignored.

Problems in using extinction are:

1. Procedure must be carried out with great consistency because even occasional reinforcement may cause the behavior to recur at a high rate. All teachers and staff must consistently engage in the extinction program; even one incident of inadvertently reinforcing the undesirable behavior can cause the behavior to start occurring again.
2. It can be difficult to determine exactly which event is reinforcing the undesired behavior in some manner.
3. Some behaviors, in themselves, may be reinforcing (such as a student who engages in self-stimulatory behavior), and the function is not tied to getting attention.
4. Some behaviors are too dangerous to ignore.
5. When some students see peers performing undesirable behaviors without any adverse consequences, they may imitate the undesirable behaviors.
6. There is limited generalization with extinction. The undesirable behavior may occur just as frequently in settings where extinction is not in effect.

Time Out

Time out is a punishment procedure in which positive reinforcement is withdrawn for a prespecified period of time following the performance of an undesirable behavior. Time out does not necessarily mean that the student is removed from the classroom or learning situation. With nonexclusionary time out, the student remains in the learning environment but is not eligible for reinforcement during the time out period. With exclusionary time out, the student is removed from the learning environment.

Time out procedures will include the following common characteristics:

1. High density of reinforcement is in educational setting. Time out will work **only** if the environment is more interesting and reinforcing than the time-out situation or environment.
2. No reinforcement is available during time-out period. Time out will work only if teacher can control that no reinforcement is delivered to the student during the time out.
3. Duration of the time out period has been prespecified and is brief.
4. Student is not released from timeout if the undesirable behavior is still occurring when the time out period ends. This does not mean that the entire time out period is restarted if the student is still engaging in the undesirable behavior at the end of the time-out period, but that the time period is extended.
5. Time out is applied immediately following the undesirable behavior.
6. Verbal interactions with the student are brief, to the point, and calm. Student is ignored when in time out.
7. Detailed records are kept.
8. Time out does not involve taking away any reinforcers from the student.
9. When the student returns, he or she is treated exactly like the other students. Reinforcement should be no easier or harder than it is for other students (i.e., don't hold a grudge).
10. The student is taught an alternative desirable behavior that can be engaged in for reinforcement so that the student does not have to engage in the undesirable behavior.

Exclusionary Time Out

With exclusionary time out, the student is removed from the situation for a specified amount of time. Exclusionary time out should be used sparingly and only for chronically and seriously undesirable behaviors.

The time-out environment should be boring and nonreinforcing for the student. The student should be removed to an area where he or she will not be seen (and preferably not heard) by anyone except the person administering the time out. It is very important that the student be monitored during the time out so that other undesirable behaviors do not occur (such as the student leaving the school).

Nonexclusionary Time Out

With nonexclusionary time out, the student is allowed to remain in the classroom or learning environment but is not allowed to receive reinforcement for a specified amount of time. For example, the student may be removed to a specific time-out area of a classroom where he or she can still see the lesson, or the teacher may say, "You can earn points again after you have been working at your desk for five minutes." This could also be as simple as the teacher not reinforcing by turning away from the student. The big advantage to nonexclusionary time out is that the student is not removed from the learning environment and can still receive academic instruction.

Criticism of Time Out Procedures:

Time out has been criticized because:

1. It fails to teach functional and desirable behaviors.
2. It decreases the student's opportunity to learn more appropriate behavior as well as academic skills by removing the student from the learning environment.
3. It removes the student from the staff's attention when the student needs the attention the most.
4. It may have paradoxical effects, functioning as a negative reinforcer of undesirable behavior or as an escape mechanism when difficult or unpleasant tasks exist in the "time-in" environment.

Difference between Extinction and Time Out

The difference between extinction and time out is that with extinction, reinforcement is withheld for a specific behavior that had been previously reinforced. With time out, the student is not eligible for reinforcement for any behavior for a specific amount of time.

Response Cost

Response cost is when points, tokens, privileges, or other reinforcers already given to a student are removed contingent on instances of a specific behavior or behaviors. Response cost is best used with undesirable behaviors that: (1) have been difficult to decrease or eliminate through the reinforcement of competing behaviors, and (2) are not excessively dangerous to other students or materials in the environment.

For example, Rapport, Murphy, and Bailey (1982) worked with second-grade "hyperactive" students who had poor attentiveness, had high rates of disruptive behavior, and did not complete their academic work. The students received 20 minutes of free time for working on their tasks without disruption but lost one minute for each instance of inattentiveness. The teacher had numbers from 1 to 20 listed on cards and flipped the cards to the next lower one (from 20 to 19) with each instance of inattentiveness.

Response cost can be used when time out or extinction is not a possibility. Another advantage is that it can be administered more quickly than time out for positive reinforcement. Response cost is often used with token economies (see Chapter 7 for information on token economies). When used accurately, response cost rarely produces the extreme emotional behavior often seen as a side effect of other punishment procedures.

Use the following guidelines when using response cost:

1. Specify ahead of time the undesirable behaviors that will be fined. This is useful in reducing the ambiguity that may exist when teachers provide consequences for student behavior.
2. A single fine should not significantly deplete (bankrupt) the total number of tokens or points.

3. If a student is being fined many times, the size of the fine is probably inadequate.
4. Initial introduction of the fining procedure needs to be carefully explained and rehearsed with students. This will help to avoid an undue amount of instructional time spent arguing over fines and trying to collect them.
5. The response cost should occur quickly and calmly.
6. At the time of the fine, the student should be told they are losing points, how many points, and how they can be earned back.

The disadvantages for using response cost are:

1. Fining may be conducted in a capricious manner if contingencies are not well planned and set.
2. Teachers may fine too heavily or too much at one time.
3. Student may become upset or defiant if having to surrender tokens or other items.

BEST PRACTICE RECOMMENDATIONS

1. Punishment procedures should always be combined with positive reinforcement and the teaching of desirable alternative behaviors that serve the same function.
2. If the undesirable behavior does not quickly diminish, then the punishment intervention is not effective and should be discontinued.

DISCUSSION QUESTIONS

1. What is the difference between punishment and aversive interventions?
2. Is it ever okay to harm students when using punishment procedures?
3. Are punishment procedures by definition not harmful?
4. Can all undesirable behaviors be decreased without the use of punishment?

CLASSROOM AND SCHOOL ACTIVITY SUGGESTIONS

1. Observe in a classroom and record the undesirable behaviors that are occurring. List the ones that would best benefit from the use of punishment and ones that would not.
2. Interview adults about the use of punishment in their own schooling to see whether they thought specific instances helped or hindered their academic and social behavior. What influences did punishment have on their adult lives?
3. Observe in a classroom and take frequency data on the teacher's use of reinforcement and punishment. Analyze which appears to be most effective in that classroom and why.

REFERENCES

Benoit, R. B., and Mayer, G. R. (1974). Extinction: Guidelines for its selection and use. *The Personnel and Guidance Journal, 52*, 290–296.

Farmer, A., & Stinson, K. (2009/2010). Failing the grade: How the use of corporal punishment in U.S. public schools demonstrates the need for U.S. ratification of the Children's Rights Convention and the Convention on the Rights of Persons with Disabilities. *New York Law School Law Review, 54*, 1035–1069.

Horner, R. H. (2002). On the status of using punishment: A commentary. *Journal of Applied Behavior Analysis, 35*, 465–467.

Horner, R. H., Dunlap, G., Koegel, R. L., Carr, E. G., Sailor, W., Anderson, J., Albin, R. W., & O'Neill, R. E. (1990). Toward a technology of "nonaversive" behavioral support. *Journal of the Association for Persons with Severe Handicaps, 15*, 125–132.

Jones, V., & Jones, L. (2007). *Comprehensive classroom management: Creating communities of support and solving problems* (8th ed.). Boston, MA: Pearson.

Kazdin, A. E. (2001). *Behavior modification in applied settings* (6th ed.). Belmont, CA: Wadsworth/Thomson Learning.

Lee, D. L., & Axelrod, S. (2005). *Behavior modification: Basic principles* (3rd ed.). Austin, TX: Pro-Ed.

McGinnis, E., & Goldstein, A. P. (2003). *Skillstreaming in early childhood: New strategies and perspectives for teaching prosocial skills.* Champaign, IL: Research Press.

Rapport, M. D., Murphy, H. A., & Bailey, J. S. (1982) Ritalin vs. response cost in the control of hyperactive children: A within subject comparison. *Journal of Applied Behavior Analysis, 15*, 205–216.

Repp. A. C., & Singh, N. N. (1990). *Perspectives on the use of nonaversive and aversive interventions for persons with developmental disabilities.* Sycamore, IL: Sycamore Publishing Company.

Chapter 6

CLASSROOM STRUCTURE

Key Point Questions

1. What are classroom rules?
2. What are classroom guidelines?
3. What are classroom procedures?
4. What are guidelines for adults in classroom?

WINDOW OF THE WORLD CASE STUDY 1

Mr. Morreau teaches in a middle school. Returning to class from recess or lunch can sometimes be difficult for his students due to disagreements or altercations that may have been experienced during those times. Even calming down from physical "highs"–from running around and being excited–can be difficult. Mr. Morreau established a routine where when students enter the classroom, the lights are off (except for a lamp at his desk), quiet classical music is playing, and Mr. Morreau is ready at the door to greet and direct students to their desks. This allows students to transition to a quiet setting where they can calm down, and for Mr. Morreau to deal with any problems before students enter the classroom.

Once the students are at their desks, Mr. Morreau turns on the lights, then turns off the lamp and then the music. Students know this routine and have a blank piece of paper and pencil ready. Mr. Morreau then puts a question about the upcoming academic content on the smart board. Students have three minutes to write a paragraph of three to five sentences about the question. Mr. Morreau then gives a consistent signal (the phrase "Time is up, put your pencils away, and give your paper to the collectors") ending the activity. Two students, who are designated for the week as "collectors," gather the papers, put them in a collection tray on Mr. Morreau's desk, and return to their seats. Mr. Morreau praises the students for their behavior, reaches into a jar (containing slips of paper with each student's name), pulls out two names, and announces, "Jared and Samantha win five points each for being at class on time, completing their work, and putting their materials away quickly. Please give yourself 5 points on your self-management point card." Then he draws another slip and says, "Now Katisha has 60 seconds to tell us a joke." Katisha smiles, stands up, and quickly tells her joke (since students know the routine, they are prepared with a joke). Everyone laughs, she takes a bow, and Mr. Morreau asks the students to raise their hand if Katisha should get five points for the joke being funny. Everyone raises their hands, and Mr. Morreau tells Katisha to put five points on her self-management point card, which she does. Mr. Morreau then transitions right into the academic content for that class period.

This process, which happens at the beginning of every class period, has taken only five minutes! The process established clear procedures for students when they enter the class, involved academic engagement with the writing activity, allowed Mr. Morreau to reinforce two students for their specific desirable behaviors, and concluded with a "fun" activity that students enjoyed. Moreover, the process decreased opportunities for undesirable behavior and increased opportunities for desirable behaviors that Mr. Morreau can reinforce.

WINDOW OF THE WORLD CASE STUDY 2

Ms. Inafuku teaches high school sciences classes. She has 30 to 35 students in each class period. When students enter her classroom, they sign in for attendance using a clicker with the smart board. Any student not signed in when the bell rings is automatically counted as late. These results are sent electronically to the office, as well as to any parents who have requested this information. Ms. Inafuku has a web site, blog, and social media site where information regarding class rules, homework assignments, chapters being covered, related books on the topic being studied, and suggested web sites are posted and available to students and family members.

Once the bell rings, Ms. Inafuku puts up on the smart board two questions she has prepared from the reading assignment and one she has selected from those posted by students on the web site. Students use their clickers to answer the multiple-choice questions, and their answers are electronically recorded. After two minutes, Ms. Inafuku tells students to put their clickers away (they know that they only have two minutes each day to answer three questions). She posts the results on the smart board (these are automatically scored and recorded), which gives her the percentage of students who answered correctly, as well as the percentage of incorrect answers. This gives Ms. Inafuku an opportunity to immediately go over the questions with the students and discuss why a choice was correct or incorrect. Additionally, individual student scores and group responses are emailed to parents so that they can see the results and go over the material with students who are having difficulty.

Ms. Inafuku then posts on the smart board what will be covered academically the rest of the class period, including the format of instruction (today is group work, then brief group reports with feedback from Ms. Inafuku). This is followed by a presentation by Ms. Inafuku regarding vocabulary words and reading instructions for the upcoming chapter. Ms. Inafuku then directs the week's assigned student "setter uppers" to get materials ready for the groups. As they do so, she goes over the group work rules, transition rules, and how group work results should be reported to the class. Students are then cued to go to their work groups. During the group work session, Ms. Inafuku circulates among the groups, checking for on-task behavior and group cooperation (which she praises), and answers any content-related questions.

Ms. Inafuku is known as a no-nonsense teacher where not a minute of class time is wasted; consequently, students know that they have to be ready to go as soon as the bell rings. At the same time, she is known as a teacher who has fun and engaging activities. School-wide assessment results show students in her class do well academically, have strong test scores, and often get into very good colleges.

Key Point Question 1: What Are Classroom Rules?

Class rules that are clear and positive are needed for every classroom. The purpose of these rules is to communicate teacher expectations regarding student behavior. Without classroom rules, anarchy is likely to rule, with little academic instruction taking place. These classroom rules provide a basis for student accountability, as well as for catching the students "being good." The rules should be specific and refer to observable student behavior. For instance, the rules "be on time with materials" or "focus on work" are observable behaviors, while the rules "be responsible" or "do your best" are not.

Involving students in setting the classroom rules helps with their understanding of the rules and also their "buy in" to the rules. Teachers should guide this process as it is important that students not be allowed to set their standards too high. Once the classroom rules are set, rules should be shared with parents and other family members. This sharing will provide the family with clarity on expected conduct, understanding if rules are violated, and knowing what desirable behaviors to reinforce at home.

Characteristics of good classroom rules include:

1. Keep rules to a minimum (3–4) for any classroom situation.
2. Keep the wording of the rules simple, such as, "Keep hands and feet to yourself." Table 6.1 provides examples of classroom rules.
3. State the rules positively. This is very important as it serves to tie reinforcement systems to the classroom rules by letting students know which behaviors will be reinforced. Stating the rules positively allows the focus to be on desirable behaviors that the teacher wants students to do, not on what not to do (undesirable behaviors). For instance, it would be easy for a teacher to reinforce students who are keeping hands and feet to themselves.
4. Post the rules in a prominent location where the rules are easily visible to students.
5. Go over and practice the rules repeatedly, especially at the beginning of the school year and also when new students enter the class during the school year. Mere posting of classroom rules is ineffective. These practice sessions should explain the reasoning behind the rules and can be short, providing guidelines and skill

Table 6.1
Examples of Classroom Rules

---

1. Follow teacher directions first time given.
2. Raise your hand and wait for permission to talk.
3. Be respectful of others and their property.
4. Clean up your area.
5. Be kind and show respect.
6. Be prepared.
7. Be at class on time.
8. Bring what you need with you.
9. Listen to the teacher.
10. Be kind to others.
11. Be ready to work when the bell rings.

---

building for actual situations that are likely to arise. For instance, what does the rule "Keep hands and feet to yourself" mean in practice? Provide examples and nonexamples so that students can distinguish between the two and practice the desired behavior. This also allows students to be reinforced for demonstrating the desired behavior during the practice session, as well as during other class times (Paine, Radicchi, Rosellini, Deutchman, & Darch, 1983).

Key Point Question 2: What Are Classroom Guidelines?

Classroom guidelines refer to the physical layout of the classroom as well as how other adults besides the teacher should behave in the classroom.

How the Classroom Space Should be Physically Arranged

Teacher's Desk and Teacher Behavior

The teacher's desk should be in a corner of the room facing students, which gives the teacher the ability to easily scan the room from his or her desk. If there is a classroom assistant or a desk for other staff, this desk should be on the opposite side of the room from teacher's the desk, again to allow for easy scanning of the room (Paine et al., 1983).

Whereever in the classroom the teacher is, he or she should sit or stand at all times so that, with peripheral vision, he or she can see as much of the classroom as possible (known as having eyes in the back of the head). Teachers should scan the room on a frequent basis to check on potential problems and also to reinforce students for desirable behavior.

Teaching Stations

Teaching stations can best be placed in the corners of the room. The student chairs should face the wall to reduce distractions. The teacher's chair should face the room, making it easier to monitor other areas of the room (Paine et al., 1983).

Student Desks and Learning Areas

Student desks can be arranged in rows, groups or clusters, semi-circles, or as long tables. Seating can be open or assigned. There is no one way that necessarily is best. Variables such as the students' age and sophistication, the teaching style, and the area of room available all influence which strategy might work best in a specific classroom.

The advantage of desks in rows is that all students are facing the instructional presentation area, making it easy for the teacher to see students' faces. Disadvantages are that it is difficult to do group work and difficult to monitor students at the back or end of rows. Having desks in groups has the advantages of being set up for group learning activities and making it easy for the teacher to move among and interact with student groups. Disadvantages are that the teacher cannot see all student faces, and, likewise, it is harder for some students to see the teacher during instructional presentation.

Students and teacher should have easy access to and from their desks and learning areas. It is important to analyze "traffic patterns" for determining how students and teacher can easily go to and from different classroom areas without bumping into each other. For example, student desks could be arranged in rows in a semi-circle, where students enter the desk rows from the right side and exit to the left side. This creates designated ways for students to get to and from their desks and minimizes situations that may cause delay or conflict.

Classroom Materials

Frequently used teaching materials and supplies should be in an area, or areas, that are readily accessible. Storage cabinets, smart boards, and class dividers should be set up so that they are at the walls, if possible, and should not block the teacher being able to visually scan areas of the classroom.

Classroom Structure

In a review of the literature, Simonsen, Fairbanks, Briesch, Myers, and Sugai (2008) report that classrooms with more structure promote more appropriate academic and social behavior, greater task involvement, better peer interactions, and more attentive behavior. Simonsen et al. (2008) recommend that classrooms should be designed to minimize crowding and distractions and that active supervision positively impacts student behavior in different settings, including classroom and nonclassroom areas (e.g., hallways).

In the classroom, it is often a good idea to have quiet areas (pillows, books, or other headphones with music) and reinforcement areas (with games, puzzles, art materials) for students to go to as needed (or when finished with work).

In the classroom it is possible, and often very advantageous, to have roles assigned to students (on a daily, weekly, or monthly basis). These roles can include messenger, greeter, phone answerer, material distributor, attendance taker, encourager, and token distributor. Having students in these roles can increase student engagement, teach responsibility, and allow positive role models for other students. If possible, every student in the class should always have a role assignment and these assignments can be rotated on a regular basis.

Key Point Questions 3: What Are Classroom Procedures?

General Routines

Establishing routines is important for students as they will have to engage in these classroom behaviors repeatedly throughout the day, as well as throughout the school year. Having clearly established routines, with students repeatedly practicing them, will make expected

Table 6.2
Classroom Routines that Need to be Established

1. Entering class.
2. What to do if tardy.
3. Notes from home.
4. Taking seat.
5. Taking of attendance.
6. Transition to activities, staff, or settings.
7. How to seek help or ask questions.
8. Restroom rules.
9. What to do when work is finished early.
10. Paper/work distribution.
11. What to do when teacher is busy.
12. Use of smart phones and other electronic devices.
13. What to do if need to leave class or cannot cope with situation.
14. Water and/or snack rules.
15. Clothing rules (hats, hoods, etc.).
16. Cleaning up materials and areas.
17. Exiting class.

behaviors clear to students and allow the teacher opportunities for reinforcing students to engage in these behaviors. Table 6.2 provides examples of classroom routines that need to be established.

Getting Student Attention

It is necessary that there be a specific strategy for getting students' attention in the class. It should be used consistently and be understandable to the students. This signal could be a phrase ("Class, your attention please"), a bell, flicking of the lights, music, or a hand signal (such as holding up two fingers). Students are then reinforced for responding appropriately to the signal.

Numbering System

Numbering systems are where each student is assigned a number. This can make it easier and quicker for activities, such as getting lined up by number for recess (start with number 1, then the next day number 2, etc.). It can also make it easier to get groups ready (numbers 1–4 to work station #1, numbers 5–8 to work station #2, etc.).

Academic Work

Policies for academic work should be clearly laid out for students and their family; they should be specified in a course syllabus, posted on web sites, or shared through email or social media. Such policies might involve how certain issues are handled for students, such as late work, makeup work, extra work, and reporting of student progress and grades. Publically posted class/day's schedule can help students understand and plan for the sequence of activities that will be occurring. Visuals can be used to clarify what is expected of students (pictures, short video clip, diagram, power point, etc.) or to give a visual time warning or countdown (10 seconds until groups are to start).

It can be beneficial to start day/class with a student-preferred activity as this reinforces students for being to school/class on time and encourages participation. During class times, as well as days, it is often a good idea to alternate least-preferred activities with most-preferred activities (Axelrod, 1977).

Down Time

Down time should be kept to an absolute minimum. Time fillers (also known as sponge activities) should be set up and ready for quick use. These time fillers can be interesting academic activities, such as math problems, puzzles, worksheets, etc. These can also be used for extra points or other reinforcement. For example, the principal comes to the door of Ms. Parker's room with an urgent problem that cannot wait. Ms. Parker quickly switches her smart board to math problems, telling students to get out a piece of paper, put their name on it, and work quietly and individually, and that each student will receive one bonus point for each problem answered correctly. She waits until the students are engaged in the problems and then steps into the doorway (not into the hallway where she cannot monitor the classroom) and talks with the principal. This transition took less than one minute, had no down time, and provided no chance for students to go off task or to get into trouble.

Transition Procedures

Transitions, whether they are from task to task, setting to setting, person to person, or behavior to behavior, can be fraught with poten-

Table 6.3
Common Transition Problems and Possible Solutions

Transition Problem	Possible Solution
Students talk at beginning of period and interrupt teacher.	Establish beginning of period routine. Have content activity ready and begin class at once with this activity.
Students talk too much during transition, or students do not begin their work after transitioning.	Post assignment and rules where all students can see them. Have students practice seat work transition and reinforce successful transitions and work.
Students stop work before they should.	Establish that students work until signal from teacher and then clean up area.
Students leave their seats or work areas at inappropriate times.	Define appropriate behavior during transition times, practice, and reinforce the occurrence of the desirable behaviors.

Adapted from Emmer and Evertson (2013).

tial problems. Table 6.3 provides some common transition problems and possible solutions. Nelson, Benner, and Mooney (2008) recommend that with transitions:

1. Have clear avenues for students to move to designated areas.
2. Have a signal to indicate that there is a transition about to happen.
3. Secure student attention and remind them of expectations regarding talking, noise, travel direction, and personal space issues.

General Procedures to Put in Place

Identify generic positive desirable behaviors and reinforce them. What are the generic behaviors that you want students to do?

Independence.

Appropriate social behavior.

Completing work.

Following school and classroom rules.

Minimize reinforcement for undesirable behaviors.

Give students clear rules.

Define system for undesirable behavior (what will happen when undesirable behavior occurs).

Remember to include rules for staff to follow.

Key Point Questions 4: What Are Guidelines for Adults in the Classroom?

Other Staff, Students, and Adults in the Classroom

It can be beneficial to involve other students, staff (administrators, speech therapists, mobility specialists, inclusion specialists, behavior specialists, janitors, etc.), and adults (parents and other volunteers) in academic instruction and other activities in the classroom. It is advantageous to have rules posted for staff and adults so that they are clear on classroom rules. These individuals can do things such as:

- Listen to students read.
- Drill basic facts such as math, history, or vocabulary.
- Drill students on difficult reading words.
- Direct small-group activities.
- Develop and supervise art, music, and cooking projects.
- Send "good day" notes home.
- Make positive phone calls to parents.
- Teach students something unique (fact, foreign language phrase, sign language, magic trick, joke, etc.).
- Praise students.
- Let students help with their duties.

Setting Rules for Adults in Class

1. The adults need to be instructed on:
   a) what to do,
   b) when to do it,
   c) where to do it,
   d) who to do it with, and
   e) how to do it (Paine et al., 1983)
2. Don't allow staff or other adults to interrupt during direct teaching times. Have them leave a note or contact during prep times.

3. If interruption must occur, use a sponge activity for students. Do not talk to the person until all students are working independently on the task.
4. If the adults are involved in instruction, set up time with them, before hand, where you can demonstrate the activity, provide a chance for them to practice it, and receive your constructive feedback.

BEST PRACTICE RECOMMENDATIONS

1. Have classroom rules, directly teach rules, and reinforce these rules.
2. Have clear routines and procedures for students, and teach and reinforce these.
3. Have rules and guidelines for all adults in the classroom.
4. Position yourself to be able to scan all sections of the room.

DISCUSSION QUESTIONS

1. Is it better for teachers to set their own classroom rules or have students involved in the process?
2. What flexibility should occur with set classroom routines?
3. Should teachers stop routines or academic instruction to deal with undesirable behaviors?

CLASSROOM AND SCHOOL ACTIVITY SUGGESTIONS

1. Go to multiple classrooms and observe whether classroom rules are posted, whether they are easily visible to students, and ask students to tell you what the rules are and whether they can provide examples of the rules.
2. Observe and take frequency counts on the number of times that three students in the class follow class rules and also the number of times that they are then reinforced for following the rules. Analyze whether reinforcement is occurring frequently enough for following the class rules.

3. Visit a classroom and analyze the procedures and routines for students. Do they enhance academic instruction? In what ways? If not, how do they impede academic instruction?

REFERENCES

Axelrod, S. (1977). *Behavior modification for the classroom teacher.* San Francisco: McGraw-Hill Book Co.

Emmer, E. T., & Evertson, C. M. (2013). *Classroom management for middle and high school teachers* (9th ed.). Boston, MA: Pearson.

Nelson, J. R., Benner, G. J., & Mooney, P. (2008). *Instructional practices for students with behavioral disorders: Strategies for reading, writing, and math.* New York: Guilford Press.

Paine, S. C., Radicchi, J., Rosellini, L. C., Deutchman, L., & Darch, C. B. (1983). *Structuring your classroom for academic success.* Champaign, IL: Research Press.

Simonsen, B., Fairbanks, S., Briesch, A., Myers, D., & Sugai, G. (2008). Evidence based practices in classroom management: Considerations for research to practice. *Education and Treatment of Children, 31,* 351–380.

Chapter 7

PREVENTATIVE PROCEDURES AND INTERVENTIONS

Key Point Questions

1. What are ecological modifications?
2. What is goal setting?
3. What are token economies?
4. What is the Good Behavior Game?
5. What is relaxation training?
6. What are curriculum modifications?
7. What is anger control training?
8. What are pretask requests?

WINDOW OF THE WORLD CASE STUDY 1

Zelia is a high school student who does well academically and is generally well behaved but is known to have "rage" at the drop of a hat if she believes that peers and teachers are disrespecting her. These rages include verbal aggression and threats and can sometimes escalate into physical aggression. Zelia's teachers are very concerned about this behavior and for Zelia's future. At a student study team meeting, the school psychologist, Ms. Huber, is assigned to come up with a plan for helping Zelia.

After meeting with Zelia and each of her teachers, Ms. Huber decides that several interventions need to be immediately implemented to develop skills for Zelia. Zelia realizes her rage behavior is a serious problem, and she is worried that she will end up in the Juvenile Justice System. Since Zelia is willing to work with Ms. Huber, Zelia agrees to meet individually with Ms. Huber for 10 minutes before school each day. During this time, Ms. Huber teaches Zelia relaxation skills (visualization, deep breathing, and muscle tense/relax). Second, Zelia joins an anger management group meeting several times a week during lunch time. Because Zelia is not the only student at school who is having problems controlling anger, it is beneficial for a group to meet and develop positive social skills to replace the anger behaviors. Third, Ms. Huber and Zelia set up a self-reinforcement system where Zelia self-monitores her behavior to help her not respond to triggers or provocations from peers. Reviewing the self-monitoring recorded data, both Zelia and Ms. Huber are surprised to see the number of times per day that Zelia is provoked by peers. Each time that Zelia does not respond to these triggers, she makes a mark on a card; then for every ten times that she did not respond she reinforces herself by downloading a song onto her smart phone. She also briefly meets with Ms. Huber at the end of each day to commiserate on the behavior of Zelia's peers. In this way, Ms. Huber supports and praises the changes in Zelia's behavior. Fourth, Ms. Huber meets with the teachers in the school for some training on teacher behaviors that students perceived as disrespectful. This allows the teachers to change their behavior and not unintentionally illicit undesirable student behavior.

Because of these interventions, Zelia's rage behavior decreases significantly. Zelia now has positive behaviors replacing her rage behavior and peer support in her anger management group. Further, with the changed behavior of her teachers, she is having fewer situations that are likely to set off her rage behavior.

WINDOW OF THE WORLD CASE STUDY 2

Mr. McAdoo's was having a hard time controlling his class. Teaching middle-school students academic skills was hard enough, but he was even more frustrated because he rarely had an opportunity to actually teach. One day after school, he had a long talk with another teacher, Ms. Stiffler, who rarely had any discipline problems in her class and was known for how well her students did academically. Ms. Stiffler came into Mr. McAdoo's class several times during her prep periods.

Ms. Stiffler had a number of suggestions for Mr. McAdoo. She talked with him about the need to reinforce the desirable behaviors that he wanted to see from students. She suggested that he implement the Good Behavior Game as it involved students working in groups, competing with other groups for prizes, and the chance to earn extra free time to hang out as a group (activities she knew students liked to do). Second, she suggested that he implement a token economy for specific individual behaviors that he wanted students to do. After thinking it over, he decided on a point system where each student could earn points for being ready when the bell started (one point), having homework completed (five points), having all materials with them (five points), and being focused on work (one point that he distributed using a Variable Interval schedule). Third, she talked with Mr. McAdoo about several students who were struggling academically. She suggested that he implement more activity-based lessons, change his instructional style to be faster paced, and combine visual and verbal instruction. Finally, she suggested that he frequently intersperse questions into his presentations and use cue response cards to increase student involvement, thus giving him immediate feedback on their understanding of the information.

Mr. McAdoo was grateful for these recommendations and immediately put them into practice. He was pleasantly surprised at how effective these strategies were, especially for the students who were struggling academically and presented the most challenging behaviors.

Key Point Questions 1: What Are Ecological Modifications?

Ecological manipulation includes the systematic use of environmental variables in order to promote positive behavior change (Cowick & Storey, 2000). Teachers have control over a number of factors that may affect students, such as physical settings and setting structure, staff-student and student-student interactions, instructional methods and goals, task difficulty, and scheduling of activities. Teachers need to maximize positive interactions between adults and students in the classroom. Through ecological manipulations, it is possible to prevent undesirable behaviors from occurring and also to promote positive replacement behaviors in a way that results in greater generalization and maintenance. Table 7.1 presents examples of ecological manipulations. These ecological manipulations may involve focus on the following factors.

Broader Aspects of a Student's Life

It is important to look broadly at a student's life to evaluate factors to change for increasing desirable behavior in that student. This evaluation may include factors such as:

1. Changing schedules or routines.
2. Resolving physical or medical issues.
3. Increasing positive social contacts in and/or outside of school.

Setting Factors

Setting factors may increase the probability of desirable or undesirable behaviors and may influence the student's ability to cope with the environmental variables. For instance, having a student sit next to certain peers may influence the behavior of that student (if he or she likes or dislikes the peers or how close he or she is to the peers). If Veruca is struggling socially, then it would be desirable to have Veruca paired with students who have good social skills and who can serve as desirable role models (rather than pairing her with other peers who are having social difficulties).

Factors to evaluate are:

1. Places where desirable and/or undesirable behaviors are occurring.
2. Persons with whom desirable and/or undesirable behaviors are occurring.
3. Activities where desirable and/or undesirable behaviors are occurring.

Opportunities to Respond (OTRs)

Conroy, Sutherland, Snyder, and Marsh (2008) define OTRs (also known as active student responding) as a questioning, prompting, or

Table 7.1
Examples of Ecological Manipulations

Function Is to Obtain Desirable Event:
Increase interest level of activity.
Change activity.
Break activity into smaller segments.
Provide free time in classroom involving movement.
Provide outside activities that involve climbing, running, pushing, pulling, or lifting.
Allow for students to choose position for working, including standing and lying on floor.

Function Is to Obtain External Stimulation:
Sitting with a peer.
Pairing with a peer.
Review classroom discussion content ahead of time.
Public acknowledgment of student successes.
Information to access resources (e.g., counseling help, medical assistance).
Schedule regular conferences/check ins.
Pairing with advocate to maximize social involvement.
High reinforcement ratio/social praise.
Provide extra responsibilities in classroom/school.

Function Is to Obtain Attention:
Counseling services.
Social skills instruction.
Cooperative learning activities.
Use of older peer tutors.
Use of volunteers and school staff.

Function Is to Escape/Avoid:
Provide quiet space for calming down .
Provide isolated area of release of anger.
Journal writing.
Structured play situations.
Prompting initiations and appropriate interactions.
Use of cooperative learning activities.
Use of peer models and peer tutoring.
Curriculum modification.
Use of clear/precise directives.
Provide high-probability requests prior to low-probability request.
Clearly established rules and routines.
Clearly established consequences for both desirable and undesirable behavior.
Brief activities.
High interest activities.
Provide choice of activities.
Use a safety signal to indicate that activity is about to end contingent on appropriate behavior (e.g., we're almost finished).

Adapted from Cowick and Storey (2000).

cueing technique that begins a learning trial (e.g., "What number comes after 10?"). OTRs increase the frequency of student responses leading to increased correct responses, increased student engagement, and a decrease in undesirable behaviors (Conroy et al., 2008; George, 2010). OTRs include:

1. Frequent teacher instructional talk that includes a variety of cues and prompts for student responding.
2. Presenting information in a manner that increases correct student responding (also known as errorless learning). For example, the teacher could say "2 plus 2 equals 4. What does 2 plus 2 equal?"
3. Frequent checks for individual student understanding and accuracy ("Neil, what does 2 plus 2 equal?").
4. Providing corrective feedback for student errors.
5. Providing reinforcement for correct student responses.

Task-Related Factors

Many undesirable behaviors occur in task-related situations, so often a teacher's first interpretation is that the student is being noncompliant. An alternative explanation is that there is something about the task that is problematic for the student. For example, by being aggressive, the student gets out of something that he or she considers nonfunctional (or easy, boring, or too difficult).

Interventions that may alleviate task-related factors are:

1. Breaking the task down into smaller steps.
2. Giving the individual extra assistance on certain steps that may be more difficult.
3. Changing the scheduling.
4. Changing everything (or as much as possible).

Response Interruption

Response interruption prevents an undesirable behavior from continuing (the behavior has to first occur before it can be stopped) by interrupting the behavior. These interruptions can include:

Prosthetic device (such as the use of a helmet for a student with severe self-injurious behavior).

Manual blocking (the teacher standing between an aggressive student and the intended victim).

Verbal cues ("Eva, you need to stop clenching your fists and take a deep breath").

Physical Exercise

Exercise has many benefits for students, such as lowering stress levels, enhancing moods, boosting blood flow to the brain and helping it to receive oxygen and nutrients, improving sleeping at night, and increasing cognitive performance (Archer & Kostrzewa, 2012; Hillman, Erickson, & Kramer, 2008). Since many students do not get adequate amounts of exercise in or outside of school, the use of quick and simple exercises in classrooms can be beneficial for academic and social behaviors.

Key Point Questions 2: What is Goal Setting?

Goal setting (also known as student contracts) involves the student in setting specific academic or behavioral goals he or she will meet and the specific reinforcement he or she will receive for meeting that goal (Jones & Jones, 2007; Lassman, Jolivette, & Wehby, 1999). The trick is to have a goal that is realistic, is achievable, and requires student effort. This can enhance student motivation and reduce the occurrence of undesirable behaviors. It is recommended that the goal/contract include:

1. Academic material the student plans to learn or the behavior in which he or she will engage.
2. Specified activities and/or specific behaviors in which the student will engage (defined and positively worded).
3. The degree of proficiency the student will attain.
4. How the student will demonstrate that the learning has occurred.
5. What the time dimensions are for the goal.
6. How the goal will be measured and evaluated. Performance feedback must be used to provide ongoing information about student behavior (whether they are making progress toward the goal).

7. The role and responsibilities for each person (student, teacher, and others such as family members).
8. A written contract that is signed by all parties involved.
9. Short term goals should be initially used for quick reinforcement.
10. The goal intervention ties into self-management strategies.

Key Point Questions 3: What are Token Economies?

A reinforcement system based on tokens is referred to as a token economy. Tokens function in the same way that money does, where tokens are used to purchase back-up reinforcers. Tokens are conditioned reinforcers (they can be exchanged for a variety of objects or activities, e.g., back-up reinforcers). Tickets, stars, points, or checkmarks are commonly used.

Advantages to using a token economy are:

1. Tokens/points can be distributed quickly and unobtrusively.
2. Reinforcement with tokens can develop high rates of desirable behavior.
3. Tokens can bridge the delay between the desirable behavior and the delivery of the back-up reinforcement.
4. Since tokens are backed up by a variety of reinforcers, they are less subject to satiation than other reinforcers.
5. Tokens can be delivered without interrupting instruction.
6. Tokens do not require consumption of treats or performance of behaviors that may interrupt instruction.

Table 7.2 provides general guidelines for the implementation of token economies.

Key Point Questions 4: What is the Good Behavior Game?

The Good Behavior Game encompasses a variety of strategies where students are divided into teams, competing against the other teams, or to meet a specific goal to earn points for their team (all teams can win). The Good Behavior Game has been evaluated in classrooms (Barrish, Saunders, & Wolf, 1969) and other school settings, such as the lunch room (McCurdy, Lannie, & Barnabas, 2009). The Good Behavior Game has been effective for both decreasing undesirable behaviors

Table 7.2

General Guidelines for the Implementation of Token Economies

1. Explain the behaviors that receive or lose points as well as the system, posted point values (cost or price), reinforcement menu, and redemption times and rules.
2. Instruction and role playing regarding desirable and/or undesirable behaviors, as well as for redeeming and/or losing points, should occur before initiating the token system.
3. Claiming reinforcers should involve a minimum of discussion and record keeping.
4. A regular routine for distribution and redemption should be developed to minimize interruption of instruction.
5. Pair praise with delivery of tokens.
6. Redemption and exchange periods may be scheduled hourly, daily, and/or weekly.
7. Menu of reinforcers should specify the reinforcer options and costs and be specified in advance.
8. There should be a variety of reinforcers with a variety of prices so that everyone can purchase at least one reinforcer.
9. A store, lottery, and/or auction may be used for redemption of tokens, in addition to sale of reinforcers on an individual basis.
10. Tokens may be given for individual, group, or class behavior.
11. Tokens can be based on a monetary system so that students can learn functional skills (counting, banking, interest accumulation, etc.) in conjunction with the token economy.
12. Students should not be able to obtain tokens from other sources or be able to counterfeit tokens.

Adapted from Kazdin (2001) and Myles, Moran, Ormsbee, and Downing (1992).

and increasing desirable and academic behaviors (Tingstrom, Sterling Turner, & Wilczynski, 2006). For example, Kleinman and Saigh (2010) examined the effectiveness of the Good Behavior Game in a multiethnic New York City public high school. Classroom rules were posted, and students were divided into two teams. A reinforcement preference questionnaire was used to select daily and weekly prizes. The classroom teacher placed a check on the board after every rule infraction (while naming rule violators and their infractions). The team with the fewest marks at the end of each day became the daily winner and received prizes. The team with the fewest marks for the week was recognized as the weekly winner and received additional prizes. The use of the game resulted in marked reductions in the rate of seat leaving, talking without permission, and aggression.

The generic strategy of the Good Behavior Game is:

1. The class is divided into teams (if one student tries to sabotage team, then that student may be his or her own team).

2. The teams compete to see which can earn the most points in a class period, day, week, month, semester, and/or year. All of these contingencies can potentially be in play at one time, which increases the opportunities for reinforcement.
3. Competitions (in which teams receive reinforcement) may be on a daily basis, weekly, in a league, etc.
4. May set up a criterion (a point goal) so that all can end up winners. For example, every team that gets five points during a class period receives reinforcement.
5. May be used for academic performance and/or student conduct. For instance, every team member who turns in his or her homework earns one point for the team, and every student who is at class on time earns one point for the team.
6. Back-up reinforcers are provided for winners (such as activities, prizes, etc.).

Key Point Questions 5: What Is Relaxation Training?

School can be a stressful and anxiety-generating place for students for a variety of reasons, such as tests, crowded hallways, undesirable peers, and mean teachers. This stress can negatively impact academic and social performance. Thus, strategies for reducing or eliminating stress can be beneficial for students.

Relaxation training involves a variety of strategies, such as visualization, worry control, coping skills, nutrition, and exercise (Davis, Eshelman, & McKay, 2008; Shapiro & Sprague, 2009). The goal is for the student to develop skills and strategies that reinforce behavior that is incompatible with anxiety and is a coping skill for stress. Relaxation skills can be taught to an individual student, a group of students, or a whole class. As with any intervention, not all students will respond successfully to relaxation training. Some of the most common relaxation methods are:

1. Tensing and relaxing muscle groups (also known as deep muscle relaxation or progressive muscle relaxation), such as tensing and then relaxing hands or shoulders.
2. Deep breathing (also known as diaphragmatic breathing) involves expansion of the abdomen rather than the chest when breathing.

3. Squeeze objects. These can be balls, modeling clay, or "koosh" objects.

These strategies can be used individually or together. For instance, students could be taught to tense and relax three muscle groups and to take deep breaths for 30 seconds before starting a test. This could help them to reduce their stress level and to become more focused before starting to answer questions.

Key Point Questions 6: What Are Curriculum Modifications?

Making changes or modifications to academic instruction can be a key component of positive behavior support. Many students engage in undesirable behaviors due to difficulty in their academic performance, and, for this reason, changes or modifications can decrease undesirable behavior. Curriculum modifications are often appropriate for all students, and they are part of "good teaching" (Halverson & Neary, 2009; Murphy, 1996).

The terms *accommodations* and *modifications* are often used interchangeably, but they represent two different changes to the curriculum. Accommodations provide different ways for students to take in (access) information or communicate their knowledge back to the teacher. The changes basically don't alter or lower the standards or expectations for a subject or test. Accommodations do not substantially change the instructional level, the content, or the performance criteria for the student. The use of Braille, oral tests, taped lectures, recorded text, note taker, preferential seating, and modified directions are all examples of accommodations.

Modifications are changes in the delivery, content, or instructional level of subject matter or tests. They result in changing or lowering expectations and create a different standard for some students. For students with disabilities, curriculum modifications are often developed formally through the Individualized Education Plan process. Modifications do change the instructional level and/or content for students. Modified tests, use of a calculator, alternate materials, and shortened assignments are examples of modifications. Table 7.3 provides examples of curriculum modifications.

Table 7.3
Examples of Curriculum Modifications

A. *Change the Structure of the Instruction:*
  1. Can the student's participation be increased by arranging the lesson in:
  Cooperative groups?
  Partner learning?
  Peer tutors or cross-age tutors?
  2. Can the student's participation be increased by changing the lesson format?
  Activity-based lessons?
  Experiential lessons?
  Community-based lessons?
  3. Can the student's participation and understanding be increased by changing the
  delivery of instruction or teaching style?
B. *Change the Demands of the Task and Criteria for Success:*
  4. Will the student need adapted curricular goals?
  Adjust performance standards
  Adjust pacing
  Same content but less complex
  Similar content with functional/direct applications
  5. Will changes be needed in the evaluation system?
  Arrange criterion-referenced or personalized evaluation.
C. *Change Elements in the Learning Environment:*
  6. Can changes be made in the classroom environment or lesson location that will
  facilitate participation?
  Environmental/physical
  Social
  Lesson location
D. *Change the Way the Task Is Done:*
  7. Will different materials be needed to ensure participation?
  Same content but variation in size, number, or format
  Additional or different materials or devices
E. *Change the Support Structure:*
  8. Will assistance from others be needed to ensure participation?
  From peers or other support staff such as an inclusion specialist?

Adapted from Putnam (1993).

Wright (2005) has provided information on nine types of adaptations for curriculum modification:

1. *Size:* Adapt the number of items that the student is expected to learn or complete. This might be the length or portion of an assignment, a demonstration, or a performance that learners are expected to complete.
   Examples: Reduce the number of social studies terms a student must learn at any one time. Reduce the length of report to be written or spoken, the number of references needed, and/or the number of problems to be solved.

2. *Time:* Adapt the time allotted and allowed for learning, task completion, or testing.
   Examples: Individualize a timeline for completing a task, and adjust the pace of learning (increase or decrease) for some students.

3. *Level of Support:* Increase the amount of personal assistance with a specific student.
   Examples: Assign peer buddies, teaching assistants, peer tutors or cross-age tutors, and cooperative learning groups to provide support.

4. *Input:* Adapt the way instruction is delivered to the student.
   Examples: Use different visual aids, videos, and field trips; plan more concrete examples; provide hands-on activities; and place students in cooperative groups.

5. *Difficulty:* Adapt the skill level, problem type, or rules on how the student may complete the work.
   Examples: Allow the use of a calculator to figure math problems, simplify task directions, and change rules to accommodate student needs.

6. *Output:* Adapt how the student can respond to instruction in terms of demonstrating understanding and knowledge.
   Examples: Instead of answering questions in writing, allow a verbal response. Use a communication book for some students and/or allow students to show knowledge with hands-on materials.

7. *Participation:* Adapt the extent to which a student is actively involved in the task.
   Examples: In geography, have a student hold the globe while others point out locations. In cooperative learning groups, a student may be an "encourager."

8. *Alternative/Modified Goals:* Adapt the goals or outcome expectations while using the same materials.
   Examples: In social studies, expect one student to be able to locate just the states while others learn to locate capitals as well. In a written language activity, a student may focus more on writing some letters and copying words rather than composing whole sentences or paragraphs.

9. *Adapted Curriculum:* Provide different instruction and materials to meet a student's individual goals.
   Examples: In a foreign language class, a student may develop a play or script that uses both authentic language and cultural knowledge of a designated time period, rather than reading paragraphs or directions.

Key Point Questions 7: What Is Anger Control Training?

Many students in school settings are angry, which can lead to poor academic performance, aggression, and other undesirable behaviors. One strategy with strong empirical evidence of effectiveness is Aggression Replacement Training (ART), which is an intervention designed for aggressive students (Goldstein, Glick, & Gibbs, 1986). ART teaches alternative skills to anger and aggression.

The three components of ART are:

1: *Skill Streaming,* which teaches a curriculum of ProSocial, interpersonal skills (i.e., what to do instead of aggression). Skill streaming is covered in more detail in Chapter 10.

2: *Anger Control Training (ACT),* which teaches students what to do, as well as what not to do, if provoked. The goal of ACT is to teach students self-control of anger. In ACT, students bring to each session a description of a recent anger-arousing experience that they record in a binder. Table 7.4 provides an example of ACT steps. For ten sessions, the students receive instruction in responding to their frustrations with a chain of behaviors that include:

1. Identifying triggers (i.e., those external events and internal self-statements that provoke an anger response, such as being too close to a particular peer or having one's space suddenly invaded).
2. Identifying cues (i.e., those individual physical events, such as tightened muscles, flushed faces, and clenched fists, which let the student know that the emotion he or she is experiencing is anger).
3. Using reminders (i.e., self-statements, such as "stay calm," "chill out," and "cool down," or nonhostile explanations of others' behavior).
4. Using reducers (i.e., a series of techniques that, like the use of reminders, is designed expressly to lower the student's level of anger, such as deep breathing, counting backward, imagining a peaceful scene, or imagining the long-term consequences of one's behavior).
5. Using self-evaluation (i.e., reflecting on how well the frustration was responded to by identifying triggers, identifying cues, using reminders, and using reducers and then praising or rewarding oneself for effective performance (Goldstein & Glick, 1994).

Table 7.4
Example of Anger Control Training Steps

Avoiding Trouble with Others
STEPS
1. Decide if you are in a situation that might get you into trouble.
2. Decide if you want to get out of the situation.
3. Tell the other people what you decided and why.
4. Suggest other things you might do.
5. Do what you think is best for you.

Adapted from Goldstein, Glick, and Gibbs (1986).

3: *Moral Reasoning Training,* which promotes values that respect the rights of others and helps students to want to use the interpersonal and anger management skills taught. The goal of moral reasoning training is to have students think about moral issues from different perspectives and examine their judgments, as well as those of others.

Moral reasoning training generally involves group meetings where relevant examples of moral dilemmas are presented. Each student in the group is asked to describe the proper behavior the person in the dilemma should do, and why (Goldstein et al., 1986).

Key Point Question 8: What Are Pretask Requests?

Pretask requests (also known as behavioral momentum) is a procedure designed for situations in which an adaptive pattern of responding competes with undesirable behaviors. Pretask requests are an antecedent strategy in that the procedure is used to keep the undesirable behavior from occurring. Pretask requests can be effective in transitions, acquisition of skills, and breaking a chain of undesirable behaviors.

For example, Singer, Singer, and Horner (1987) used pretask requests with four elementary students with moderate to severe disabilities who had extensive histories of noncompliance to teacher requests. The pretask requests were used when the students came in from recess at three different times during the day. During baseline, when the students came in from recess, the teacher met each student at the door and delivered the request, "Go to group now," while pointing to the appropriate set of chairs in the classroom. The students demonstrated low rates of compliance (17% to 33%) during this phase of the study. During the pretask requests phase, the teacher met the students at the door and delivered an individualized set of pretask requests for each student (i.e., "Give me five," "Shake hands," "Say your name") before saying "Go to group now." If the students complied within three seconds, they received verbal praise from the teacher. The results from the study indicated that each of the student's compliance increased to or near 100% levels when the pretask requests were used.

Pretask requests involve identifying three to five simple responses that:

1. The student can already perform,
2. Require a very short time to complete,
3. Are from the same response class as the targeted, desirable behavior, and
4. Have a high probability of being performed following presentation of a teacher request.

They are then followed by a "difficult" request that the student has not performed successfully and is likely to resist via undesirable behavior. A request consists of an instruction to complete a task in which the student frequently engages in undesirable behavior.

There are three main situations in which to use pretask requests. The first is during "transitions" to avoid what is confusing or inappropriate. When a student is changing from one task to another, pretask requests can be used to facilitate appropriate responding during the transition. This avoids giving the student an opportunity to engage in undesirable behaviors. For example, when Shirley is changing from a group lesson to snack time, when the lesson ends, her kindergarten teacher immediately says, "Shirley, stand up, give me five, say your name, then go to the snack table." This avoids giving Shirley the opportunity for undesirable behaviors (not going or saying I don't want to go to snack) and immediately gives her desirable behaviors to engage in that they lead to her going to the snack table.

The second situation is to strengthen the durable responding (or acquisition of skills) by the student. In this situation, pretask requests are interspersed in with tasks that the student has trouble performing or is still learning. This allows the student to make a high density of correct responses and receive reinforcement while learning new tasks. For instance, Vostal and Lee (2011) used pretask requests in a continuous reading task for three adolescents identified with Emotional Behavior Disorders who were instructed on fifth grade reading material. Results indicated that when students read a third grade paragraph immediately before a fifth grade paragraph, they decreased the latency to initiate reading of the fifth grade paragraph and increased words read correctly per minute on the first ten words of the fifth grade paragraph.

In the third situation, pretask requests are used to interrupt a chain of behaviors that typically lead to undesirable responding. Delivering the pretask request early in such a chain increases the likelihood that the undesirable behavior will be avoided, and when the student starts to engage in undesirable behaviors, the pretask requests are delivered so that the student is engaging in desirable behavior. This desired behavior is likely to continue rather than the undesirable behavior. For example, if Leon has an escalation sequence of behaviors when he is presented with math work sheets that involve making an exasperated noise, looking angrily at the teacher, banging his hand on his desk, sitting in his chair with the front legs off the floor, making a rude remark to a peer, and then crumpling his paper and throwing it at the teacher, his teacher could use pretask requests at the beginning of this chain of behaviors. When she gives him the sheet and he makes an exasperated noise, she could ask him to take a deep breath, get out his pencil, put the pencil on the desk, give her a bump with his hands, put his hands on the desk, and take another deep breath. She could then praise him for complying, remind him that he did well yesterday doing math problems, remind him of their secret signal if he needs help, and remind him of the points he will receive for problems answered correctly.

Guidelines for Using Pretask Requests

Pretask requests should only be used if there is a high enough level of reinforcement and antecedent practice for desirable behavior. Otherwise, pretask requests can inadvertently reinforce undesirable behavior. The teacher first needs to decide whether one of these three situations is occurring. If so, then pretask requests may be effective. If not, then another strategy is called for.

Second, the teacher must assess whether the student is bored or frustrated during teaching sessions, is going from a more to a less reinforcing situation, is unclear about the transition, or if there is a chain to the inappropriate behaviors that the student is displaying.

Third, the teacher must determine what behaviors the student reliably performs that may be used in the pretask requests (i.e., "take this," "put it on the table," "come here," etc.). For task variation, it is necessary to establish tasks that the student knows how to perform and enjoys doing.

Fourth, the student must be reinforced for following the requests.

Finally, the teacher must establish the pretask requests as part of the student's school day. It is important to emphasize that pretask requests are a preventative strategy and should not be used as a punishment procedure that follows undesirable behavior.

BEST PRACTICE RECOMMENDATIONS

1. Preventative procedures are focused on antecedent interventions that build student skills that then prevent undesirable behaviors from occurring.
2. Changing the classroom structure and environment can also be an effective preventative procedure.
3. A variety of preventative procedures can be combined as an effective intervention.

DISCUSSION QUESTIONS

1. How do you decide what type of intervention will be most successful with a student or group of students?
2. Does it unnecessarily single out a student to use an intervention, such as relaxation training or pretask request, when other students are not receiving that intervention?
3. Is it likely that these intervention procedures will lead to generalized increases in desireable behavior or decreases in undesireable behavior?

CLASSROOM AND SCHOOL ACTIVITY SUGGESTIONS

1. Observe in a classroom and list the types of undesirable behaviors you see. Match the type of preventative procedure that would be most effective as an intervention for each listed behavior.
2. Interview students about which preventative procedure(s) they would find most appropriate and beneficial to use.

REFERENCES

Archer, T., & Kostrzewa, R. (2012). Physical exercise alleviates ADHD symptoms: Regional deficits and development trajectory. *Neurotoxicity Research, 21*, 195–209.

Barrish, H. H., Saunders, M., & Wolf, M. M. (1969). Good behavior game: Effects of individual contingencies for group consequences on disruptive behavior in a classroom. *Journal of Applied Behavior Analysis, 2*, 119–124.

Conroy, M. A., Sutherland, K. S., Snyder, A. L., & Marsh, S. (2008). Classwide interventions: Effective instruction makes a difference. *Teaching Exceptional Children, 40*, 24–30.

Cowick, B., & Storey, K. (2000). An analysis of functional assessment in relation to students with serious emotional and behaviour disorders. *International Journal of Disability, Development and Education, 47*, 55–75.

Davis, M., Eshelman, E. R., & McKay, M. (2008). *The relaxation and stress reduction workbook* (6th ed.). Oakland, CA: New Harbinger Publications.

George, C. L. (2010). Effects of response cards on performance and participation in social studies for middle school students with emotional and behavioral disorders. *Behavioral Disorders, 35*, 200–213.

Goldstein, A. P., & Glick, B. (1994). Aggression Replacement Training: Curriculum and evaluation. *Simulation & Gaming, 25*, 9–26.

Goldstein, A. P., Glick, B., & Gibbs, J. (1986). *Aggression replacement training: A comprehensive intervention for aggressive youth.* Champaign, IL: Research Press.

Halverson, A. T., & Neary, T. (2009). *Building inclusive schools: Tools and strategies for success* (2nd ed.). Upper Saddle River, NJ: Pearson.

Hillman, C. H., Erickson, K., & Kramer, A. F. (2008). Be smart, exercise your heart: Exercise effects on brain and cognition. *Nature Reviews Neuroscience, 9*, 58–65.

Jones, V., & Jones, L. (2007). *Comprehensive classroom management: Creating communities of support and solving problems* (8th ed.). Boston, MA: Pearson.

Kazdin, A. E. (2001). *Behavior modification in applied settings* (6th ed.). Belmont, CA: Wadsworth/Thomson Learning.

Kleinman, K. E., & Saigh, P.A. (2010). The effects of the good behavior game on the conduct of regular education New York City high school students. *Behavior Modification, 35*, 95–105.

Lassman, K. A., Jolivette, K., & Wehby, J. H. (1999). "My teacher said I did good work today!": Using collaborative behavioral contracting. *Teaching Exceptional Children, 31*, 12–18.

McCurdy, B. L., Lannie, A. L., & Barnabas, E. (2009). Reducing disruptive behavior in an urban school cafeteria: An extension of the Good Behavior Game. *Journal of School Psychology, 47*, 39–54.

Murphy, D. M. (1996). Implications of inclusion for general and special education. *The Elementary School Journal, 96*, 469–493.

Myles, B. S., Moran, M. R., Ormsbee, C. K., & Downing, J. A. (1992). Guidelines for establishing and maintaining token economies. *Intervention in School and Clinic, 27*, 164–169.

Putnam, J. W. (1993). *Cooperative learning and strategies for inclusion.* Baltimore, MD: Paul Brookes.

Shapiro, L. E., & Sprague, R. K. (2009). *The relaxation and stress reduction workbook for kids: Help for children to cope with stress, anxiety and transitions.* Oakland, CA: New Harbinger.

Singer, G. H. S., Singer, J. H. G., & Horner, R. H. (1987). Using pretask requests to increase the probability of compliance for students with severe disabilities. *Journal of the Association for Persons with Severe Handicaps, 12,* 287–291.

Tingstrom, D. H., Sterling Turner, H. E., & Wilczynski, S. M. (2006). The good behavior game: 1969–2002. *Behavior Modification, 30,* 225–253.

Vostal, B. R., & Lee, D. L. (2011). Behavioral momentum during a continuous reading task: An exploratory study. *Journal of Behavioral Education, 20,* 163–181.

Wright, D. B. (2005). *Teaching and learning.* Sacramento, CA: Resources in Special Education.

Chapter 8

COOPERATIVE LEARNING AND PEER TUTORING

Key Point Questions

1. What is cooperative learning?
2. What is peer tutoring?

WINDOW OF THE WORLD CASE STUDY 1

Ms. Flynn was a middle-school teacher who taught earth science among other subjects. She was very enthusiastic about the subject, but a teacher doing a peer review mentioned that Ms. Flynn talked most of the time, and there was little student involvement. Ms. Flynn decided to take some data on her behavior and her lecturing. She was a little mortified to find out that she was talking for almost 95% of the class time! Obviously her enthusiasm for the subject was letting her get carried away, and it was not making students enthusiastic about the subject. After hearing about cooperative learning from some other teachers and after doing some reading about it, she thought that cooperative learning would be an effective strategy to use with her students. There were always a few students in every class who didn't do so well academically, were isolated socially, or had some undesirable behaviors. Her analysis of the classes was that cooperative learning would benefit these students as well as the other students who were already doing well.

129

Ms. Flynn decided that she would initially try cooperative learning in one class to see how it worked. She decided to use the Student Teacher-Achievement Divisions Group Investigation strategy in her second period class, as this was the class in which her students were having the most academic and social problems. She introduced the strategy to the class and for two weeks spent the first part of classes teaching group learning skills to students. She had students model and practice the skills in some short group activities before the whole class. She then decided to implement the strategy for teaching ecosystems as this was a complex topic, and students often disliked and struggled with the material. Ms. Flynn assigned students to their groups so that she balanced the academic and social needs of the groups. While the groups worked, she was surprised to be so busy going from group to group with answering questions, asking questions to see whether students were understanding, and reinforcing desired group work skills. She was pleasantly surprised to see how motivated the students were for making their groups work and to see their improvement in grasping the academic material.

WINDOW OF THE WORLD CASE STUDY 2

The students in Mr. Pflueger's third-grade math classes generally did well academically and socially. Mr. Pflueger was always on the lookout, though, for improving his instruction. He decided that his math classes could sometimes get a bit "dry" and that students were not as engaged as he thought they could be. Three students (Vincent, Molly, and Carmen) tended to "cut up" during these "dry" times, which disrupted the whole class and brought the instruction to a halt. After reading through some books on instructional strategies, he decided that peer tutoring would be a good way to liven things up and increase opportunities for students to actively respond to math calculations and memorization.

Mr. Pflueger decided to use the "Teams-Games-Tournaments/Classwide Peer Tutoring" strategy. He initially did some teaching of peer tutoring skills, having students practice in front of the class and then with peers. Mr. Pflueger then divided the class into teams that competed with each other on a weekly basis. He assigned students within each team to tutoring pairs. Within the pair, students reversed being the tutor and the tutee. For the math problems, the tutee would "say and write" the response, and the tutor would then award two points for each correct response. For incorrect responses, the tutor would provide the correct answer, require the tutee to write the answer three times, and award one point if the tutee corrected the mistake. Immediately after the tutoring session, the students totaled their daily points and recorded them on a scoreboard in the front of the classroom. Students also took a weekly quiz individually, and they earned five points for their team for each correct answer. At the end of the week, all points, including bonus and test points, were totaled, and the winning team was able to redeem its points for special prizes (lunch with Mr. Pflueger, special reading time with the librarian, getting to line up first for the week, special achievement certificates sent home from the principal, etc.).

Mr. Pflueger was very pleased with the active responding of the students, how motivated they were to get points, their academic improvement, and how little time there was for undesirable behavior to occur. This was especially true for Vincent, Molly, and Carmen as they were now actively engaged as both tutors and tutees, and they wanted to do well for their teams.

Key Point Question 1: What Is Cooperative Learning?

The term *cooperative learning* refers to a family of instructional practices in which the teacher gives various directions to groups of students and has them work together on learning academic material (Johnson & Johnson, 2013). Cooperative learning is a flexible method that can be used in a variety of ways and has been shown to be an effective instructional strategy with a wide variety of students (Putnam, 1998). From a Positive Behavior Support perspective, cooperative learning is beneficial for connecting students with peers in a positive way and for developing academic skills, both of which increase desirable behaviors and decrease undesirable behaviors. The purpose of cooperative learning is to enhance academic learning in groups rather than on their own or in competition with other students. This learning has been summarized as:

Table 6.1
Advantages of Cooperative Learning:

---

1. Academic Achievement.
2. Improved Self-Esteem.
3. Active Learning.
4. Social Skill Development.
5. Peer Acceptance and Friendship.

Cooperation, compared with competitive and individualistic efforts, tends to result in higher achievement, greater long-term retention of what is learned, more frequent use of higher-level reasoning (critical thinking) and meta-cognitive thought, more accurate and creative problem solving, more willingness to take on difficult tasks and persist (despite difficulties) in working toward goal accomplishment, more intrinsic motivation, transfer of learning from one situation to another, and greater time on task. (Johnson, Johnson, & Smith, 2007, p. 19)

Table 8.1 provides advantages of cooperative learning strategies.

How Does Cooperative Learning Work?

In cooperative learning, the class typically is divided into groups of three to six students usually of the same age, but differing in ability, ethnicity, and gender. The teacher's directions are designed to have the students work together as a team on an academic task. The students learn to cooperate to follow the teacher's instructions; however, cooperation itself, while a worthwhile objective, is not the principal objective in cooperative learning instruction. When students work together toward a common goal, their mutual dependency often motivates them to work harder to help the group, and thereby themselves, to succeed. In addition, they often must help specific members of the group do well, and they can often become more accepting of (and value) the members of the group.

Cooperation is more than just sharing materials, sitting around a table together, helping another student with assignments, or discussing ideas. Cooperative learning is more formal, and its primary characteristic is interdependence. It is collaboration among students working together toward a common goal. The rewards that are achieved in this type of interaction are based on the work of the group. All of the members of the group receive the same score and reinforcement for the group's efforts. The group is thus affected by each student's contributions. Examples of this type of student to student interaction include preparing a group presentation on a cultural artist, completing a group social studies project, and performing a play (Berry, 2003).

Certain conditions facilitate cooperative learning efforts to be more productive than competitive and individualistic efforts:

1. Clearly perceived positive interdependence.
   A. Students "sink or swim together."
   B. Students in the group have two responsibilities: learn the assigned material and ensure that all members of the group learn the assigned material (no "free riders").
   C. Teachers may add joint reinforcers (e.g., if all members of the group score 90% correct or better, each receives five bonus points).
2. Considerable group interaction.
   A. This positively influences efforts to achieve academic performance, committed relationships and roles within the group, psychological adjustments, and social competence.
3. Clearly perceived individual accountability and personal responsibility to achieve the group's goals.
   A. Keep the size of the group small. The smaller the size, the greater the individual accountability may be.
   B. Give an individual test to each student.
   C. Randomly examine students orally by calling on one student to present the group's work to the teacher (in the presence of the group) or to the entire class.
   D. Observe each group and record the frequency with which each member contributes to the group's work.
   E. Assign one student in each group the role of checker. The checker asks other group members to explain the reasoning and rationale underlying group answers.
   F. Have students teach what they learned to someone else. When all students do this, it is called simultaneous explaining.
4. Frequent use of the relevant interpersonal and small-group skills.
   A. Getting to know each other.

B. Communicating accurately and unambiguously.

C. Accepting and supporting each other.

D. Resolving conflict constructively.

5. Frequent and regular processing of current group functioning to improve the group's future effectiveness.

A. Describing what member actions were helpful and unhelpful.

B. Making decisions about what actions to continue or change.

Guidelines for Implementing Cooperative Learning Groups

It is critical that the teacher reinforce a student **only** when all members of the group succeed in learning the assignment or, in the case where a teacher assigns the students different parts of a complicated task, only on the basis of the group's overall achievement and not according to the merit of any individual student's contribution to the group's effort. Also, the teacher must ensure that the contributions of all members of the group are genuinely important so that the group's success cannot be attributable merely to the work of one or two students. If the teacher merely instructs the students to work together and to help each other, the academic gains are generally no greater than had the students worked alone on the task. These guidelines are summarized in Table 8.2.

Table 8.2
Guidelines for Establishing Cooperative Learning Groups

---

1. Organize the groups.
2. Mix together students of varying motivation and ability levels within a group so that the students learn from each other.
3. Model techniques.
   -Actively teach the cooperative learning skills to students.
4. Gradually increase the responsibility for planning and implementing the tasks to the students.
5. Give groups enough time to work together (a few days, a week, a month)
   -Each group member must be held accountable.
   -Facilitate but do not manage the groups.
   • Provide each student with a strategy card. This card reminds each student the behaviors for being in the group. The card can include: What is the reason for working in group? Do I understand instructions? If I do not understand, ask members for understanding. If members don't understand, ask teacher. Self-monitor progress by asking myself if I am listening and helping. When finished, I ask myself what I have learned.

Adapted from Berry (2003); Goor, Schween, Eldridge, Mallein, and Stauffer (1996); and Sonnier-York & Stanford (2002).

Specific social skills may need to be taught: As with any school situation involving social interactions, students may need to be taught social skills that are specific to making the cooperative learning groups successful. Teachers cannot assume that students necessarily have these skills or that they will use them in the cooperative learning environment. By specifically letting students know the social skills that are expected of them and by teaching those social skills (see chapter 9 for information on social skills instructional strategies), teachers can help ensure that the students have the skills and are able to use them in the group. Table 8.3 provides an overview of special social skills that may need to be taught.

Table 8.3
Specific Social Skills for Cooperative Learning, Which May Need to Be Directly Taught

Contributing ideas.
Asking questions.
Expressing feelings.
Encouraging members to participate.
Providing constructive feedback.
Disagreeing without criticizing.
Elaborating on a comment or an answer.
Checking for understanding.
Using humor to enhance group cohesiveness.
Expressing support and acceptance toward ideas.
Expressing warmth and empathy toward group members.
Exhibiting self-control.
Sharing materials.
Perspective-taking.
Active listening.
Summarizing.
Paraphrasing.
Staying on task.
Staying with the group.
Turn-taking.
Resolving conflicts.
Asking for help.

Arrange the cooperative learning environment: As with any classroom arrangement, it is necessary that careful consideration be given to the physical environment in the classroom for the cooperative learning. Student desks may be arranged in circles or clusters, students may work at a large table, and/or students can work online or through social networking sites. In the classroom, it is important to keep sufficient space between groups to reduce distractions (visual and auditory) as much as possible.

Explain the criteria for academic and social success: It is very important that students understand the performance expectations for individuals and the group as a whole. The teacher needs to make clear any distinctions between group goals and individual accountability. It can be helpful for the teacher to provide examples, models, and role-playing of the desired skills.

Provide closure to the lesson and evaluate the product and progress of group work: At the conclusion of the lesson, the teacher should facilitate a review of the desired outcomes for each group. Direct feedback should be provided to the students regarding the quantity and quality of their work. Reinforcement can then be delivered to individuals and groups as appropriate.

Cooperative learning practices: There are five attributes which are considered "critical" for successful cooperative learning include

1. A common task or learning activity that is suitable for group work.
2. Small-group learning.
3. Cooperative behavior within the group.
4. Interdependence within the group.
5. Individual accountability and responsibility.

Learning Together: Common tasks or learning activities suitable for group work can occur at all grade levels; however, more conceptual learning requires more discussion, explanation, and elaboration. Cooperative behaviors within the group are emphasized. Students work together, discuss, listen, question, explain, elaborate, share ideas and materials, and encourage each other. Within the group, positive interdependence is interpreted as the perception that one is linked with others so that one cannot succeed unless the other team members also succeed. Equal participation in the group is stressed (see Table 8.4 for activities that promote equal participation). Groups are structured so students seek outcomes that are beneficial to everyone within the group. Within the group, individual accountability or responsibility is attained by students checking responses on individual worksheets, the teacher randomly selecting one group member to explain, or the teacher giving individual quizzes or tests. Group members are to hold one another accountable for their learning.

Table 8.4
Activities that promote equal participation:

- Timed Pair Share: Students work in pairs. One student speaks for one minute on topic or question, then the other person speaks for one minute on topic or question
- Rally Write: Students take turns writing answers (e.g., on a worksheet, answer to a question).
- Find Someone Who: Students circulate finding information from classmates or filling out a mind map.
- Numbered Heads Together:
1. Students form teams and count off numbers so each student has a number.
2. A topic is posed to the students.
3. The students are asked to "put their heads together" to share with each other what they know about the topic.
4. The teacher calls out a number, and students with that number stand up and provide one point on the topic that others (with same number) have not yet already shared.

Adapted from Kagan (1990).

Grouping typically is done heterogeneously by mixing gender, race/ethnicity, and achievement levels (i.e., high, medium, low). However, a teacher may sometimes form homogenous groups of students who need to work on a specific skill, procedure, or set of facts.

Positive interdependence is structured in multiple ways. Goal achievement by students is positively correlated–that is, students perceive that they can reach their learning goals if, and only if, group mates also reach their goals. The multiple learning goals are to learn the assigned material and make sure that all group members do the same. Tasks require students not only to agree on answers, but to be able to explain their group's reasoning or strategies. Resource materials can be limited to one copy per group or jigsawed, with each member having different materials. Division of labor sometimes occurs for suitable tasks. Roles are assigned and rotated frequently. Each member is assigned a role that is essential to the group's functioning (e.g., reader, checker, relater/elaborator, accuracy coach, summarizer, encourager, confidence builder). Reinforcers may be given in the form of bonus points if all members of a group achieve preset criteria of excellence.

Reflection (processing) on social skills, academic skills, and group dynamics should occur regularly after group work is completed. Students should discuss how well group members are learning and maintaining effective working relationships. They can also identify helpful or unhelpful behaviors of members and behaviors to continue or to change. It is possible to have shared leadership occur through assigning and rotating roles essential to a group's work.

While cooperative groups are at work, the teacher's role is complex and varies in different phases of the lesson. The teacher specifies academic and social objectives, explains the academic task and cooperative goal structure, monitors and intervenes during group work, evaluates learning and facilitates processing, and provides reinforcement.

Specific Types of Cooperative Learning Groups

Student Teacher-Achievement Divisions

1. Students are grouped heterogeneously based on past achievement, race, ethnicity, and/or gender.
2. Groups are called "teams" in order to transfer some of the motivational dynamics of team sports into the classroom arena.
3. Typically, the teacher follows a cycle of teacher presentation/ direct instruction, team study and practice, individual quizzes, and team recognition.
4. Individual students receive grades based on their own quiz scores.
5. Teams also receive points based on individual members' improvement over past performance (i.e., individuals earn improvement points that are used solely for team recognition).
6. The task for group work is for all members to practice and master facts and skills, as well as solve problems in math and identify main ideas in literature.
7. Student interaction occurs in small teams of four or, occasionally, five members. Students often practice in pairs within their teams.
8. Cooperative behaviors include students discussing the problems or questions together, comparing their answers, and explaining and correcting any misconceptions or mistakes. Peer norms support academic effort and achievement.
9. Positive interdependence occurs when teammates encourage each other to do their best; individual learning is important for team success. The only way for the team to succeed is to concentrate on the learning of every team member.
10. Tasks require discussion and mutual help for all team members to succeed.

11. Explicit teaching of social skills does not occur unless there is a specific need for it.

12. Reflection (or processing) on team functioning is not highly emphasized.

13. Group leadership is not specified; no single leader is selected for a team.

14. The teacher's role varies in different phases of the instructional cycle. The teacher presents information; circulates among and praises the teams; computes base scores, improvement points, and team improvement scores; and presents certificates or other reinforcers to high-performing teams.

Student Teacher-Achievement Divisions Group Investigation:

1. A complex topic is divided into multiple subtopics to be studies by different research groups.

2. The class determines subtopics and organizes into research groups.

3. Groups plan their investigations, what they will study, how they will go about it, and how they will divide the work among the group members.

4. Groups carry out their investigations. Members of each group gather, organize, and analyze information on their subtopic.

5. Groups plan their presentations. Members share and discuss their data with their group and plan the group report together.

6. Groups make their presentations. Reports are delivered to the entire class in a variety of forms and with the participation of all group members.

7. Teachers and students evaluate the group investigation individually, in groups, and as a class. There are varied means for assessing contributions of individual members as well as the group presentation as a whole.

8. The common task or learning activity is to investigate a complex topic divided into subtopics for groups to research. The task should allow all group members to readily participate and have an opportunity to talk, and it should require members to make choices and group decisions.

9. Small-group learning takes place in research groups with no more than four or five members.

10. Cooperative behavior includes jointly planning the investigation using detailed suggestions given for cooperative planning. Students work together and sometimes individually; they assign roles and divide the tasks among themselves, exchange materials, ideas, and information, plan their presentation together, and give feedback to their classmates.

11. Positive interdependence begins with the identification of a broad problem of common concern to the class, which then leads to jointly planning, coordinating, and conducting the investigation. Interdependence takes different forms and different phases of the complex undertaking.

12. Individual accountability or responsibility occurs when students divide up and take responsibility for a part of the task, carry out their investigations, present their findings with all members taking part, receive feedback and/or writing evaluations of their work, and take individual tests.

13. Grouping procedures include random assignment, common interest in a topic, and student or teacher selection. Factors to include in grouping include individual student characteristics, task characteristics, and duration of the group investigation.

14. Explicit teaching of cooperative skills often occurs prior to the investigation. In addition to establishing a climate for interactive talk, the teacher may conduct skill-building exercises to develop students' skills in discussion and reaching consensus. Cooperative skills are taught during the investigation only if a need arises.

15. Reflection by the group members may occur in the final stage of the investigation by students identifying and analyzing what happened, generalizing their learning outcomes to different situations, and setting goals for the improvement of group behavior. Students may be asked to reflect on their own academic and social learning, as well as on the presentations of others.

16. Group structure is not made explicit by the teacher, but is determined by the student groups at different stages of the investigation.

17. The teacher's role changes at different stages in the investigation. The teacher leads exploratory discussions to determine subtopics; helps groups formulate their plans; helps maintain cooperative norms; helps students find information and use study skills;

coordinates planning, presentations, and feedback; and evaluates learning of information, higher level thinking, and cooperative behavior.

Jigsaw Groups

These groups "jigsaw" (divide up) academic content among group members, and each student is then responsible for teaching the other group members about their information section. The learning environment is specifically structured so that the only access any member has to the other content is by paying close attention to the reports (Aronson & Patnoe, 2007).

To increase the chances that each report will be accurate, the students doing the research do not immediately take it back to their jigsaw group. Instead, they meet first with students who have the identical assignment (one from each jigsaw group). For example, students assigned to the topic of Abraham Lincoln's childhood and young adult life meet as a team of specialists, gathering information, becoming experts on their topic, and rehearsing their presentations (the "expert" group). It is particularly useful for students who might have initial difficulty learning or organizing their part of the assignment, for it allows them to hear and rehearse with other "experts." Table 8.5 provides guidelines for implementing Jigsaw groups.

Once each student has mastered his or her content material, the jigsaw groups reconvene in their initial groups. The expert in each group teaches the other group members about his or her content information. Students are then tested on the academic content (e.g., Abraham Lincoln's life).

Benefits of the Jigsaw instruction are:

1. Efficient way to learn the material.
2. Encourages listening, engagement, and empathy by giving each member of the group an essential part to play in the academic activity.
3. Group members must work together as a team to accomplish a common goal. This facilitates interaction among all students in the class, leading them to value each other as contributors to their common task (Aronson & Patnoe, 2007).

Table 8.5
Guidelines for Implementing Jigsaw Groups

1. Divide students into groups of five or six students. The groups should be diverse in terms of gender, ethnicity, race, and ability.
2. Appoint one student from each group as the leader. Initially, this person should be the most mature student in the group.
3. Divide the day's academic content into five or six segments (matching the number of students in the group). For example, if you want history students to learn about Abraham Lincoln, you might divide a short biography of him into stand alone segments on his: (a) childhood and young adult life, (b) family life with Mary and their children, (c) work as a lawyer, (d) political career before 1861, and (e) presidency.
4. Assign each student to learn one segment, making sure students have direct access only to their own segment.
5. Give students time to read over their segment at least twice and become familiar with it.
6. Form temporary "expert groups" by having one student from each jigsaw group join other students assigned to the same segment. Give students in these expert groups time to discuss the main points of their segment and to rehearse the presentations they will make to their jigsaw group.
7. Bring the students back into their jigsaw groups.
8. Instruct each student to present his or her segment to the group. Other students in the group are encouraged to ask questions for understanding and clarification.
9. Move from group to group, observing the process and intervening when necessary.
10. At the end of the session, give a quiz on the material to provide accountability for student learning and performance.

Adapted from Aronson and Patnoe (2007) and Walker and Crogan (1998).

Key Point Question 2: What is Peer Tutoring?

Peer tutoring involves the use of student peers to provide academic instruction for students. Peer tutoring is another method for developing positive social relationships as well as academic skills. Peer tutors may be of the same age or may be older students. As with any learning activity, it is extremely important that the peer tutors be taught necessary skills before they begin the actual tutoring.

Benefits for Tutors

Not only do the students getting tutored benefit academically and socially, but often the tutors do as well. These benefits have been summarized by Galbraith and Winterbottom (2011):

Tutors' perceptions of their role motivated them to learn the material, and their learning was supported by discussion and explanation, revisiting fundamentals, making links between conceptual areas, testing and clarifying their understanding, and reorganising and building ideas, rehearsing them, and working through them repeatedly, to secure their understanding. When tutors employed long answer questions, there was evidence of reflection on their learning and links made between conceptual areas. When preparing to tutor, tutors could focus on key points and engage with basic ideas from alternative perspectives. Mental rehearsal of peer tutoring episodes helped them appreciate weaknesses in their own subject knowledge. (p. 321)

Guidelines for Implementing Peer Tutoring:

1. Determine the roles for tutors. Will they provide instruction, provide reinforcement, take data, be role models?
2. Determine what skills tutors will teach such as academic skills, study skills, or social skills.
3. Recruit and select tutors (not all volunteers should necessarily be used). Tutors can be older or same-age peers, high or low academic achievers, and of the same or different characteristics (gender, ethnic background, cultural background, language spoken, etc.).
4. Tutors need to be trained. Time needs to be taken to train, model, and provide feedback.
5. Tutors need to be supervised after training and be reinforced and provided feedback as necessary (Paine, Radicchi, Rosellini, Deutchman, & Darch, 1983).

Types of Peer Tutoring

Teams-Games-Tournaments/Classwide Peer Tutoring: This strategy combines components of the Good Behavior Game, Cooperative Learning, and Peer Tutoring (Delquardi, Greenwood, Wharton, Carta, & Hall, 1986; Maheady, Harper, & Mallette, 1991).

1. Four major components:
   A. Weekly competing teams.
   B. Highly structured teaching procedures.
   C. Daily point earning and public posting of scores.
   D. Direct practice of functional academic skills.
2. Each week class is randomly divided into two competing teams.
3. The teacher then assigns students within each team to tutoring pairs.
4. One student in the pair serves as the tutor for 10 to 15 minutes, while the other student is the tutee.
5. Then roles are reversed for an equivalent amount of time.
6. While working in dyads, students must follow prescribed teaching procedures:
   A. Tutor presents an instructional item (e.g., spelling word, math problem, social studies question), and the tutee must "say and write" the response.
   B. If the answer is correct, the tutor awards two points.
   C. If the tutee responds incorrectly, the tutor (a) provides the correct answer, (b) requires the tutee to write the answer three times, and (c) awards one point if the tutee corrects the mistake. If the tutee refuses or fails to correct the answer, no points are awarded.
7. The object of the game is to complete as many items as possible in the allotted time.
8. While the peer tutoring is in effect, the teacher moves about the classroom and awards bonus points for "good" tutor and tutee behavior. Behaviors that may be reinforced include: (a) clear and succinct presentation of materials, (b) appropriate use of points, (c) correct use of the error correction procedure, and 4) supportive comments and assistance.
9. Immediately after the tutoring session, students total their daily points and record them on a scoreboard in the front of the classroom.
10. Tutoring sessions typically occur two to four times per week and are followed by a weekly quiz.
11. Students take tests individually, however, and earn five points for each correct answer.
12. At the end of the week, all points, including bonus and test points, are totaled, and the "Winning Team of the Week" is announced.

Weekly results, as well as outstanding individual efforts, are posted in classroom or school bulletins and through achievement certificates.

Pointers

1. Teach students to use CWPT.
   A. Teacher models appropriate tutoring serving as tutor with student as tutee.
   B. Roles are then reversed.
   C. Teacher makes mistakes (provides both positive and negative examples) so students can see how the error-correction procedure works.
   D. Dyads are formed with the rest of the class, and pairs are given practice tutoring and role reversing.
   E. Dyads are monitored closely.
2. Monitor and award bonus points.
   A. Students may fail to benefit from CWPT if procedural components (e.g., error-correction procedure) are not used correctly.
3. Use CWPT often, at least twice per week with 25 to 30 minutes per session.
4. Monitor student and class progress and adjust the CWPT program as necessary.
   A. Too few practice sessions, insufficient length of tutoring sessions, inappropriate use of tutoring procedures, etc.

Why does CWPT work?

1. Ensures high rates of accurate responding.
2. Includes both massed and distributed practice.
3. Requires active engagement of the tutor and tutee.
4. The practice task matches the criterion task (e.g., weekly spelling test).

Peer Assisted Learning Strategy (PALS)

In PALS, students partner with peers, alternating the role of tutor and tutee. Students engage in a variety of structured academic activi-

Table 8.6
Benefits from PALS Instruction

1. Actively involves all students in tasks they can perform or learn to perform successfully.
2. Increases student opportunity to read and practice academic skills.
3. Motivates students to do better academically.
4. Provides for positive and productive peer interaction.
5. Creates opportunity for students who are having academic difficulty to assume an integral role in a valued activity.
6. Helps teachers accommodate academic diversity.

Adapted from Fuchs, Fuchs, and Burish (2000); and Fuchs, Fuchs, Mathes, and Simmons (1997).

ties such as reading aloud, listening, and providing feedback. PALS is typically implemented three times a week for 30 to 35 minutes (Fuchs, Fuchs, & Burish, 2000; Fuchs, Fuchs, Mathes, & Simmons, 1997). Benefits from PALS are provided in Table 8.6.

In the implementation of PALS:

1. Students are assigned to pairs,
2. Students have clear responsibilities. For example for reading in Grades 2 to 6, the tutee will read for 5 minutes, the tutor will follow along and correct mistakes as needed. The tutee will work on academic skills such as comprehension strategies, retelling, summarizing, and predicting with assistance from the tutor.
3. The pairs are part of teams.
4. Points earned by pair are merged with their team and teams can earn a variety of reinforcers.

Why PALS works

1. High response rate.
2. High levels of on-task behavior.
3. Immediate feedback on performance.
4. Tied into token economy system.

BEST PRACTICE RECOMMENDATIONS

1. Group skills must be directly taught to students before the implementation of cooperative learning interventions.

2. Peer tutoring skills should be taught to both the tutor and tutee before the implementation of the tutoring. Reinforcement by the teacher should be delivered to both the tutor and tutee.

DISCUSSION QUESTIONS

1. How much cooperative learning is appropriate in a class?
2. What academic subjects are best taught with cooperative learning?
3. How much peer tutoring is appropriate in a class?
4. What academic subjects are best taught with peer tutoring?

CLASSROOM AND SCHOOL ACTIVITY SUGGESTIONS

1. In a classroom in which cooperative learning, peer tutoring, and teacher-led instruction take place, take frequency data on undesirable student behaviors and active student responses during these three conditions.
2. Interview teachers and students to see which learning condition that they prefer and why.

REFERENCES

Aronson, E., & Patnoe, S. (2007). *The jigsaw classroom: Building cooperation in the classroom* (2nd ed.). New York: Longman.

Berry, R. L. (2003). Creating cooperative classrooms. *Education Digest, 69*, 39–42.

Delquardi, J., Greenwood, C. R., Wharton, D., Carta, J. J., & Hall, R. V. (1986). Classwide peer tutoring. *Exceptional Children, 52*, 535–542.

Fuchs, D., Fuchs, L. S., & Burish, P. (2000). Peer-Assisted Learning Strategies: An evidence-based practice to promote reading achievement. *Learning Disabilities Research and Practice, 15*, 85–91.

Fuchs, D., Fuchs, L. S., Mathes, P., & Simmons, D. (1997). Peer-Assisted Learning Strategies: Making classrooms more responsive to student diversity. *American Educational Research Journal, 34*, 174–206.

Galbraith, J., & Winterbottom, M. (2011). Peer tutoring: What's in it for the tutor? *Educational Studies, 37*, 321–332.

Goor, M., Schween, J., Eldridge, A., Mallein, D., & Stauffer, J. (1996). Using strategy cards to enhance cooperative learning for students with learning disabilities. *Teaching Exceptional Children, 28,* 66–68.

Johnson, D. W., & Johnson, F. (2013). *Joining together: Group theory and group skills* (11th ed.). Boston, MA: Pearson.

Johnson, D., Johnson, R., & Smith, K. (2007). The state of cooperative learning in postsecondary and professional settings. *Educational Psychology Review, 19,* 15–29.

Kagan, S. (1990). A structural approach to cooperative learning. *Educational Leadership, 47,* 12–15.

Maheady, L., Harper, G. F., & Mallette, B. (1991). Peer mediated instruction: A review of potential applications for special education. *Reading, Writing, and Learning Disabilities, 7,* 75–103.

Paine, S. C., Radicchi, J., Rosellini, L. C., Deutchman, L., & Darch, C. B. (1983). *Structuring your classroom for academic success.* Champaign, IL: Research Press.

Putman, J. W. (1998). *Cooperative learning and strategies for Inclusion.* Baltimore, MD: Paul Brooks.

Sonnier-York, C., & Stanford, P. (2002). Learning to cooperate. *Teaching Exceptional Children, 34,* 40–44.

Walker, I., & Crogan, M. (1998). Academic performance, prejudice, and the jigsaw classroom: New pieces to the puzzle. *Journal of Community and Applied Social Psychology, 8,* 381–393.

Chapter 9

SELF-MANAGEMENT STRATEGIES

Key Point Questions

1. What is self-management?
2. Why are using self-management strategies advantageous for students?
3. What are the types of self-management strategies?
4. How are self-management skills taught?
5. How can self-management strategies be used to increase a student's positive behavior?

WINDOW TO THE WORLD CASE STUDY 1

Martin is a middle-school student who attends an "inclusive school" where all students, regardless of whether they receive special education services, are educated together in general education classrooms. Martin does receive special education services due to the impact of a mild learning disability on academic progress. This impact is specifically observed in his organizational ability. One area in particular with which Martin struggles is organizing his homework assignments in his backpack, which is beginning to cause both academic and behavioral problems. When in class, Martin follows directions to write his homework down, which is done on a piece of paper from his loose leaf binder. Once his homework is written down, Martin stuffs the homework assignment paper in his backpack, along with any related home-

149

work handouts. Once at home and ready to work, Martin has difficulty finding his homework materials and assignments for each of his four academic classes. He dumps out the contents of his backpack, which usually consist of crumpled up school papers, lunch wrappings, broken pencils, and various collected gadgets. When the homework papers are found (often in a jumbled ball), they are usually torn, wrinkled, and unreadable. This has caused such frustration and anxiety that Martin will often refuse to do or complete his homework. On some occasions, he's so upset he will lock himself in his bedroom refusing to attempt any homework.

Both Martin's parents and teachers are worried about Martin's lack of organization skills as it is preventing his progress in all his classes and beginning to cause some behavior problems both at home and school. A meeting was held with Martin, two of his teachers, and Martin's parents to see what could be done to help Martin. It was decided that Martin needed a better strategy for how he records his homework and how he stores homework handouts in his backpack (other than the haphazard strategy he's currently using). It was also discussed that due to the fact that Martin moves from class to class, he needs a way to learn to manage this task independently, yet be able to receive feedback from his teacher and parents that his management system is working.

Martin thought it was a good idea when his teachers proposed the use of a self-management system for organizing his backpack that he could use at both school and home. For this system, Martin and his father went shopping and bought four different colored spiral notebooks, one notebook for each class. Additionally, each notebook came with a two-sided pocket page. Martin agreed that he would write down his homework for each class in the designated color-selected notebook (green for math, red for social studies, etc.). He would also put any handouts for each class in the notebook's pocket page. Martin's history teacher offered to design a daily check-off list with the step-by-step instructions Martin would follow, and Martin promised to carry this check-off list in his loose leaf binder, which he carried between school and home. This daily check-off list provided a section for each class. After each class, Martin would assess whether he followed the steps on the checklist for organizing his homework materials and check off the boxes indicating completion for each completed step. If he missed a step, he would go back and complete it. Once this was done, he would seek out the teacher to confirm he had used the system correctly. The teacher would confirm by signing the section filled out for that class. Everyone agreed that in order to have a well-organized backpack, the following steps would be on the form:

- homework written in notebook,
- handouts and/or materials placed in notebook pocket,
- notebook put in backpack,
- book, if needed, put in backpack
- pens, pencils (whole and broken), and erasers in side backpack pocket,
- other items and gadgets in inside backpack pocket,
- all wrappers and garbage thrown in trash.

Also included on the form is a line for each teacher and one parent to sign and date confirming that Martin correctly followed instruction along with any comments for corrective feedback, if needed. This way both teachers and parents would be able to communicate to Martin and each other about how the system was working.

At home, Martin's mom and dad agreed that one of them would sign the form when homework had been completed and the checklist steps followed for returning work into the correct notebook pocket and all materials into the backpack. For a further incentive, mom had Martin make a list of special rewards he liked. On Fridays, mom and Martin would review the week's self-management forms, and if Martin was successful in most classes (75%) on four out of five days, he would choose a reward from the list.

For the first three weeks, Martin would recruit feedback from each class teacher confirming that he had correctly used the checklist after each class. After three weeks, if Martin had successfully used the system, he would recruit teacher feedback only on Fridays. Everyone agreed that if Martin mastered the strategy for four weeks and was successful with homework completion, he would fade out teacher feedback by using the system on his own, omitting the teacher signatures.

WINDOW TO THE WORLD CASE STUDY 2

Marisha is a freshman in high school and considered a successful and respectful student by all of her teachers. She is well liked by her peers and enjoys drama and music. For the first semester of ninth grade, she received a 3.5 grade point average on her report card. At the beginning of the second semester, Marisha suddenly became withdrawn and appeared unhappy in her classes. Teachers began to comment to each other that they were concerned about her. The geometry teacher, in particular, was observing that Marisha appeared to be arguing with classmates during class, and her grades on class assignments were not passing grades. The other teachers expressed the same observation of Marisha not getting along with peers, but she was still getting good grades on assignments in other classes. The geometry teacher realized that it was time to find out from Marisha what was going on as it appeared it might be related to the geometry class (the only class where academically she was not doing well). The geometry teacher met with Marisha after class one day. The geometry teacher knew that academic problems can often cause students to behave poorly, especially when they don't understand material and are too shy to seek out help. So, rather than asking Marisha about her arguments with classmates, she decided to ask Marisha about how she felt about geometry and what she was learning. The teacher thought Marisha looked relieved when asked the question. Marisha readily admitted that she often did not understand what was being asked in the math questions and therefore could not figure out what equations to use to solve the problems. She also did not want her classmates to see her always asking for help. The teacher offered to provide Marisha with a guide sheet with equations matched with information on what type of problems to use them with. Additionally, she would embed at the bottom of the guide sheet a reminder for Marisha, if still needing help after reviewing the guide sheet, to put a pink sticky note on the corner of her desk indicating to the teacher to come to her desk to provide more help. This way by being able to review information she was forgetting, without constant teacher help, she could work more independently yet still have access to the teacher's help, if needed. Marisha liked the idea of managing her learning more on her own and having a "teacher help" system that would not focus too much classmate attention on her. After using the guide for two weeks, Marisha found that only occasionally did she need to talk to the teacher, and it was very similar to the occurrence rate other students needed teacher help. Additionally after two weeks, Marisha's teachers all commented on how Marisha's unhappiness and arguing behavior had disappeared.

Key Point Question 1: What Is Self-Management?

Self-management broadly refers to specific procedures used by an individual to influence his or her own behavior (Browder & Shapiro, 1985). Terms such as *self-regulation, self-monitoring, self-control, self-evaluation,* and *self-reinforcement* are often used interchangeably with the term *self-management.* Self-management may be viewed as giving the student specific skills and strategies to control his or her actions. In school settings, control is transferred from teacher to student through teaching the student skills and specific strategies to control or modify his or her own behavior. Ideally, the self-management process will involve a student (and/or teacher):

(1) Recognizing there is a problem,
(2) Seeing the problem as consisting of behavior(s) that need altering or changing,
(3) Determining the natural contingencies currently controlling the behavior,
(4) Arranging and/or changing those natural contingencies for supporting the desired behavior(s) to occur (Baer, 1984).

Through this self-management process, the chance of changing the behavior that has caused the problem will be increased. For example, in the Windows of the World Case Study 1, Martin's inability to complete homework was caused by his behavior of just throwing his papers randomly in his backpack. By changing the behavior of how he puts homework assignments in his backpack, he was able to complete his homework. Using a self-management checklist, Martin was able to respond to a cue (each step on the checklist) and self-record by placing a check next to completed steps.

Key Point Question 2: Why Are Using Self-Management Strategies Advantageous For Students?

The self-management process is useful when students have become dependent on teachers for prompts, cues, instructions, or reinforcement for completion of school work and tasks. Self-management procedures can provide the student with a positive means of transforming the need for external reminders and/or instructions from the teacher to independently using a self-managed prompt delivery process, thus taking control of their own learning process.

The first advantage for students using self-management strategies is that it involves students in their own behavior change. Rather than the teacher imposing structure for students to behave a specific way, students use a self-management strategy that guides them to change their own behavior. The result is that students are able to do tasks more independently, thus giving them more control over their learning. Being able to decide about how one learns, track one's own progress, and have more "say so" gives the student more "empowerment" or "buy in," power and flexibility in the learning process. For example, if a student has trouble remembering the directions for a class assignment, a step-by-step task analysis checklist on the desk can be used to list the order of the steps for the assignment. Once each step is completed, the student can check off the completed step. This allows the student to be more independent while working and less dependent on constantly asking the teacher for help. It is also important that this independence also decreases passivity or learned helplessness in students.

The second advantage is that the successful use of the self-management strategy in one setting can often be easily used in another setting (e.g., generalization across settings), such as using the homework checklist not only for math class but also for history and language arts classes. A checklist could also be used for physical education class to show steps in dressing for gym or posted in a school locker listing what books and materials to take to each class.

Self-management strategies can be generalized with another behavior, such as using a tally sheet to keep track of the times one is "raising hand" in class instead of calling out; likewise, a tally sheet can be used for recording "keeping quiet while the teacher is talking instead of talking to a classmate." Most self-management strategies can be designed to be used any time of the day or in any situation. Keeping with the checklist strategy example, if a student has learned to use a checklist for monitoring homework, he or she could also use it at home for doing chores, and so on.

Its use can also be generalized across people (e.g., a self-managed weekly behavior contract for general work completion can be used with all the student's teachers). These examples provide a picture of the versatility of a self-management strategy by showing that the use of a self-management strategy can be generalized to other classes, situations, behaviors, teachers, or times of the day to monitor and assess one's own behavior. If a student learns to successfully use a self-management process in these ways, he or she is more likely to continue using it in the future. Self-management strategies provide great benefit to both the student and the teacher due to the reduced student need for repeated instructions, teacher reminders, and teacher micro-management.

A third advantage is that the student may keep track of progress and assess whether the strategy is working. For example, using a step-by-step task analysis for completion of work, a student can determine whether a step has been completed or missed. Doing so increases the likelihood that assignments will be complete and helps the student to know whether a step in the task needs more clarification.

Use of self-management strategies may allow for behaviors to come under control of naturally occurring cues or stimuli (e.g., the discriminative stimulus) and decrease the need for teachers to tell students when to move to an assignment's next step or change tasks. An example of a stimulus in self-management is the use of a digital timer on a smart phone to alert the student when it's time to change subjects or tasks. The timer can be set two minutes before a class session is over to signal to the student to finish up the step in progress and prepare for the next subject or activity.

Initially, teachers may find that setting up a self-management process for a student may be time consuming as an increase in "up front" teaching may be required. However, once a process is in place, the student's use of the strategy often frees up a teacher's time by not having to help that student and enables the student to work more independently. Additionally, the student can use the strategy in multiple classes and settings and use it as a self-assessment tool for monitoring his or her own progress, thus being able to decide on any needed future modification to the strategy. For example, a student who is working on raising his or her hand and waiting for the teacher to call on him or her to answer a question instead of shouting out the answer could use a checklist to tally the occurrence of "raising hand and waiting to be called on" in each class. For every time the student raises his or her hand and waits, the student puts a check on the tally card. The tally card is taken from class to class through the entire day. At the end of the day, the student tallies the checks for the day. At the end of the week, the student graphs the tallies for each day. The student then is able to see the progress or lack of progress and assess how to improve the behavior. If the student is providing herself with a reinforcer at the end of the week for good progress, she might decide (after assessing her weekly progress in each class) to reinforce immediately after a particular class where the occurrence of shouting out has not decreased, such as giving herself a reinforcer after math class for "raising her hand" just once or when there is any increase beyond her past performance, but not reinforce in the writing class where her tally has indicated that most of the time she is raising her hand.

Key Point Question 3: What Are the Types of Self-Management Strategies?

Self-management strategies need to be tailored to the needs of the student and the appropriateness for the environment and the situation. The following are types of self-management procedures.

Antecedent Cue Regulation

Antecedents are information or stimuli provided before the behavior is to occur. Antecedent cue regulation involves the use of prompts that lead the student to the correct response. The antecedent prompt occurs before the student behavior is supposed to occur. The prompt (cue) signals the student to perform the target behavior. Prompts may be in verbal, written, physical, audio, symbolic, or pictorial form. Examples of pictorial prompts for young students might include pictures glued to the top of their desk depicting the items needed every day for learning (e.g., pencils, supply box, name card, etc.). Students look at the pictures when they come to class and obtain the items shown. The pictures (antecedent) remind the students to gather together the items. Initially, the teacher may verbally prompt the students to look at the pictures, but as the behavior for using the pictures is repeatedly built into the routine, the teacher prompts will fade out, allowing the students to become independent in completing this task. For older students, a small calendar on the desk indicating the subjects and materials needed for each day of the week and the specific time of day can be used.

Using a checklist with written step-by-step instructions for completing an assignment, posting a chart listing classroom rules as a student reminder, or providing checklists for math or science formulas to guide the student to a correct response are quick and easy self-management examples. Checklists may be on note cards, sticky notes, a computer screen or digital device, or in notebooks. If desired, pictures or symbols can be used in place of words. A task analysis consists of written step-by-step instructions that lead the student to a correct response (Storey & Miner, 2011). For example, a self-management system might list the items to be put away at the end of class using icons (pencil, paper, books, and worksheets). These icons can be listed with check boxes next to them. The checklist can be used for leading a student to perform every step within a task (such as getting assignments and materials ready for taking home), perform an entire task looking up information on a topic such as the Angor civilization of Cambodia, and making note cards with relevant information on their buildings and temples) or to perform a series of tasks in correct order over a longer period of time (writing an essay by "chunking" out the sections that need to be completed and in what order).

Clocks and time-keeping devices (analog or digital) set to provide a tone as a reminder to perform an activity at a specified time, such as taking medication or eating a snack. A clock face can be modified to replace a number on a clock face with a symbol for a specific task. This is advantageous when a task is done at the same time each day, such as having lunch at 12:00 p.m. A picture of a lunch pack or sandwich and drink can be shown where the 12:00 hour is, cueing the student that it is time to have lunch.

Recording devices (smart phones, laptops, or other electronic devices) can be prerecorded to deliver an audio cue. The student listens to the prompt, performs the task, listens to the next prompt, and so on. Examples for using this type of recorded prompting are: following recipe steps, following directions for cleaning up an area of the classroom at the end of the day, or following steps for a science experiment. Many students find auditory cues more understandable than written instructions (or need both the written instructions and the auditory instructions paired together). This is especially helpful when learning a new task where correct sequence is important, such as learning long division, following job tasks when working in the cafeteria, or building a model in subjects such as science. Computer text to speech software can be used to read the prompts for each step, allowing the student to click on the next step. Many applications for delivery of visual and/or auditory prompting are now available to be downloaded into smart phones, mobile handheld devices, or other electronic devices that can be used for prompting and self-management strategies (www.iprompts.com).

Many students find it useful to have a list of steps to follow when they are angry or upset. For these situations, students may keep a card in their desk to pull out and read to help them reduce the agitation. Teaching students to use self-verbalization and self-monitoring in upsetting social situations can help them from losing self-control and responding impulsively (Lerner & Johns, 2009). Students write questions on a card to help them "stop and think" before responding. They can create their own questions to follow. An example of this could be:

WHAT IF ?
What Happened?
How did it make me feel?
Are there good reasons I need to tell someone who can help?
Try counting to ten backward to calm down.
If I am still upset and can't work, I will talk to the teacher or a supervising adult.

Pictures, icons, symbols, and graphic organizers also provide antecedent cues to a student. For example, a checklist using pictures or icons could also be used for physical education class to show steps in dressing for gym. Each icon depicts the next garment to put on in the dressing process. An icon checklist can also be posted in a school locker illustrating which books and materials are needed for each class. Additionally, pictures or icons can be used to show procedures such as actions to follow in a fire drill as shown:

Graphic organizers serve as a visual representation of the learning process (steps in creating a project, studying for a test, writing a paper) and providing a reminder to stay on task. Graphic organizers are useful self-management tools as they provide "cues" to stimulate newly learned information or help students organize information. Graphics should be simple, use minimal text, and eliminate unnecessary detail to keep the message concise and clear (Lever-Duffy & McDonald,

2011), such as a planning matrix illustrating a schedule for homework due in each class for each day of the week or month. Another graphic such as a planning tree can be used to show the goals and subgoals of a project with the sequence of tasks listed in each appropriate goal box (Forte & Schurr, 1996). See Figure 9.1 for example of a planning tree.

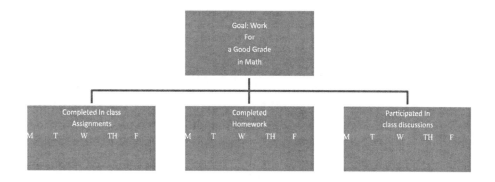

Figure 9.1. Planning Tree for Obtaining a Good Grade in Math Class

Self-Monitoring and Self-Recording as Part of the Self-Evaluation Process

Self-Monitoring and Self-Recording: Self-monitoring and self-recording involve students evaluating whether they have performed a behavior (self-monitoring) along with creating a written record of each time the behavior is performed (self-recording). In this process, the self-monitoring provides the opportunity for the students to become aware of their performance (when they **are** performing the behavior as well as when they **are not** performing the behavior). If students want to increase their success rate for completing their homework by keeping a daily record to see which days they complete homework, then they may find it useful to see whether there is a pattern for the noncompletion, such as particular days when homework is not completed (see Figure 9.1). If Tuesdays turn out to be nonhomework completion days, the student can analyze the cause (perhaps every Tuesday is a three-hour after school sports practice day, leaving little time for homework, along with feeling extreme fatigue in the evening). In this example, knowing when homework is not being completed becomes valuable information in assessing how to address the problem. Knowing the possible cause helps the student devise a solution that could be to arrange with the math teacher to do two assignments on Monday (and none on Tuesday) or complete the Tuesday math assignment during a study period. In this example, knowing when the behavior was not occurring was valuable information for changing the behavior. Table 9.2 provides an example of a student monitoring their being focused on teacher instruction.

Self-Evaluation: The self-recording of the data provides the tool for students to self-evaluate their performance to an educational standard or a self-selected goal (Storey, 2008). These two steps–self-monitoring and then self-recording–become part of a self-evaluation process providing students with the information on whether the behavior has occurred or whether the targeted goal has been met; in this way, it gives students an active role for assessing their own progress. Additionally, this self-evaluation can often serve as a reinforcing activity because it is completed independent of the teacher and gives the students feedback on the degree of success achieved on the targeted task. A useful and simple assessment tool for this is a checklist. A checklist helps students identify key criteria for a task, such as reviewing their own writing work against listed criterion writing standards, and provides information for any needed revisions. This same checklist can serve as a conference tool with the teacher in order to receive further feedback on progress (Culham & Wheeler, 2003). Besides academics, targeted behaviors can be self-evaluated. An example of a simple self-evaluation strategy for young students to im- prove getting along with others is to have a small card on the desk for students to circle a happy face next to a picture or icon of children sharing when they have shared during an activity and to circle a sad face when they have not shared. Initially, the criteria chosen might be that the student will share at least once during a given activity, and when this is accomplished, the criterion is increased for future activities. After the activity, the student gives the card to the teacher for feedback and reinforcement.

Self-Recruited Feedback, Self-Determined Reinforcers, and Choice of Reinforcers

Mank and Horner (1997) define self-recruited feedback as involving people in their own intervention and involves three components: (a) self-monitoring of the specific behavior, (b) self-evaluation of performance against a predefined criterion, and (c) recruitment of contingent feedback from the external environment. An example of self-recruited feedback is when a student completes a specific task, self-evaluates her behavior, scores it, and then shares the information with the teacher for feedback and reinforcement. A clear example of self-recruited feedback is the student scoring her sharing behavior with happy or sad faces next to the sharing icon and then taking it to the teacher for feedback. Once the teacher and student review the scoring, reinforcement is delivered. Reinforcement can be of many different types. For some students, the teacher's attention and comments may be sufficient reinforcement. However, some students may initially only be satisfied with an additional tangible reinforcer. This reinforcer could be in the form of tokens or points traded in later for an item from a selection of prizes. If the student uses self-reinforcement (which is always combined with self-evaluation or self-monitoring), then the reinforcer would be administered by themselves. In this process, they decide on a reinforcer such as a treat they give themselves from their desk or a token they put in their pencil box for redeeming a self chosen prize later. An advantage of self-reinforcement is the immediacy of reinforcement delivery as teachers are often not available to reinforce in a timely manner. Involving students in choosing the evaluation criteria (self-determined criteria) is a further step for supporting students in becoming independent in their learning. Student determine the criteria for success (e.g., two happy faces for each activity). An example for using this process is shown in Table 9.1

Table 9.1
Self-Monitoring, Self-Evaluation, Self-Determined Reinforcement
Example for a Classroom Setting.

Student daydreams in his math class not focusing on instruction.	Identification of the problem
Student needs to be focused on teacher instruction.	Determining behavior to be changed
Student uses a timer (smart phone in pocket that vibrates) to go off every two minutes to alert him to be focused on teacher instruction.	Determining a solution
When the timer goes off, student observes whether he is focused on teacher instruction. If he is on task, he uses a tally sheet listing the time intervals and puts a plus mark next to that interval if he was focused on teacher instruction, or a minus mark if he was not focused on teacher instruction when the timer went off.	Self-monitoring of target behavior
Student decides that to start he will need one plus mark for math class. When achieved he will increase by one the number of plus marks needed for next class session.	Self-determined criteria
At the end of the class session, student tallies up the plus marks; if there are one or more checks, he then provides himself with a reinforcer from a menu of preferred activities.	Self-evaluation of performance
Student has achieved his self-determined criteria and chooses to reward himself by going to the school library to read his favorite magazines after school (included on his self-reinforcement menu).	Self-Reinforcement

Table 9.2

Self-Monitoring Form for a Single Behavior Example for the Classroom

Time Intervals Math Class: 10:00–10:35 Date:	Desired Behavior: Focused on teacher instruction When the timer goes off, decide whether you are focused on teacher instruction. Put a + for focused on teacher instruction. Put a 0 for not being focused on teacher instruction.	
10:02	+	
10:4	+	
10:6	0	
10:8	+	
10:10	0	
10:12	+	
Total +	4	
Self-Determined criteria	4	
Met Goal?	YES	NO
Choose self-determined reinforce?	YES	NO
Keep Goal:	YES	NO
Decrease Goal	YES	NO
Increase Goal	YES TO: 5	NO

Self-Punishment and Self-Management

If self-punishment is utilized in a self-management strategy, it may involve a "response cost" procedure, where students would lose points, tokens, or privileges already embedded in their school program. The intent for using a response cost system would be to target a behavior that needs to be decreased, such as spitting, destroying property, yelling at the teacher, and so on. An example of using a response cost in a self-management system would be when a student gives herself ten tokens at the beginning of the day and takes away a token each time she performs the target behavior to decrease. The teacher and student can determine ahead of time how many tokens (eight, nine, or ten tokens) she must keep to receive the "free time" or other chosen privilege at the end of the day. It should be remembered that students typically are more motivated to succeed when they are obtaining something they want rather than when they are losing something. However, using a response cost system in a self-management strategy can be effective for decreasing undesired behaviors when the process is used in conjunction with strategies that build new desired behaviors through the use of positive reinforcement. An example of this would be teaching the student who yells at the teacher (behavior to be decreased) to count to ten before responding when angry (alternative behavior) and then to use a calm voice to respond (desired behavior). When students perform the desirable alternative behavior, they are positively reinforced with a compliment or a stronger reinforcer, such as points or a tangible reinforcer, if needed. If students do yell at the teacher, then they would fine themselves a certain number of points.

Key Question 4: How Are Self-Management Skills Best Taught?

Snell and Brown (2006) outline the combination of components needed to set up a self-management tool such as deciding on the goal (what behavior needs changing), choosing a manner in which progress will be recorded (self-monitoring), evaluating whether progress is being made (self-assessment), and deciding on a reward for progress made (self-reinforcement).

The following steps outlined by Koegel, Koegel, and Park (1992) are helpful for setting up a self-management program:

A. Getting Ready
    a. Define behaviors
    b. Measure behaviors

     c. Choose a reinforce

     d. Select an initial goal

  B. Teaching Self-Management

     a. Get materials

     b. Teach identification of the behavior

     c. Record the behavior

     d. Reinforce self-management

  C. Creating Independence

     a. Increase the amount of time the individual self-manages behavior

     b. Fade reliance on prompts

     c. Increase the number of response necessary for a reinforce

     d. Fade the presence of the teacher.

Function of Behavior and Environment in Developing Self-Management Systems

The first step in designing the self-management system is for the student to be able to describe and/or demonstrate the target behavior to change. Additionally, the student and teacher must understand the factors that influence the behavior in order to develop a self-management plan that will actually address the target behavior. Depending on the function (reason) for the behavior, a self-management system may or may not be the correct tool to meet the student's need. Understanding the function of a behavior can also help determine situations when a self-management tool may not be the correct choice for intervening. If the functional assessment indicates that the antecedents involve a student not understanding the task, not learning the task, or not being attentive to or responsive to cues or consequences, then a different strategy should be chosen. An example of this would be where a student cannot check off the systematic steps for writing a short story because he doesn't understand the curricular terms stated in the steps describing the writing process. Once those terms are directly taught, then the student can use the checklist. In those cases where a student is not responsive to cues and consequences (reinforcers), the functional assessment process provides a means to delve deeper into assessing the student's specific behavioral needs for determining the best choice of interventions.

Teaching Self-Management

Students need to understand that a behavior is an action they perform They need to be aware of what it looks like or feels like in order to monitor whether the behavior has occurred. It is important to understand that teachers will often need to directly teach the self-management strategy, demonstrate it, and provide guided practice for the student. Direct teaching of the self-management strategy is extremely important. This can be done through the teacher initially modeling for the students the strategy's components: recording, monitoring, and reinforcing (example could be the teacher using a checklist as a reminder to take attendance, monitoring his progress at the end of the week, and buying ice cream at Friday lunch for 100% weekly attendance taking). Role play would be another way to have the student practice the strategy by moving through each component in a short period of time just to practice the skill (teacher might create a lesson plan on how to use the strategy using examples of typical student expected behaviors such as raising hand to answer questions, lining up quietly to leave classroom, etc.). Only describing to the student how to use the self-management strategy may not be enough for the student to then successfully use the system. Student independent practice of the self-management strategy should include teacher supervision with delivery of reinforcement for using the strategy. Teaching should include reinforcement, prompts of encouragement, and corrective feedback, when needed. In time the frequency of reinforcers might be decreased to allow the natural occurring stimuli to control the desired behavior.

Key Question 5: How Can Self-Management Strategies Be Used Effectively to Increase a Student's Positive Behavior?

Involving the student directly in the self-management process is the most effective way to increase a student's desirable behavior. For this reason, self-management strategies such as keeping a written record of behaviors performed during a specific time and place are often easy to use. Whether self-management strategies are designed for a single targeted behavior response (raising hand to speak in class) or for a series of steps in a behavior (how to get ready for class), the design should be as simple and clear as possible for student understanding and ease of

Table 9.3
Self-Monitoring form for a Chain of Behaviors Example for the Classroom

Steps to Be Ready for Class	Completed Step: Circle Yes or No
Personal belongings put away	YES NO
Tool box on top of desk	YES NO
Activity folder on top of desk	YES NO
Quiet and sitting at desk, looking at teacher	YES NO

use. Figure 9.2 illustrates a self-management form for a single behavior, and Table 9.3 illustrates self-management steps in a chain of behaviors.

Once a student has been directly taught a new skill, he or she can use a task analysis self-management form, where each step in the new skill is listed and designed for the student to check off each step once performed. This is an ideal way for students to practice the new skill on his or her own without missing a critical step and causing an error in learning the skill. Additionally, a task analysis form may be used to help the student review a previously learned skill to maintain or relearn it.

A self-evaluation form can be used by students to show how well they performed on a learned skill or how well they are mastering a target behavior that needs improving. A self-evaluation form is an effective way for students to monitor their own progress and review the results with teacher for feedback (see Table 9.4)

Most importantly, self-management processes should be adapted to meet the individual needs, learning styles, and preferences of the students. For example, a student may prefer a notebook to a checklist on the desk to keep track of tasks; some students may find a visible self-management procedure embarrassing or stigmatizing.

The following steps are provided for teachers to follow when setting up a self-management process:

- Involve students in the process.
- Collaborate with student for each step in process and engage them in the design of the self-management form.

Table 9.4
Self-Evaluation Form for a Chain of Behaviors Example for the Classroom

Follow Steps to be Ready for Class	Completed Step: Circle Yes or No	Teacher Feedback
Personal belongings put away	YES NO	YES NO COMMENT:
Tool box on top of desk	YES NO	YES NO COMMENT:
Activity folder on top of desk	YES NO	YES NO COMMENT:
Quiet and sitting at desk, looking at teacher	YES NO	YES NO COMMENT:

- Adapt process to learning style and preference of students.
- Model the strategy.
- Have students practice the strategy with teacher monitoring.
- Provide praise and corrective feedback.
- Have students use the strategy independently periodically checking for accuracy.
- Once students are competent in using strategy, allow independence. An occasional reminder to use it in appropriate situations may be needed.

Younger students may be more limited in their involvement in creating the process, but they should be given as much choice as possible in the creation of the form and procedure.

Self-management strategies promote learning in a less supervised setting (such as the lunchroom or quad) and facilitate as much independence as possible for students. Independence gives students the opportunity to control how they learn and the pace of learning. For the teacher, increasing the use of self-management strategies fades out student reliance on the teacher, reducing the need for constant prompting by the teacher and instructional staff, thereby freeing up their instructional time to support other students. Further advantages for teacher and student are outlined in Table 9.5

Table 9.5
Advantages for Students and Teachers using Self-Management

Advantage for Student	Advantage for Teachers	Steps for Implementing a Self-Monitoring Strategy	Example
Monitor and adjust own behavior	Provides remedies for noncompliant or disruptive behaviors	Choose one behavior to focus on (e.g., completing assignments)	Student will complete in class assignments
Use of strategy increases appropriate behavior	Strategy transfers management of the student's behavior to the student	Consider the type of antecedent prompting that was needed to get student to complete the task and the reinforcement being used.	Student uses a self-monitoring chart showing 5-minute interval boxes that can be checked off indicating whether he or she is on task or off task at end of each interval.
Improves academic work and social skills	Increases positive attitude of teacher toward student	Design a self-monitoring strategy to replace the needed teacher prompting.	A digital timer along with the self-monitoring chart can be used. The digital timer on the desk is set to alert the student every 5 minutes to evaluate whether he or she is working on the assignment. At the end of each 5-minute interval,

Continued on next page

Table 9.5 *cont.*

Advantage for Student	Advantage for Teachers	Steps for Implementing a Self-Monitoring Strategy	Example
			the student assesses whether he or she is on task or off task and checks the yes or no box.
Student perceives him or herself as capable and successful	Increases time spent on other needed instructional tasks	Collaborate with the student on the use of the strategy. Clarify the behavior being self-monitored and the advantage to the student in using self-monitoring.	Student needs to stay focused on working in order to complete assignment. Monitoring her or himself will eliminate the constant teacher prompting, which can be stigmatizing and disruptive to other students.
Student takes ownership of monitoring and evaluating her or his own behavior	Reduces need for constant supervision of student	Teach the student how to self-evaluate her or his on task or off task behavior when the timer goes off. Give examples of what the "on-task" behavior looks like, along with examples of what "off-task" behavior looks like.	When the 5-minute timer goes off, student checks the "on" box if she or he is thinking about the problem, writing out the problem, and working quietly and independently on the problem. Student checks the "no" box if he or she is out of seat, talking to classmates, daydreaming, or doing anything other than the assignment.
Removes teacher reminders that may be embarrassing in front of peers	Relieves teacher from constant prompting	Practice using the self-monitoring form in a simulation.	Teacher should model the use of the strategy. It may

Table 9.5 *cont.*

Advantage for Student	Advantage for Teachers	Steps for Implementing a Self-Monitoring Strategy	Example
			be necessary to simulate or play act "on-task" and "off-task" behavior while using the self-monitoring form with the timer set shorter time intervals. After the teacher models the use, have the student practice a short time.
Use builds confidence, independence, and self-determination (e.g., feelings of "I'm smart. I can do this myself")	Increases feelings of success for both student and teacher	Monitor closely the first use of self-monitoring strategy.	During first use, monitor the process to make sure timer is working and student is correctly using the form. Be available to help the student with the process, if requested. Otherwise, allow student to manage the process on his or her own.
Allows student to correct any errors, building confidence	Allows teacher to prevent future errors from occurring	Meet with student to review first use and make any necessary adjustments.	Discuss how well the strategy worked with student. Answer any questions and give corrective feedback and reinforcement.
Builds feelings of self-mastery	Frees teacher time from supervision	Instruct student on how to count and record the on-task time achieved.	Record the time amount of "on-task" behavior achieved. A total of 30 minutes (6 intervals for 5 minutes each) for on-task behavior is possible.

Continued on next page

Table 9.5 *cont.*

Advantage for Student	Advantage for Teachers	Steps for Implementing a Self-Monitoring Strategy	Example
Builds confidence at each step and promotes feelings of success	Initial investment of planning and time can result in student learning to work on task thereby enabling teacher to provide instruction to other students	Decide on a success level for reinforcement. Initially, any level of success in the use of the strategy should be reinforced. The level of reinforcement can be faded as student masters the strategy. In time, the feeling of independence and success in completing school work may become the only necessary reinforcement.	Reinforcement can be a choice of a preferred activity or an item from a preset class rewards list or from a "tailored to student" choice list created by student and teacher. Initially (perhaps, for first the week) reinforce every day any use of the strategy. Second week, each day reinforce for ten minutes "on task." Third week, each day reinforce for 20 minutes "on task." Fourth week, each day reinforce for 30 minutes "on task."

BEST PRACTICE RECOMMENDATIONS

1. Self-management strategies should be an integral part of a teacher's instructional "tool kit" and be incorporated in both academic and behavioral instruction.
2. When developing a self-management strategy, consider using it in the beginning, middle, and ending phases of instruction. Introducing self-management to a student in the beginning of learning a new skill may reduce errors in learning the task or process incorrectly.

3. Carefully assess the student's learning needs, learning style, preferences, and learning environment before developing a self-management strategy to determine the appropriateness of the strategy. There may be considerable adaptation of a self-management strategy needed for a student or a different instructional approach needed altogether.

DISCUSSION QUESTIONS

1. Should teachers instruct all students in self-management strategies or just students who are having difficulty in certain academic or behavioral areas?
2. How can technology support students' use of self-management in setting their own goals? In managing their own learning? In assessing their own progress?
3. How can using self-management strategies for academic areas become a positive behavior support in addressing troublesome student behavior?
4. In what ways can teachers provide self-management strategies to students without their use being stigmatizing for the students?
5. Should students always fade out the use of a self-management system once the original problem is resolved and/or the goal has been met?

CLASSROOM AND SCHOOL ACTIVITY SUGGESTIONS

1. Visit a class and observe at least one or more students who are having trouble with behavior and/or academic work. Make a list of two or three self-management strategies that might help each of these students. Analyze your list and choose one strategy for each student that best addresses the student's need. Write this need in the form of a goal for this student.
2. Interview a student who is having trouble with a behavior or an academic task. With the student, determine a self-management strategy that involves (a) defining the behavior for creating a self-management goal, (b) choosing a system for monitoring the

behavior, (c) designing a form for recording data and assessing progress of the behavior, (d) creating a list of self-reinforcers, and (e) devising a timeline plan for the teacher and student to review if the self-management plan is working or needs adjustment.

REFERENCES

Baer, D. M. (1984). Does research on self-control need more control? *Analysis and Intervention in Developmental Disabilities, 4,* 211–218.

Browder, D. M., & Shapiro, E. S. (1985). Applications of self-management to individuals with severe handicaps: A review. *Journal of the Association for Persons with Severe Handicaps, 10,* 200–208.

Culham, R., & Wheeler, A. (2003). *40 reproducible forms for the writing traits classroom.* New York: Scholastic Teaching Resources.

Forte, I., & Schurr, S. (1996). *Graphic organizers and planning outlines for authentic instruction and assessment.* Nashville, TN: Incentive Publications, Inc.

Koegel, L. K., Koegel, R. L., & Parks, D. R. (1992). *How to teach self-management to people with severe disabilities: A training manual.* Santa Barbara, CA: University of California, Santa Barbara.

Lerner, J., & Johns, B. (2009). *Learning disabilities and related mild disabilities; Characteristics, teaching strategies and new directions.* Boston: Houghton Mifflin Harcourt.

Lever-Duffy, J., & McDonald, J. B. (2011). *Teaching and learning with technology.* Boston: Pearson.

Mank, D. M., & Horner, R. H. (1987). Self recruited feedback: A cost effective procedure for maintaining behavior. *Research in Developmental Disabilities, 8,* 91–112.

Snell, M. E., & Brown, F. (2006). *Instruction of students with severe disabilities.* Upper Saddle River, NJ: Pearson.

Storey, K. (2008). Systematic instruction: Developing and maintaining skills that enhance community inclusion. In K. Storey, P. Bates, & D. Hunter (Eds.), *The road ahead: Transition to adult life for persons with disabilities* (2nd ed., pp. 51-72). St. Augustine, FL: Training Resource Network, Inc.

Storey, K., & Miner, C. (2011). *Systematic instruction of functional skills for students and adults with disabilities.* Springfield, IL: Charles C Thomas Publisher, Inc.

Chapter 10

SOCIAL SKILLS INSTRUCTION

Key Point Questions

1. Why are social skills important?
2. Is having social competence the same as having good social skills?
3. How does one assess social skills?
4. What are instructional strategies for teaching social skills?

WINDOW OF THE WORLD CASE STUDY 1

Matera is a fifth-grade student who gets good grades and is extremely popular with her classmates. The only concern Ms. Salter has for Matera is that she does not take direction well from Ms. Salter. Just yesterday, Ms. Salter asked her to rewrite her story using the provided rubric, and Matera angrily replied that she didn't want to do anymore work on it, and then she walked away. This was not the first time an incident like this had happened where she was sassy and defiant at the teacher's request. Adding to this concern about Matera's behavior, Ms. Salter had noticed that other girls in the class were beginning to imitate Matera's defiant response to her requests. She wasn't sure of the cause for this behavior (perhaps spring fever or summer vacation on the horizon), but regardless of the cause, Ms. Salter decided that it was important to take immediate action and that the behavior should not be ignored. Returning to the classroom, she located a lesson from

175

the Skillstreaming program on Responding to Difficult Requests. She knew she could appropriately include a role-play for "responding to teacher requests" into the lesson scenarios. The Skillstreaming lesson was included in the social studies period right after lunch break when the students enjoyed the active role-plays. Ms. Salter was ready when the students returned to class after lunch. After having students provide examples of difficult requests (luckily one example included a teacher asking a student to do an assignment over). Ms. Salter modeled the steps to use for responding. These steps were: (a) listen to what the other person is requesting, (b) restate back what you understand the person is asking, (c) if you disagree, ask the other person to explain anything you don't understand, (d) if you still disagree, politely provide the person with the information and reason you feel or think differently, and (e) Stop and think about the person's response and the best way to handle the situation. Ms. Salter guided students through the role-plays and provided immediate corrections if steps were missed. The next day, Ms. Salter took advantage of "teachable moments" when students could be reminded to use this new skill in responding to difficult requests throughout the school day, and she provided the students with praise. On Friday, she gave the students a ten minute popcorn break at the end of the day for their excellence in responding to her requests.

WINDOW OF THE WORLD CASE STUDY 2

Mr. Cameron was concerned about Willard, his second grader, who was not getting along with others on the playground. He was getting daily reports from classmates about Willard's disruption to classmates' games at recess. He would often disrupt any ball game by taking the ball and running away, but there were also reports of Willard running through hopscotch and taking game pieces away from students playing board games. He did not observe this kind of behavior from Willard in the classroom. Willard was a good student and shared well when working in cooperative groups. When Mr. Cameron asked Willard why he ran away with the ball, he answered, "I want to play." Mr. Willard would say, "Did you ask if you could join the game?" "Oh, yes," Willard would say. Mr. Cameron would get the same response from Willard when he asked about the same behavior with hopscotch and board games. Mr. Cameron was pretty sure students weren't intentionally excluding Willard, but he decided it would be a good idea to review with the whole class how to include their classmates in a game on the playground. He thought if he worked with all the students on how to invite someone to join a game, or ask to join in a game, he could address Willard's behavior problem at the same time. Mr. Cameron started by reading a story book that was exactly about a child not being included in recess games at school. In the story, the young school children learned how to invite someone to join a game, and they also learned how to appropriately ask to join a game. The class discussed the problem in the story and discussed how they could use the "asking" in both situations. To make sure they really learned "how" to ask from the story, Mr. Cameron conducted a role-play. First he modeled the asking, and then he called on students to model it. Willard also had a turn and asked perfectly in both role-plays. Pretty sure this was going to work, Mr. Cameron continued on with class. However, Mr. Cameron was shocked to hear after the lunch recess that Willard was stealing the ball from the kick ball game. Once again when asked, Willard replied that he did ask to join the game. However, his classmates said he didn't, and they added that they had asked him before they started the game to join, just like they practiced in the classroom. The next day at recess, Mr. Cameron (after checking with the principal and careful not to be seen) caught on his smart phone Willard ignoring the classmates' invitation to join the game, stealing the ball, and not asking at any time to join the game (Mr. Cameron only used this video of Willard for his own baseline records). Over the next few days, he videotaped volunteer students who were good role models for "asking" to join ball games. In the classroom, Mr. Cameron played the videos for the whole class, and together they critiqued how well the "asking" went, and some editing went on until they all felt it was a good role model video of the skill. Mr. Cameron met with Willard at the beginning of each recess for a week, and together they watched the video. During the video watching, Mr. Cameron pointed out to Willard (who was highly focused on the video) the steps he was seeing modeled. With the help of the video and some reminders from his classmates, Willard's disruptive behavior did decrease (Mr. Cameron made sure to check in with all of the students about their asking behavior at recess and to praise and reinforce all of the students with good behavior coupons for asking appropriately to join in games), and in a couple of weeks Willard could be seen joining in games at the beginning of recess, just like his peers. Mr. Cameron was able to videotape Willard using his new learned social skill. Willard's Success Video became part of the class library video role model collection. The collection was kept on the class bookshelf so students could look at them at any time. The video turned out to be popular as the children loved to watch themselves. At the end of the year, Mr. Cameron had a large collection of student-made videos teaching the social skills they had learned through the year.

Key Point Question 1: Why Are Social Skills Important?

Just about every situation that a student experiences with other people will require a socially appropriate response. Acceptable social skills are necessary for successful interactions in almost all domains of living (in school, at home, in community settings, on a date, and at work). Since the amount and variety of social skills needed increases as we age due to the increased environments and groups of people we need to adapt to, learning successful social skills can become a lifelong process. Children learn social skills through social interactions, and these skills continue to develop and be refined as they grow. For example, a child quickly learns a set of behaviors (smiling, laughing, crying, babbling) she can use to gain approval and reinforcement from other people (usually mom and dad, at first, and then with siblings and familiar others). As a child grows older, her behaviors change to adapt to the expectations of significant people around her (such as parents expectations for developmentally age-appropriate behaviors; a 5-year-old should act like a 5-year-old and not a 2-year-old). The child's social interactions are shaped by the responses of those around her. If her mom smiles back and gives her a tickle, she will continue to use that "smile" to obtain mom's positive reinforcement. These early simple interactional behaviors are continuously built on until a complex system or repertoire of social behaviors is developed. However, social skills don't stop developing at a certain age. How we interact with others is constantly being influenced by other people's reactions to us. If a reaction to a particular behavior (someone thanks us for helping them) is reinforced, we will be more likely to continue to use that behavior (help them or others). If a reaction is not favorable (we are yelled at for picking something up for someone), this punishment may cause us to be less likely to use that behavior again with that person. Notice the words "that person." Success with specific social behaviors varies across people, places, time, and social situations. These varying factors add complexity for understanding and choosing the appropriate behavior to use in a specific circumstance. Schumaker and Hazel (1984) define a social skill as "any cognitive function or overt behavior in which an individual engages while interacting with another person or persons. Cognitive functions include such capacities as empathizing with or understanding another person's feelings, discriminating and evaluating consequences for social behavior. Overt behaviors include the nonverbal (e.g., head nods, eye contact, facial expression) and verbal (e.g., what the person says) components of social performance." For example, if Mavita is criticized by her friend, Jamine, for not playing with her at recess, Mavita will listen to what Jamine says, decide how to react, defend herself, if needed, and tell Jamine she will not exclude her in the future and she is glad Jamine told her. This interaction involved decision-making capacity—processing and evaluating what is said and deciding how to respond. It also involved Mavita's nonverbal behavior in standing near Jamine as she spoke to her, having a serious expression on her face, using a serious tone of voice when responding, and making eye contact.

Key Point Question 2: Is Having Good Social Competence the Same as Having Good Social Skills?

Social Competence

Generally, a student is considered to have social competence if his or her interactions with others result in a positive effect–in other words, how good the student is at interacting with others (Foster & Ritchey, 1979). A socially competent person would be judged by others (peers, teachers, etc.) to be skilled at using specific social behaviors in specific social interactions. There is not one definition for "social competence," yet most definitions span from general attributes such as empathy and cooperativeness of the student to describing specific desired social behaviors such as taking turns, making polite remarks, or doing a kind act for someone (Sugai & Lewis, 1996).

Social Skills

As we can see from the definition above, social skills can be considered a component of social competence. Most of the professional literature agrees that social skills are learned, either directly (the teacher instructing students what to say when they accidently bump into a peer) or indirectly (raising of hand in class and politely asking a question after observing other peers perform the behavior and being reinforced by the teacher). Although positive social skills are often learned without instruction, sometimes students will only learn specific social behaviors with instruction. This social skill instruction should be direct, be systematically planned, and teach specific social behavior that results in the student's behavior being considered (a) a positive interaction (with peers, teachers, etc.), and (b) judged a positive social skill by peers, teachers, and parents (Gresham, 1986). Social skills include both verbal behaviors and nonverbal behaviors (e.g., physical mannerisms such as how to stand or make eye contact). If a student says, "Thanks a lot" (verbal), but has a sneer on his or her face (nonverbal), the nonverbal behavior has changed the meaning of the exchange from a message of gratitude to a message of sarcasm. It's important, then, that teachers include nonverbal behaviors when teaching social skills.

Poorly developed social skills, lack of social skills, or students not using social skills they have learned can present a barrier to success in both academic performance and social inclusion. Research has show that students with poor peer and adult social relationships are more likely to develop behavior problems that can lead to academic failure, involvement with the criminal justice system, need for mental health services, and difficulties in adult life in both relationships and maintaining employment. Since the opinion and actions of other adults and students can have a significant influence on the behavior of an individual student, it is important for the teacher when planning for the assessment and instruction of social skills to keep in mind that students or individuals, besides the target student, will be an important component of the assessment and intervention. For this reason, using assessment strategies that rate the opinions of others on how important it is to learn a particular social skill, or to what degree the target student already has mastered the social skill is necessary for determining what to teach. Also, focusing on teaching skills that help build student friendships and create opportunities for students to use these skills with peers is a critical component in social skill teaching. For instance, teaching a student how to carry on a conversation is an important skill needed in making friends. Teachers can have students practice this skill with each other conducting a social skill lesson, which provides students with a model format for asking and answering questions in a conversation. After the lesson, students use a checklist to keep track of when they use their new learned conversation skills in other settings, such as the cafeteria, playground, before school, or after school. Once students have recorded having a conversation at three different times, they turn in their list for a special treat from the teacher.

Key Points Question 3: How Does One Assess Social Skills?

There are many different ways to assess what social skills need to be taught (such as observing the student, asking the student, asking peers, teacher ratings, etc.). Sometimes a variety of assessment tools will be used in order for the teacher to exactly pinpoint the skill deficit. When assessing social skills, it is important to take into consideration what is typical behavior for the student's age, gender, peer group, and any other cultural or societal behavioral norm. The decision about what instructional methods to use should always be directly related to the results of the assessment. Social skill assessment needs to be systematic and provides teachers with the following information:

1. A complete understanding of the social skill problem (skill deficit), including what social skill the student needs to learn (skill building) or whether the skill is already known but not being used (performance deficit), and what practice opportunities and reinforcement for using the skill can be provided,
2. How and where the skill should be taught,
3. The modality for how to teach it (using a teacher-made lesson, a social skills curriculum, incidental teaching, planned class);
4. How to evaluate whether the new social skill has been learned (a system for measuring skill acquisition and use as outlined in Chapter 2),
5. A plan to monitor the student for on-going performance (maintenance) of the social skill; and

6. Is the social skill occurring in the criteria environment (the classroom) or situation (greeting others) as well as in generalization of student's interactions with others. Knowing who, what, where, when, and why a student is performing a desired behavior can provide information for developing effective interventions (Sugai & Lewis, 1996).

Direct Observation

It is important to know the student's strength in the social skill area, what social skills the student already successfully performs, and which social skills the student needs to develop. Determining these factors can be done through direction observation methods (see descriptions in Chapter 2) or a systematic functional assessment process involving direct observation (see description in Chapter 3), where information concerning the social skill is collected and measured. The purpose of the measurement is to identify positive social skills that are lacking (greeting peers appropriately), understand the specific social behavior presenting problems (using wrong words in greetings), identify replacement social skills (specific words to use in greetings), help with planning instruction for teaching the new social skill (such as role-playing with the teacher and peers), monitor its use (frequency counts of appropriate greetings), and evaluate the effectiveness of the instruction (are appropriate greetings increasing?). Without this systematic approach to evaluate and address the target social skills, the intervention may not actually teach the student the desired skill and could result in an ineffective and inefficient solution (Horner, O'Neill, & Flannery, 1993) and a waste of valuable teacher time.

Social skill assessment can be used for both an individual student and groups of students to identify social skill deficits. There are many possible reasons that a student may be having difficulty in any particular social context. For example, it is possible that the student has not learned a specific skill (rules for lining up) or does not know in what situations to use it. For example, a student might cut in front of a student in the cafeteria lunch line because he or she wants to be with a friend, not realizing that the rules for lining up in the classroom also apply in the cafeteria. It could also be that the student knows a skill but is inconsistent in using it (a student knows how to ask to play a game of checkers but instead sometimes quickly sits down in front of another student), or due to insufficient practice of the skill and lack of strong reinforcement for using it, cannot use it effectively (a student has self-rehearsed how to respond to name calling by another student, but in the actual situation only a small part of the rehearsed response is said, making the response ineffective). Also, another behavior in the student's repertoire of behaviors could interfere with the student being able to successfully use the skill (a student knows to walk away from provocation to fight, but heightened anxiousness may prevent the student to actually move away from the conflict).

Walker and Stieber (1998) recommend the following components as part of an assessment for students who have social skills deficits: (a) teacher and parent ratings of aggression, ADHD, and social skills; (b) ratings by peers to ascertain social status and possible rejection; (c) direct observation of student–peer social exchanges in free play settings; and (d) review of school records for disciplinary referrals and teacher statements about social skill deficits.

Teacher Rankings

One tool used for identifying students with social skills problems is teacher rankings. A teacher ranking assessment involves teachers ranking their students in a most to least order, requiring the teacher to record and measure the frequency of the target behavior. For example, to identify students who would be the most chosen for a game, a teacher might rank students from most chosen to least chosen by peers after measuring the frequency of this social interaction for all students. With this information, the teacher could determine whether a specific social skill's lesson on including others and making new friends would benefit the class, or if specific skills such as how to ask to join a game needs to be directly taught to some students. Of course, this provides only general information about groups of students and does not identify social behavior problems of specific students. However, it may be useful as a starting point for assessing which social situations need social skill intervention.

Peer Nominations

This method involves asking students to choose their preferred peers for certain activities/situations. These can involve positive nominations (someone you would definitely want to play with) and negative nominations (someone you would definitely not want to play with). Some examples of questions might be, "Who would you most (least) like to sit next to at lunchtime in the cafeteria?" or "State one student you would definitely like to invite to your house and one student you would not want to invite to your house." Peer nominations also provide a general screening on how students perceive their peers (best or worst friend, least and most popular). A teacher could use this as a screening tool to learn which students are being rejected and which students could be tapped for leadership roles. A teacher can create a peer nomination sociogram with the collected data (see Figure 10.1), which can be used for determining appropriate interventions (Elksnin & Elksnin, 2006). For example, if two students currently don't interact very frequently but indicate they would like to play with each other (reciprocal nominations), the teacher could create opportunities for them to interact, such as through the use of a cooperative learning strategy or having them do a school activity together such as volunteering in the library.

Rating Scales

A more in-depth measurement is detailed ratings by adults, peers, and/or others (such as playground supervisors) of target behaviors (works cooperatively in groups, socializes with peers, and makes positive conversation). A list is made of desired social behaviors, and others rate the degree to which the student demonstrates the behavior. This scale can produce information about specific social behaviors that need improvement and also provide a comparison of the student's social skills in a variety of settings. For example, if, through the ratings completed by parents and other adults working on the school campus, a teacher discovers that a student who argues excessively with him in the classroom does not behave this way with parents at home or with other adults in different school settings (cafeteria, playground, etc.), then this teacher would know to focus on the nature of the student–teacher interactions and assess what antecedents, setting events, or consequences might be influencing this behavior. For example, the teacher collects functional assessment data over a week's time, observing and recording when the student becomes excessively argumenta-

Figure 10.1. Sociogram for Forming Learning Partners

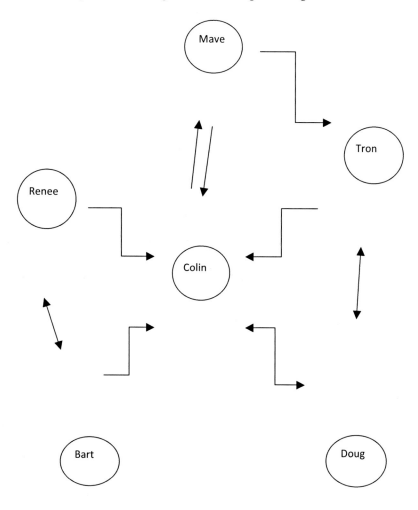

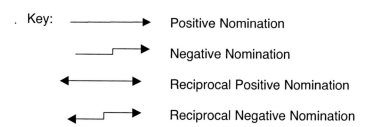

Each student in the learning group was asked to select one student they would want to partner with and one student they would not want as a partner. **Name**	**Positive Nomination**	**Negative Nomination**
Colin	1	3
Renee	1	0
Mave	0	0
Tron	2	0
Bart	1	0
Doug	1	1

In reviewing this sociogram, the teacher may decide to partner Doug and Tron, Renee and Bart, and Mave and Colin. Further assessment of why Colin is least preferred is indicated.

tive. The teacher's assessment of the data indicates that the student becomes aggressively argumentative only in math class when he receives less than 100% on his graded math papers. With this information, the teacher now knows it is a response to a specific event (grade) in a specific setting (in math class).

The Walker-McConnell Scale of Social Competence and School Adjustment (Walker & McConnell, 1995) provides an elementary rating scale and an adolescent rating scale assessment tool for identifying students who require social skills instruction. These two separate tools provide assessment items that a teacher identifies as preferred behaviors, such as "shows sympathy for others" and "attends to assigned tasks." These ratings can be useful in predicting social needs and potential future problem areas. For example, in a longitudinal study of 80 at-risk males, teacher ratings of social skills recorded in Grade 5 were shown to predict contact with police or arrest through Grade 11 (Walker & Stieber, 1998).

Interviews

An interview can be a written or an oral assessment providing information that cannot be obtained through other measurement systems. Interviews can be conducted with students, teachers, parents, or peers and provide information through anecdotes and descriptions of specific situations as to why a student behaves in a certain way. These data can provide information on the context in which the behaviors are occurring, help define the behavior of concern, and help choose appropriate social skill interventions. Interviews are considered an indirect measure as they are conducted after the behavior has occurred and most likely in a different setting (as opposed to an observation, where one is directly assessing the behavior as it happens and where it is happening) and the influences that may increase the occurrence of the behavior.

Elksnin and Elksnin (2006) provide the following interview guidelines:

1. Establish the goal for the interview. Is the goal to obtain information, get cooperation, or establish rapport?
2. Based on the goal, develop a list of potential questions to ask.
3. Identify ways the interviewee's perspective may differ from yours.
4. Identify sensitive topics to avoid during the interview.

Role-Play

Role-play is another way to identify whether a student can perform a specific social skill. In-role play assessment, the student practices a specific social skill required in a given scenario. For example, a student would participate in a role-play where he or she has to decide whether to attend a class or cut class with peers. The role-play would allow the student to demonstrate whether he or she can defend his or her choice to peers to comply with school rules instead of giving into peer pressure to cut class with peers to hang.

Scenarios are practiced in classroom or other settings such as the lunch room or in the quad (individual or small-group instruction) and directed and controlled by the teacher. Teachers can create role-play situations that require the use of the targeted social skill. Different settings (home, school, community, employment) where the student may need to use the skill should be included in the scenarios. McGinnis and Goldstein (1997) have created a commercial social skills program, Skillstreaming, which incorporates the role-play strategy. Preference should be given to assessing the student's ability to perform social skills in the criterion setting (the classroom, lunchroom, quad, etc.) where any competing contingencies might be occurring. If that is not possible, then role-play in the classroom setting.

Key Point Question 4: What Are Instructional Strategies For Teaching Social Skills?

Preparing a teaching plan to teach social skills is the same process as preparing a teaching plan to teach academic skills. There should be instructional goals and objectives, a planned direct instructional sequence, an opportunity for the student to demonstrate the behavior, and a systematic assessment process to determine whether the skill has been learned or whether the student needs more instruction (Sugai & Lewis, 1996). There should also be planned extension (generalization) activities for the student to practice the new social skill in other settings (home, places outside of school, and in different school settings), with other people, across times, and across behaviors with positive reinforcement provided. The use of the new social skill should be periodically monitored over weeks and months to see whether students are still using the behavior successfully. Positive reinforcement should always be provided at these monitoring times to strengthen the skill use.

Published Social Skill Curricula

Examining the numerous published social skills curricula can serve as a starting point to teach commonly desired social behaviors. A list of available programs to consider is provided in Table 10.1. Although many of the skills in these programs are generic, more intensive instruction for students who are having serious social skills deficits can be planned using the program's assessment tools. For selecting the most appropriate program, it is important to review the program content for what age group is targeted and what methods are used to teach the social skills. Table 10.2 provides guidelines for criteria to keep in mind when selecting a commercial program.

Table 10.1
Selection of Published Programs for Social Skills Instruction

The ACCEPTS Program (Walker et al.), middle to high school ages,
http://www.proedinc.com/customer/productView.aspx?ID=625&SearchWord=ACCEPTS%
20PROGRAM

ACHIEVE Stop and Think Social Skills Program (Knoff), PreK through 8th grade,
http://projectachieve.us/stop-think/stop-and-think.html

The EQUIP Program (Gibbs, Potter, & Goldstein), adolescents, 12–17 yrs,
http://www.researchpress.com/scripts/product.asp?item=4848#5134

I Can Problem Solve programs (Shure), K though 6th grade,
http://www.researchpress.com/product/item/4628/

PATHS curriculum (Kusche & Greenburg), PreK through 6th grade,
http://www.channing-bete.com/prevention-programs/paths/paths.html

The PREPARE program (Goldstein), middle and high school students,
http://www.researchpress.com/product/item/5063/

Skillstreaming Program (Goldstein & McGinnis), PreK through12th grade,
http://www.skillstreaming.com/

Teaching Social Competence to Youth and Adults with Developmental Disabilities
(D. A. Jackson, N. F. Jackson, & Bennett), Adolescents and Adults,
http://www.proedinc.com/customer/productView.aspx?ID=1428

Think Aloud (Camp & Bash), ages 6 to 8 yrs for small-group instruction and grades 1st
though 6th for classroom programs,
http://www.teachervision.fen.com/skill-builder/problem-solving/48546.html

Teacher-Designed Social Skills Instruction

Teachers can design their own social skills instruction lessons once the social skills to be taught are identified. A direct instructional approach that incorporates role-modeling, role-playing, and performance feedback can be planned (Peterson, Young, Salzberg, West, & Hill, 2006). A variety of strategies for teaching social skills should be used, and every effort should be made to teach in natural environments using authentic contexts and targeting skills the student's value (Elksnin & Elksnin, 2006).

Table 2
Guidelines for Choosing a Published Curriculum

1. What instructional components are included in the curriculum?
(a) modeling,
(b) video modeling,
(c) role play,
(d) direct instruction,
(e) measurement,
(f) rehearsal/practice,
(g) prompting/coaching,
(h) positive reinforcement/shaping, and/or
(i) opportunities to practice.
2. Are the following programming considerations covered?
(a) Are assessment procedures/instruments included?
(b) Is the curriculum adaptable to individual needs?
(c) Can the curriculum be used with small groups?
(d) Can personnel implement the curriculum without specialized training beyond that described in the curriculum?
(e) Is the cost reasonable and manageable?
(f) Are strategies included that will promote maintenance and generalization of skills?

Adapted from Carter and Sugai (1988, 1989).

Generalization

Some students may learn to use a social skill in one setting, one time, or with a person or group but will not use it in another similar situation. Helping students to generalize a new learned social skill can be done using the following guidelines (Brown & Odom, 1994; Smith & Giles, 2003):

1. Use language similar to the language the student will encounter in the natural setting in which the social skill will be used.
2. Use a variety of role models so that the student doesn't associate the social skill with only that person and thus will be more likely to generalize the skill across people.
3. Include all the behaviors in the behavior chain when teaching a social skill. For instance, when teaching "greeting" skills, besides teaching the typical response phrases for greeting, also teach the eye contact, voice inflection, and acceptable standing distance from the person. More complex skills can be added to this chain (deciding what to say next, how to ask a question to engage the

other person, how to end the conversation, etc.) as the student masters the foundational skills.

4. Avoid teaching social skills only at a specific class time. Use the teachable moments throughout the day by taking the time for incidental teaching by providing learning opportunities to use a social skill in the natural environment. Students are more motivated to use the skill in real-life situations. For example, if students are fighting at recess and return to the classroom riled up and angry at each other, this is the time for the teacher to address the situation and teach the skills for calming down, thinking aloud about what happened, and considering what other options they have, besides fighting, for handling the problem.

5. Just as reading is generalized across subjects, so, too, learning and using social skills should be incorporated in the curriculum throughout the day. Opportunities for social skills instruction can be embedded in literature lessons, social science projects, cooperative learning groups, and learning civic responsibilities, only to mention a few of these curriculum opportunities. This will also help to promote generalization of a social skill across settings and situations.

6. Once students are assessed to have mastered the targeted social skills, maintenance of the skills can be reinforced intermittently with fun activities, free time, conversation with a friend, and such (Elksnin & Elksnin, 2006).

Incidental Teaching

Incidental teaching uses situations as they occur throughout the day and the natural interactions between student and teacher to form the basis for practicing social skills (Elksnin & Elksnin, 2000). Providing explicit instruction at the moment when a social skill error is occurring is an effective way to teach students to read the social cues and respond appropriately. Teachers can point out nonverbal cues (gestures, facial expressions, voice tone, standing distance, etc.), characteristics of the environment, and any other factors present that indicate the need for an adjusted response. For instance, if a student is attending a school assembly where a speaker is delivering a speech and the student yells over to a friend across the aisle, "Hey, let's get together after school," this would be an instance for incidental teaching, where the teacher could quickly and quietly prompt the student to observe the nonverbal behavior of others (everyone looking forward to the stage, eyes focused on speaker, not talking, serious faces, body movements still) and point out that the student is in an assembly room in a situation where a student is expected to be respectful to a speaker, which involves being quiet and listening. Calling to a friend is behavior for recess, lunch, or before and after school. With practice, a teacher could be in and out of that coaching moment in seconds and has not missed the opportunity for correcting a social error and guiding the student in the expected behavior. A follow-up consultation with the student should follow the assembly, and the teacher will positively reinforce the student for complying by not continuing to call to the friend, staying quiet, looking at the speaker, and listening. It is important to review with the student again the expected behaviors used in that specific situation.

Modeling

A social modeling strategy in which teachers or peers demonstrate how to perform the social skill, provide an opportunity for the student to practice it in, and provide feedback and reinforcement has been found effective for teaching social skills. Cartledge, Gardner, and Ford (2009) report that students from culturally diverse backgrounds have had good success in social skills acquisition when peer-mediated instruction was used, and they maintained these skills through the use of self-monitoring with recording their behavior on self-recording sheets (see Chapter 9 on self-management strategies). Teachers can first teach the skill to the students through modeling the desired social skill and then train a few students, providing them with a script to reteach the skill to peers. Peer modeling can be done with one-on-one individual instruction or in small groups. Only students who have mastered the skill should be chosen to be role models. Teachers should monitor peer sessions and assess whether students are successfully learning the skills. Once the teacher has determined through this assessment that students have learned the skill, then role-plays could be used to challenge the student's ability to adapt his or her new learned skill to unpredictable situations. In this way, a teacher can provide instruction on how to cope in difficult situations. Storey and Miner (2011) provide a format to for using this "coping" modeling:

1. Stop the role play after mistakes are made and correct the error.
2. Point out what the error was and why it was made.
3. Provide instruction on how to avoid the error.
4. Demonstrate the strategy used to avoid the mistake.

Multimedia and Video Modeling

Multimedia (virtual environments, simulations, videos, pictures, and other multimedia) can be very effective strategies for teaching social skills. Video peer modeling (VPM) and video self-modeling (VSM) are visual instruction ways to teach social skills. VSM involves the target student observing her or himself on video performing a skill to be learned while VPM involves the target student observing a friend or other student on video performing the skill to be learned. There is increasing research in this area indicating that students efficiently learn target social skills using video modeling (Gül & Vuran, 2010). Video modeling eliminates teacher prompting, allowing the student to completely focus on the model being presented. Convenience is another factor for using this tool. Teachers, students, or parents are able to manipulate the camera, zooming in and out, editing as necessary, and the results can be viewed repeatedly by the student. Another advantage is that it is easy to see the antecedent–behavior–consequences relationship in a video (as opposed to hearing a story about someone performing a behavior correctly). These situations can be manipulated so that the student can see both appropriate and inappropriate demonstrations of the social skill so that they can make the appropriate discrimination. For example, a student could be videoed in a practice interview for a job. An interview error of the student frowning at times during the interview can be seen in the first recording. A second recording can show the student correcting the error and not frowning and smiling at times during the interview. The student can then compare the correct behavior of smiling to the incorrect behavior of frowning in an interview. In VSM facial expression, body language, voice tone, and emotions can be seen and monitored. VPM allows students to review together and analyze their behaviors and responses, or provide solutions as a group to a specific individual (Prater, 2007).

Cognitive Modeling

Many problem-solving strategies are part of social skills curricula wherein the particulars of a social interaction are discussed between the teacher and the student. Core elements of these strategies involve the following components: a detailed account of what the student did, what happened, whether the outcome was positive or negative, and what the student will do in the same situation in the future. Teachers should assist students in identifying the specific behaviors that result in positive solutions, in addition to identifying the behaviors that caused an undesirable outcome. For example, if a student grabs a book away from another student and a fight ensues between the two students, a teacher can help the students analyze the situation as to where the disagreement started. In this case, the teacher would guide the students through thinking about each step of the social exchange and locate the social error that caused the fight. In this case, the students would identifying that "asking" instead of "grabbing" should be used in the future to avoid a fight.

Social Stories

Social stories provide students with a narrative or script for appropriate behavior in a variety of situations and allow students to understand and rehearse the steps needed to perform a target social skill. Teachers can provide students with teacher-made or published social stories or students can create their own comic strip social stories or make video clips acting out the skill. The following is an example of a teacher-made social story for addressing raising your hand when answering a question for an early elementary student:

Raising My Hand to Answer the Teacher's Question
1. The teacher asks a question.
2. I know the answer.
3. I want to say the answer.
4. I raise my hand.
5. I wait for the teacher to call on me.
6. The teacher calls my name.
7. I say the answer.
8. When the teacher calls on someone else, I put my hand down.

This strategy allows for perspective taking and encourages the students to consider a range of responses to a specific situation. More information on social stories can be found at http://www.thegraycenter.org/Social_Stories.htm.

Behavioral Rehearsal and Role-Play

Behavioral rehearsal, embedded in social skills curricula, such as the Skillstreaming curriculum, uses role-play to provide opportunities for students to rehearse the needed social skill in social situation scenarios and receive corrective feedback and positive reinforcement. To avoid having the student practice an incorrect skill, prompting ahead of the rehearsal on what the student will do and say will (precorrection) minimize the chance of the student practicing social skill errors. Behavioral rehearsal/role-play can be effective in small-group instruction, where students who are not role-playing also have a responsibility in the role-play process. These roles could include: a director who narrates what is going on or what the actors are doing, a note taker who records a description of how the actor used the target skill, and a conflict observer role that records under what conditions the actor had to use the target skill. Concurrently while role-playing the scene, the actor can narrate what is happening and what he or she is thinking. This gives the teacher an opportunity to use precorrection and have the student use the social skill successfully. These roles actively engage all the students in the learning process and provide assessment information for the teacher in determining whether the students understand the social skill and are learning it. At end of the role-play, the teacher recaps what happened and describes the correct behaviors demonstrated. For example, for a role-play where a student demonstrates how to handle being disturbed while working in class, the teacher would comment, "Vim looked directly at his friend who was talking to him during math class and said, "I can't talk to you now. The teacher said we need to finish our math problems and not talk". It is important that the teacher avoid making comments about unrelated behaviors added into the role-play (student used wrong names, dropped something, laughed, or fell out of character) and keeping students focused on the target social skill they are learning (Sugai & Lewis, 1996).

Literature and Teaching Social Skills

Reading children's literature, particularly stories that focus on topics such as making friends, dealing with bullies, and encountering new situations, can be an effective strategy for teaching social skills (Rush & Lipski, 2009). Forgan (2002) provides a step-by-step process for using literature to help solve social problems. The steps involve:

1. Prereading. Have students look at the title and the illustrations, discuss with an adult what the book's plot is, and then relate it to their own experience. Students use the KWL chart (What do you want to **Know** about the topic, What do you **Want** to learn about the topic? What have you **Learned** about the topic).
2. Guided Reading. The teacher reads the story out loud. Students reflect on the story silently or writing in a journal.
3. Post Reading Discussion. During discussion, the students identify the main problem in the story by retelling the story and teacher guidance with probing questions.
4. Students then identify the problem and solutions using the following outline:
   I SOLVE
I	Identify the problem
S	Solutions to the problem
O	Obstacles to the solutions
L	Look at the solutions again–choose one
V	Very good. Try it!
E	Evaluate the outcome

BEST PRACTICE RECOMMENDATIONS

1. Teach social skills both formally and informally throughout the school day, focusing on targeting immediate situations when a social skill error is made.
2. Teach social skills in the same systematic way you would teach an academic subject.
3. Use a variety of methods to teach social skills but give preference to strategies that use direct teaching and active learning strategies (role-play, behavioral rehearsal, modeling), being sure to provide strong and ongoing reinforcement for correct social skills performance.

Table 3
Environmental Social Skill Observation Form

SETTING	SOCIAL SKILL	SOCIAL SKILL USED SUCCESSFULLY	SOCIAL SKILL ATTEMPTED BUT UNSUCCESSFUL	SOCIAL SKILL NEEDED (did not attempt)
Classroom	Sharing	Marve, Teresa, Jo, Krem	Forge, Wallace	Soto
	Lining up	Marve, Teresa, Jo, Krem, Forge, Wallace	Soto	
	Saying "Thank you"	Teresa, Jo, Krem, Wallace, Forge		Marve, Krem
Playground	Taking turns	Marve, Teresa, Jo, Krem	Forge, Wallace	Soto
Cafeteria	Making room at table	Marve, Teresa, Jo, Krem, Forge		Forge, Soto

Adapted from Elksin and Elksin (2006).

DISCUSSION QUESTIONS

1. How do you best decide which social skills to teach?
2. How do you decide whether you should teach a social skill in a whole-class format, small-group format, or individual one-on-one format?
3. Won't students grow out of social skills deficits as they get older and learn appropriate skills? Is it really necessary to teach social skills in schools?

SCHOOL-BASED ACTIVITY SUGGESTIONS:

1. Observe your students displaying social skills in the classroom. Make a list of social skills that you see students using successfully, social skills that are missing, and social skills that are not being used successfully. Now take this list to other environments (playground, cafeteria, and library) and check to see whether students

are using or not using the same skills. Add any new skills to this list that need to be taught to students. Use this list as a basis for selecting social skills lessons.

2. From the list above, choose two different strategies for teaching social skills. Compare the outcomes for each strategy to see which was more effective with your students.

REFERENCES

Brown, W. H., & Odom, S. L. (1994). Strategies and tactics for promoting generalization and maintenance of young children's social behavior. *Research in Developmental Disabilities, 15*, 99–118.

Carter, J., & Sugai, G. (1988). Teaching social skills. *Teaching Exceptional Children, 20*, 68–71.

Carter, J., & Sugai, G. (1989). Social skills curriculum analysis. *Teaching Exceptional Children, 21*, 36–39.

Cartledge, G., Gardner, R., & Ford, D. Y. (2009). *Diverse learners with exceptionalities: Culturally responsive teaching in the inclusive classroom.* Upper Saddle River, NJ: Pearson.

Elksnin, L. K., & Elksnin, N. (2000). Teaching parents to teach their children to be prosocial. *Intervention in School and Clinic, 36*, 27–34.

Elksnin, L. K., & Elksnin, N. (2006). *Teaching social-emotional skills at school and home.* Denver, CO: Love Publishing Co.

Forgan, J. W. (2002). Using bibliography to teach problem solving. *Intervention in School and Clinic, 38*, 75–82.

Foster, S. L., & Ritchey, W. L. (1979). Issues in the assessment of social competence in children. *Journal of Applied Behavior Analysis, 12*, 625–638.

Gresham, F. M. (1986). Conceptual and definitional issues in the assessment of children's social skills: Implications for classification and training. *Journal of Clinical Child Psychology, 15*, 3–15.

Gül, S., & Vuran, S. (2010). An analysis of studies conducted video modeling in teaching social skills. *Educational Sciences: Theory and Practice, 10*, 249–274.

Horner, R. H., O'Neill, R. E., & Flannery, K. B. (1993). Building effective behavior support plans from functional assessment information. In M. E. Snell (Ed.), *Systematic instruction of persons with severe handicaps* (4th ed., pp. 184–214). Columbus, OH: Merrill.

McGinnis, E., & Goldstein, A. P. (1997). *Skillstreaming the elementary school child: New strategies and perspectives for teaching prosocial skills* (2nd ed.). Champaign, IL: Research Press.

Peterson, L. D., Young, K. R., Salzberg, C. L., West, R. P., & Hill, M. (2006). Using self- management procedures to improve classroom social skills in multiple general education settings. *Education and Treatment of Children,, 29*, 1–21.

Prater, M. A. (2007). *Teaching strategies for students with mild to moderate disabilities* (pp. 452-453). Upper Saddle River, NJ: Pearson.

Rush, K., & Lipski, K. (2009). Teaching social skills through children's Literature. *Illinois Reading Council Journal, 37*, 20–25.

Schumaker, J. B., & Hazel, J. S. (1984). Social skills assessment and training for the learning disabled: Who's on first and what's on second? Part 1. *Journal of Learning Disabilities, 17*, 422–431.

Smith, S. W., & Giles, D. L. (2003). Using key instructional elements to systematically promote social skill generalization for students with challenging behavior. *Intervention in School and Clinic, 39*, 30–37.

Storey, K., & Miner, C. (2011). *Systematic instruction of functional skills for students and adults with disabilities.* Springfield, IL: Charles C Thomas.

Sugai, G., & Lewis, T. J. (1996). Preferred and promising practices for social skills instruction. *Focus on Exceptional Children, 29*(4), 11–27.

Walker, H., & Stieber, S. (1998). Teacher ratings of social skills as longitudinal predictors of long term arrest status in a sample of at risk males. *Behavioral Disorders, 23*, 220–230.

Walker, H. M., & McConnell, S. R. (1995). *The Walker-McConnell scale of social competence and school adjustment: Elementary version.* San Diego, CA: Singular.

Chapter 11

SCHOOL-WIDE POSITIVE BEHAVIOR SUPPORTS

Key Point Questions

1. What are School-Wide Positive Behavior Supports?
2. How do you teach School-Wide Positive Behavior Supports to students?
3. How do you reinforce School-Wide Positive Behavior Supports?
4. How do you Assess School-Wide Positive Behavior Supports?
5. How do you identify and develop interventions for students needing additional supports?

WINDOW OF THE WORLD CASE STUDY 1

Green Pines Middle School had a reputation for letting students "run wild," and many parents in Green Pines Township were complaining to the school board about the situation there. The school had already seen a frequent turnover of principals (the last one did not make it through the year, and for the last four years, a new principal had to be hired each year—two fired and two resigned). Additionally, many parents reported to the school board seeing students fighting on the playground, students being jumped on when they fell down, and teachers nowhere to be found for addressing the problems. The hallways and classrooms weren't much better. Students lingered in the halls after the bell rang, students were disrupting classes and derailing instruction, and teachers were heard throughout the day yelling at students to behave and threatening them with class detention. When teachers would threaten students with discipline, the students would just laugh and ignore the consequences. To make matters worse, teachers would call the office through classroom intercom requesting support for disruptive students, and no one would arrive. When students were sent to the office, they returned to the classroom with no consequences. In fact, teachers were told by administration to handle all problems in the classroom and not send students to the office. Parents knew there were many good teachers in the school, and they also recognized that losing so many principals indicated that some critical structure was missing for handling discipline problems. It was very important to the parents that their children were held accountable for their behavior and taught to act respectfully.

Parents, along with the Parent Teacher Association and Green Pine Valley School Board, looked into a new program, School-Wide Positive Behavior Support (SWPBS) Program, which they heard the adjacent school district was successfully using. A team of experts on positive behavior support from the state department of education agreed to work with the school in implementing this program. The new principal had positive experience with a SWPBS program in her last school and was happy to begin this program in her new school. Working with the parents, teachers, staff, and the school board, the principal led the school in forming a leadership team, training everyone in SWPBS strategies and processes, and setting up an assessment process to see whether the program was working. The students were then engaged in the process and the entire school to come up with three behavioral expectations they felt the school community should adopt. Almost unanimously, everyone agreed the first expectation would be "Be Respectful," followed by "Be Kind" and "Be Studious." The principal made sure the first period of the day was dedicated to going over the expectations and the behaviors students were expected to learn. Social skills lessons were distributed for all grade levels, and skills were taught, practiced, and reinforced throughout the day in classrooms, halls, cafeteria, media center, computer lab, and playgrounds. Students were reinforced with praise, success tickets for privileges, and weekly recognition over the public address system, and a special assembly was held at the end of the month for students who met the target goal for success tickets. Within a few months, the many reports of playground fighting and noncompliance in the classroom began to steadily decrease, academics were improving, and the administration started collecting data on office referrals (which the office now accepted). These data would be used in future months to track the effectiveness of this new program. Parents were now collaborating on how they could help in strengthening the SWPBS program at Green Pine Valley Middle School and were praising the school board for their effective efforts in turning around this school.

WINDOW OF THE WORLD CASE STUDY 2

Ms. Warner had tried many interventions to stop Violet from shouting out in the classroom. It was particularly disturbing that the "shout outs" occurred when Ms. Warner was teaching, and Violet's behavior was often reinforced with her peers laughing, which derailed the lessons. After four or five of these incidents, Ms. Warner discussed how to handle Violet's behaviors with the Teacher Assistant Team, which met weekly for teachers to collaborate on student concerns. From this meeting, Ms. Warner used the suggestions from the team. She taught Violet to raise her hand and wait to be called on before answering and made sure to reinforce her with praise. Ms. Warner also directed students not to laugh at the shout outs, which only encouraged (reinforced) Violet. In addition, Ms. Warner removed Violet's class privilege (15 minutes of free time) at the end of the day if Violet had more than two shout outs. Ms. Warner used frequency counts as a simple tracking system to determine each day whether the behavior was decreasing. However, after two weeks, Violet was still often disrupting the class with her shouting out. With no improvement indicated by her data tracking record, Ms. Warner saw no other solution but to send Violet to the office with a referral. She filled out the SWPBS team office referral form. Ms. Warner knew that "disruption" to the class was one of the six categories the SWPBS team approved as a reason for an office referral. She checked the "repeated minor infractions" box, wrote a clear description of the problem behavior, indicated how long the behavior had been going on, and the listed interventions and consequences that had been used to address Violet's shout out behavior. Unfortunately, this was the beginning of additional office referrals (the office made sure to send a copy of each office referral home), and after four referrals, Ms. Warner requested to meet with the SWPBS team. It was decided at this meeting to pursue a more intensive individualized intervention to correct Violet's chronic shouting out at the teacher. The SWPBS team met with the student, teacher, and parent, recommending Violet participate in the Behavior Education Program (BEP), where a daily progress report would be sent home for the parents to sign. Violet would check in with the school's BEP coordinator when she arrived at school and take the daily progress report to her teacher, who would record her progress during the day. At the end of the day, Violet would retrieve the progress report from the teacher and return it to the BEP coordination for a reward. A copy would be made of the BEP for Violet to take home for her parent's signature. Violet would then return the progress report to the BEP coordinator the next morning, and the cycle would continue with Violet given a new daily progress report. Ms. Warner and Violet also agreed on prompts (a special hand signal the teacher would use) to remind Violet to not shout out. Violet would also receive a prize from the class prize box on the days she had "no shout outs."

Key Point Question 1: What are School-Wide Positive Behavior Supports?

Student behaviors (both desirable and undesirable) outside of the classroom (hallways, the lunch room, the quad, etc.) can be of critical importance in influencing social and academic performance. Thus, it is just as important to focus on positive behavior supports in these areas as in the classroom. This focus is known as SWPBS, and it analyzes where undesirable behaviors are occurring on school grounds and develops school rules, skill building for students, and reinforcement systems for increasing desirable behaviors in those settings. The logic is the same as with positive behavior supports in the classroom, only applied to focusing on increasing desirable student behaviors throughout the school and thus decreasing undesirable behaviors.

A unique feature of an SWPBS Program is the leadership team-building approach it encompasses (Colvin, 2007). This team represents the entire faculty and administration with recruited input from students, school families, and community links (such as mental health services, juvenile justice, etc.) outside of the school setting. The team assesses what positive behaviors are necessary to create a positive and supportive environment where students will thrive educationally and socially. Once the team identifies these desirable behaviors (such as walking in the hallway, sharing on the playground, or waiting in line appropriately in the cafeteria), they are explicitly taught and reinforced systematically at every grade level and in all school settings. This supports teachers with "back up" in reinforcing desired behaviors throughout the school environment, not only in the classroom. By expecting students to demonstrate positive behaviors and comply with school rules in all school settings, students learn to use and generalize important social skills they will need to be successful in adult life. For a program to be effective, there needs to be school-wide staff commitment, support for SWPBS team meetings, strong administrative leadership, a guide for decision-making processes, staff recognition for their work, monitoring of implementation, reviewing data, obtaining regular feedback, and ensuring commitment to improving the SWPBS program is sustained (Colvin, 2007).

To strengthen the social validity for using SWPBS, it is important that each school adapt the SWPBS process in a way that addresses the needs of their particular school community's cultural values and beliefs. Routines and procedures should be used that actually target the specific behavioral problems the school community wants to address (Miramontes, Marchant, Heath, & Fischer, 2011). For this reason, all stakeholders (administrators, teachers, staff, students, and parents) need to participate and buy in (at least 80% of staff) to the process. The school's principal plays a critical role in providing support and leadership, along with parent involvement, training, and collaboration in structuring a successful SWPBS program. Table 11.1 provides guidelines for implementing school-wide positive behavior supports. Table 11.2 provides critical features of effective SWPBS teams.

Prior to implementation of SWPBS, the school needs to commit to four criteria:

A. SWPBS must be one of the school's top three priorities and be backed by administrative support.
B. A team should be established to provide support for students who have serious behavior problems.
C. The school must allot adequate resources and time for the team to be trained and for the team to plan, design, and implement SWPBS. Table 11.3 provides guidelines for efficient use of time by the team.
D. The school has to commit to at least three years for improving SWPBS in the school (Crone & Horner, 2003).

Table 11.1
Guidelines for Implementing School-Wide Positive Behavior Supports

1. Important that a team approach be used in building School-Wide Positive Behavior Supports. Need to have representatives from variety of areas (administration, special education, general education, etc.).
2. Very important to have the school principal as part of the behavior support team.
3. May want to use a two-tiered model (core team members and action team members for individual students).
4. May want to have nonteaching staff as part of the behavior support team (a lot of undesirable behaviors occur outside of the classroom where nonteaching staff are supervising).
5. Behavior support team needs a coordinator/referral liaison. This is a critical role for success of the team.
6. Roles (which can change/rotate from referral to referral) for the team includes:
   A. Conducting functional assessment interviews and observations.
   B. Reviewing academic records and work samples.
   C. Reporting functional assessment data to the behavior support team.
   D. Generating testable hypotheses.
   E. Designing, implementing, evaluating, and modifying behavior support plans.

Adapted from Crone and Horner (2003).

Table 11.2
Critical Features of Effective School-Wide Support Teams

A.	Efficient use of time (see Table 11.3 for guidelines for efficient use of time).
B.	High profile within the school.
C.	Consistent participation.
D.	Efficient system of documentation.
E.	Clear organizing procedure that delineates roles and responsibilities.
F.	System of accountability for responsibilities.
G.	Clearly defined system for making data-based decisions.

Key Point Question 2: How Do You Teach School-Wide Positive Behavior Supports to Students?

SWPBSs define school rules for all areas of the school as well as expectations, training about the rules, and feedback through reinforcement and punishment. There are six components for teaching SWPBS:

1. Select and define behavioral expectations.

Table 11.3
Guidelines for SWPBS Team Efficient Use of Time

1. Use the SWPBS system of behavior support to act as a screening process for referrals.
2. Determine whether each referral is valid.
3. Determine the extent of the functional behavior assessment that is necessary.
4. Generate an agenda for each meeting and distribute prior to the meeting.
5. Attach time limits to each agenda item.
6. Use a stopwatch to enforce time limits.
7. Keep notes of each meeting and materials organized in a binder.
8. Keep binder in a confidential location.
9. Meetings should be at the same time and day of week.
10. Assign a staff member to be the referral liaison.
11. Distribute a calendar to remind team members of meetings and deadlines.
12. Make use of existing school-based teams.

Adapted from Crone and Horner (2003).

2. Prevent problem behaviors by teaching behaviors directly (in all settings), providing examples of what the desired behaviors look like (positive examples) and what the undesired behaviors look like (negative examples). Actively monitor behavior in identified settings throughout the school environment.
3. Provide opportunities for practice.
4. Acknowledge appropriate desirable behavior with specific reinforcement.
5. Collect data and use them to make decisions regarding effectiveness and/or needed changes.
6. Respond to undesirable behaviors by correcting behavioral errors and enforcing consistent and fair consequences for breaking the rules. For example, if first grader Jordan is pushing the student he is following in line, the teacher would immediately point out the error, role model or have a peer model walking without pushing, monitor Jordan practice the correct walking, and reinforce the correct walking with praise. If Jordan continues to push, he is sent to the end of the line and told for the rest of the day, he will line up last. The teacher and staff continue to monitor Jordan for correct walking. Minor infractions are handled by teacher rules and consequences. Ongoing and severe infractions are addressed with an office referral.

Selecting Behavioral Expectations

Once the team has met and recruited feedback from the school community on social behaviors they feel are important and need to be taught, school-wide expectations can be formulated. This can be done at a meeting, by ballot, by survey, or an interview method. The school-wide support team will then choose three to five behavioral expectations, such as "Be Cooperative," "Be Safe," "Be a Friend," and "Be Respectful," which will be taught and reinforced across all school settings. Suggested guidelines are to use brief and positive action-based phrases. It is important to match the language to the age of the students and to choose a phrase that will easily lend itself to the specific behaviors students can be reinforced for. For example, "Be Respectful" relates to such behaviors as, "Be quiet, wait your turn, clean up after yourself, reply when you are spoken to, and walk without pushing." It is then possible to create a School-Wide Expectations Matrix as a teaching tool for students and staff to refer to for reminders and for reinforcement opportunities. A matrix should include the three to five school-wide expectations, with each setting the expectations are to be monitored in and the clearly stated behaviors expected for each setting. See Table 11.4 for an example of an SWPBS Expectations Matrix. As a teaching tool for role-playing and other instructional strategies, both the positive examples of the expected behavior and the negative examples of the behaviors are listed. See Table 11.5 for SWPBS Expectations Matrix illustrating positive and negative examples of target behaviors.

Interventions

Direct instruction can include social skills lessons, active supervision with reinforcement and corrective feedback, and tracking of skill performance (such as how many students were reinforced for standing in line appropriately in the cafeteria or how many students were referred to the school office for rule infractions). Many of the same strategies for teaching social skills discussed in Chapter 10 can be utilized for teaching the expected behaviors in the SWPBS program. Teaching the desired behaviors through role-play with peer modeling illustrating the positive and negative examples can be effective interventions. Incidental teaching is an especially important tool for providing imme-

Table 11.4
SWPBS Expectations Matrix

Sea View Elementary Kindergarten

	Classroom	Lunchroom	Hall	Playground
Sea Lions are Ready	• Listen at story time • Follow directions • Do your work • Use indoor voice	• Bring your lunch • Get your milk • Go to your table • Use indoor voice	• Walk in hall • Use indoor voice • Stay in line, don't push	• Follow teacher • Listen for bell • Line up quietly
Sea Lions Get Along with Others	• Share crayons • Make room for others at circle time • Wait your turn • Help someone who needs help • Say "Please" and "Thank You"	• Make room at the table • Talk to a neighbor • Help someone who needs help • Say "Please" and "Thank You"	• Hold buddy's hand • Say "Please" and "Thank You • Use quiet voice	• Wait your turn • Ask others to play • Share balls • Help someone who needs help • Say "Please and "Thank You"
Sea Lions Keep Safe	• Put toys away • Keep hands, legs, and arms to self • Always walk	• Wash hands before you eat • Sit with feet on floor • Eat quietly	• Stay in line • Keep hands, legs and arms to self • Always walk	• Wait your turn • Keep hands, legs, and arms to self • Put balls away • Line up quietly, don't push

Adapted from Colvin (2007).

diate corrective behavior feedback when an error is made and for reinforcing the correct performance of a skill.

Once student expected behaviors are introduced, opportunities for practice with reinforcement must be provided. Practicing the skill in the settings (the criterion environment) that the student will use the behavior is preferable (such as practicing how to line up in the cafeteria or how to walk down the hallway). Initially in the first few weeks of practice, frequent reminders to use the skills should be provided, and reinforcement should occur at high levels for desired behaviors

Table 11.5
School-Wide Behavior Expectations Matrix with Positive and Negative Examples

School-Wide Expectations

	Classroom Positive Examples	Classroom Negative Examples	**Hallway Positive Examples**	Hallway Negative Examples	**Cafeteria Positive Examples**	Cafeteria Negative Examples
Be Kind	**Invite other to join in** **Shair Class Materials** **Say "Thank You" and "Please"** **Make Positive Statments**	Say mean things about a classmate Pick a fight Laugh when someone needs help	**Help someone with their locker** **Stay calm if someone bumps into you** **Hold the door for someone**	Push someone back Get angry and yell at someone Run to be in line first	**Make a new friend at lunch** **Pick up something someone has dropped** **Let someone go first**	Talk only to your friend Steal someone's food Spill your drink on someone on purpose
Be Prepared Be a Responsible Student	**Have materials ready** **Be in seat** **Be quiet and looking at teachers**	Forget your backpack at home Wander around the classroom looking for materials	**Face forward** **Have hands and arms at side** **Lister for bell to enter classroom**	Stand in the hall so others can't pass Enter the classroom after the bell rings	**At warning bell, gather lunch disgards for garbage** **Sit quietly and wait for directions to exit**	Ignore warning bell and play under table Disturb your neighbor so they can't follow directions
	Follow directions **Finish your work** **Wait your turn** **Ask when you don't understand something**	Talk to your neighbor throughout class Ignore the teacher's directions Play with your cell phone	**Walk safely in the halls** **Keep to the right when walking** **Use inside voice**	Run and push to get to class Scream at your friend down the hall	**Pick up something you drop** **Recycle your lunch discards** **Line up orderly**	Cut in the lunch line Throw food Take more table space than you need

Adapted from Colvin (2007)

(all teachers and staff may have a certain number of cards, tokens, or other reinforcers that they must distribute within the first week to help make this high level of reinforcement occur).

Key Point Question 3: How do you reinforce School-Wide Positive Behavior Supports?

It is very important that the entire school staff (teachers, administrators, office staff, playground supervisors, etc.) be trained to teach and reinforce behavioral expectations in all the school settings. Students are positively reinforced by all staff for performing the desired behaviors in all school settings (such as office staff reinforcing a student for being polite when bringing a note to the office). Positive reinforcement can include praise, coupons, points, or good behavior bucks. Coupons or good behavior bucks can be traded in later for a privilege or an item from the school store (token economy), special recognition is given in weekly school announcements, and participation in special school assemblies is given (see Figure 11.1 for an example of a School-Wide Reinforcement Plan). Students and/or classes who are "caught" demonstrating a desired expectation behavior can become eligible for a weekly and/or monthly raffle or have their name submitted to participate in a planned activity. Using a variety of reinforcement systems provides multiple opportunities for both individual and group reinforcement.

The SWPBS team also needs to implement a consistent method for teachers and staff to address undesirable behaviors that occur outside of the classroom setting. When students are not responding appropriately to school-wide rules, an office referral is made. Office referrals are used for tracking the reason for referral, who made the referral, the minor or serious degree of the behavior, location where behavior occurred (very important for pinpointing where adults need to be at certain times of the day to be able to monitor students to discourage undesirable behaviors and to reinforce desirable behaviors), those involved in the incident, relevant information concerning the incident, and action taken by administration. Copies of the referral should be sent home to the parents and become part of the data-collection process for measuring the effectiveness of the SWPBS program.

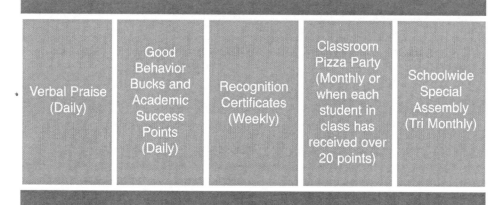

• Good Behavior Bucks are awarded for performance of positive behavior expectations.
• Academic Success Points are awarded for improvement in academic performance or special academic accomplishment.
• Good Behavior Bucks and Academic Success Points are worth 1 point toward classroom pizza party (record kept by classroom teacher).
• Good Behavior Bucks and Academic Success Points (same value as bucks) can be traded in at any time for an item in the school store.
• Recognition Certificates are awarded to students weekly who have attained more than 5 points.
• School-wide Special Assemblies are for all students in the school who received Recognition Certificates in the three-month period.
• Parents are sent a weekly announcement listing the names of students who received a Recognition Certificate

Adapted from Crone, Horner and Hawken (2004)

Figure 11.1. Example of School-Wide Plan for Reinforcement

Key Point Question 4: How Do You Assess School-Wide Positive Behavior Supports?

SWPBS is conducted on a continuum of support services involving three levels. The first level (universal support) addresses all students throughout the school. The second level (small group support) addresses the 10% to 15% of students who, in addition to the universal support, need more directed interventions for specific behaviors through small group instruction. The third level (intensive individual supports) provides a specific behavior support plan for the 5% to 10% of students who are in need of individual interventions. At every level, assessment is used to measure the effectiveness of the strategies. Three types of assessment are recommended:

1. Comparison of daily and monthly office discipline referrals,
2. Tracking the types of problem behaviors occurring by time and location, and
3. Determining whether the behavioral interventions are working by monitoring the behavior outcomes.

For example, a school is using office referrals to track the incidents of students fighting. After three weeks of tracking the office referrals, the SWPBS team determines that most of the office referrals for fighting are for the playground setting, specifically around the area with ball games such as basketball, foursquare, and tetherball. The team decides to conduct an in-service training for the playground supervisors for effective discipline practices in SWPBS for the playground and to make sure that a supervisor is always at this area. Besides office referrals, schools can track improvement in student outcomes by reviewing data on attendance, math and reading and other academic achievement, and student grades. For evaluating overall progress, Colvin (2009) provides the following guidelines for the SWPBS leadership team to follow:

1. Create a data management system or choose a web-based program (see www.swis.org for an example system to use) (see Table 11.6 for components of a data management system).
2. Assign a data entry person (could be an administrative staff person).
3. Monitor data entry weekly and create reports that are distributed to all teachers and staff.
4. Present summary graphs and reports to teachers and staff with opportunities provided for discussion and decision making.
5. At these meetings, if the data suggest a problem in a specific setting (hall, cafeteria, etc.), the faculty and staff will develop an appropriate intervention based on reinforcing desired behaviors.

Table 11.6
Components of a Data Management System

Component 1: Data Entry Functions for:
  a) Entering the type of undesirable behavior leading to referral.
  b) Entering the frequency of the behavior.
  c) Entering the location of the behavior.
  d) Entering the time of day the behavior occurred.
  e) Entering the names of students involved in the behavior.
  f) Entering the name of staff making the referral.
Component 2: System Design Capabilities include:
  a) Monitoring of data.
  b) Responding to requests for information on collected data.
  c) Generating reports for review of school-wide outcomes or targeted groups and individuals.
  d) Providing results/outcomes over a specified period of time.
  e) Located in a secure place (including web space) for confidentiality.
Component 3: System Use:
  a) Making decisions to improve discipline policies.
  b) Creating positive behavior support plans for individual students.
  c) Reporting to community and government agencies.

Adapted from www.swis.org

6. Results of data collection will regularly be presented to all stake-holders, including parents, school boards, and community as appropriate.

Key Point Question 5: How Do You Identify and Develop Interventions For Students Needing Additional Supports?

Sometimes school-wide plans are not adequate for addressing the intensive needs of some students. For students whose desirable behaviors are not improving through a school-wide discipline system, it may be necessary to consider more complex factors for deciding what targeted interventions to use. Factors to consider are:

1. Severity of the undesirable behavior.
2. How long the behavior has been going on.
3. How generalized the behavior is across settings, people, times, and behaviors.
4. How to reliably assess the function of the behavior (functional behavior assessment with direct observation may be needed as discussed in Chapter 3).

5. The intensity, complexity, and length of the treatment needed for effective behavior change.
6. The development of an appropriate evaluation measure to assess intervention effectiveness.
7. The development of an intervention plan for reinforcement, generalization, and monitoring of desired behavior (Gresham, 2005).

The targeted interventions should be continuously available to the student with rapid access (anywhere there is a teacher or staff in the school, intervention can be applied), easy for the teacher to use, consistent with the school-wide expectations, and implemented by all teachers and staff in the school (prompts can be provided throughout the day for desirable behavior and feedback along with reinforcement for desirable behaviors). Adequate resources are provided by administration or team (a system should be in place for the student to easily contact a positive support adult), and continuous monitoring and data collection are taken for assessing progress. If escape from academic tasks is maintaining the undesirable behavior, data collection can be tied to academic progress, and the intervention should include academic support. Reinforcement should be strengthened where adult and peer attention is delivered in the settings the undesirable behavior is occurring, and adult attention with a student desired tangible reinforcer (such as a coupon for movie, free time pass, etc.) should be delivered at the end of the day. Concurrently, a system for positive school contact with parents and student should be set in place (an email home, phone call, note, behavior contract shared between home and school, etc.). Whatever communication method is used, it should be timely, safe (the communication gets to the appropriate person, not lost or delayed), and reliable (everyone can count on receiving appropriate information and thus be able to provide immediate feedback, correction, and reinforcement to the student). A self-management system for increasing the student's ability to self-monitor their progress should be taught, and opportunities for making choices in their day should be increased (Crone, Horner, & Hawken, 2004).

Crone et al. (2004) provide a BEP/Check and Connect Cycle strategy, where the student receives a daily progress report to give to each teacher prior to each class period (can include other settings, too such as cafeteria, computer room, library, playground where a supervisor is present). This strategy is meant to help the 10% to 15% of students who are failing to respond to the school-wide disciplinary expectations but do not require the highest level of behavior support, yet they are at increased risk for developing serious undesirable behaviors. Crone et al. (2004) outline the key element for this program as:

1. All teachers and staff in the school along with the Behavior Support Team participate, but one person is the BEP manager.
2. Students enter the program through teacher or family nomination or student request. Students must agree to participate.
3. A BEP agreement among the student, family, and BEP coordinator is created with defining behaviors.
4. The BEP involves daily and weekly cycles. Steps in the daily cycle are:

• Student arrives at school and checks in with the BEP coordinator.
• At check in, student receives the Daily Progress Report (DPR).
• The student hands the DPR to the teacher or supervisor at the start of the day (elementary school) or start of each class period (middle or high school).
• Student retrieves the DPR at the end of each day/session, receiving feedback about the expected academic and/or social behaviors on the DPR.
• At the end of the day, the student returns the DPR to the BEP coordinator and receives a reinforcer. A copy is made for the student to take home.
• At home, the student receives positive feedback and reinforcement for success. A family member signs the form, which is returned by student to the BEP coordinator the next morning.

The weekly cycle involves the Behavior Support Team meeting to review the percentage of points the student earned (this meeting will reviews progress for all students in the BEP program) and make decisions about continued support (see Figure 11.2 for diagram of BEP process). The point system on the DPR should be kept simple; a 2 for "yes met the expectation," a 1 for "ok progress on expectation," and 0 for "not meeting behavior expectation" (see Figure 11.3 for a sample DPR). Weekly data are summarized. Data are used to decide whether students need to continue with BEP, any students need BEP modified, award reinforcers, add in new nominations to the BEP program and

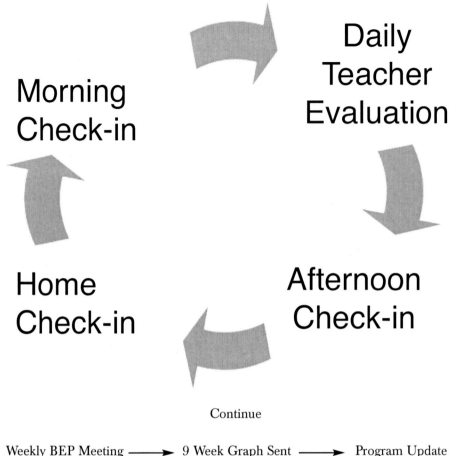

Continue

Weekly BEP Meeting ———▶ 9 Week Graph Sent ———▶ Program Update

                                                                            Exit

Adapted from Crone, Horner, and Hawken (2004).

Figure 11.2 BEP Cycle

assign any needed tasks to relevant teachers or Behavior Support Team members. Data are recorded and graphed on a weekly basis for each student and for the entire BEP program. Team reviews data weekly to determine whether progress is being made and to prioritize support for targeted students who need more help. A graph of charted progress is sent home every nine weeks or a team-decided set number of weeks.

For a small percentage of students (in the third level, approximately 5% to 10%), the BEP will not be effective in reducing their undesir-

Student Name: Mark Dibbs   Date: January 2, 2015

Expectations	Period 1	Period 2	Period 3	Period 4	Period 5
Finish work	[2] 1 0	[2] 1 0	2 1 [0]	2 [1] 0	[2] 1 0
Follow directions	[2] 1 0	[2] 1 0	[2] 1 0	[2] 1 0	[2] 1 0
Raise hand	2 1 [0]	2 1 [0]	[2] 1 0	[2] 1 0	2 1 [0]
Total points	4	5	4	5	4
Teacher initials	P.T.	R.S.	M.D.	K.S	L.H.

Points Goal: 20/30   Daily Score: 22/30

Teacher Comments:

Finished Work on time! L.H.

Remembered to raise hand! M.D

Good improvement today. K.S.

Parent Comments: Keep at it. Good Job!

Parent Signature: Mrs. Dibbs

BEP Coordinator Signature: Farminey Jones   **Student Signature:** Mark Dibbs

Adapted from Crone, Horner and Hawken (2004)

Figure 11.3. Daily Progress Report

able behavior. For these students, a functional assessment should be conducted (see Chapter 3) to determine the function of the behavior for better targeting an effective intervention, and also to assess whether the behavior needs intensive supports due to its complex or severe nature. For these students, the Behavior Support Plan must: (a) specify team members' individual responsibilities, timelines, and deadlines; (b) if possible, use an existing Student Study Team to coordinate individual PBS plans (creating a new team that has a similar function to an already existing team may be an inefficient use of time and also work at cross-purposes if both teams are addressing the same student's behavioral problem and developing different interventions for the teacher to use); (c) Provide teachers and staff with initial intensive support in implementing the BSP; and (d) make sure necessary supports are in place (behavior specialist, mentor teacher, etc.).

BEST PRACTICE RECOMMENDATIONS

1. Work first to attain teacher and staff commitments to SWPBS program before implementing program.
2. Establish a leadership team, including the school principal.
3. Define in measurable terms the expected outcomes for planned activities.
4. Use data to assess outcomes and effectiveness of interventions.
5. Put specific procedures in place, such as an annual refresher leadership meeting, to maintain the SWPBS plan and to make needed adjustments.

DISCUSSION QUESTIONS

1. What do you do if individual teachers or groups of teachers work against the goals of the school-wide behavior support team?
2. How do you arrange for planning time for teachers and staff to set up an SWPBS program?

CLASSROOM AND SCHOOL ACTIVITY SUGGESTIONS

1. Observe students behaviors in your school in three different school settings for one week. Make a list of undesired behaviors you observe in each setting each day. Tally the frequency for each behavior. Make a matrix of these behaviors to include each setting. Collaborate with your class on how to correct these behaviors by listing the desired behaviors. Teach desired behaviors through role-playing what they look like, and role-play what the corresponding undesired behaviors look like. Have the class suggest three expectations for classroom.
2. Meet with your school principal and review together the current school-side system for addressing problem behavior in your school. Share your collected observation data and discuss how an SWPBS program could benefit your school site.

REFERENCES

Colvin, G. (2007). *7 steps for developing a proactive schoolwide discipline plan: A guide for principals and leadership teams.* Thousand Oaks, CA: Corwin Press.

Colvin, G. (2009). *Managing noncompliance and defiance in the classroom: A road map for teachers, specialists, and behavior support teams.* Thousand Oaks, CA: Corwin Press.

Crone, D. A., & Horner, R. H. (2003). *Building positive behavior support systems in schools: Functional behavioral assessment.* New York: Guilford.

Crone, D. A., Horner, R. H., & Hawken, L. S. (2004). *Responding to problem behavior in schools: The behavior education program.* New York: Guilford.

Gresham, F. M. (2005). Response to intervention: An alternative means of identifying students as emotionally disturbed. *Education and Treatment of Children, 28,* 328–344.

Miramontes, N., Marchant, M., Heath, M., & Fischer, L. (2011). Social validity of a positive behavior interventions and support model. *Education and Treatment of Children, 34,* 445–468.

Chapter 12

SCHOOLS, AGENCIES, AND FAMILIES WORKING TOGETHER

Key Point Questions

1. Why is family involvement important in Positive Behavior Supports?
2. What mental health resources are available?
3. What are wraparound services?
4. How can school violence be prevented?
5. How can bullying be prevented?
6. What is the Juvenile Justice System and how does it interface with Positive Behavior Supports?

WINDOW OF THE WORLD CASE STUDY 1

Idwal was in seventh grade and a bully, no doubt about it. Tall and large for his age, he easily intimidated his peers by standing close and towering over them as he made his demand (which was usually money or for them to complete his academic work). Even his friends were intimidated and would not say anything, even if he would shove a student who was not quick enough to cough up money or his homework that they were to have done the night before. No students were willing to risk saying something to an adult for fear of retribution. Fortunately, two parents of children being bullied were monitoring their children's postings online, and, being friends, they conferred with each other and decided to bring the matter to the attention of the school principal, Ms. Rainey. Understanding the importance and urgency of the situation, Ms. Rainey immediately referred the situation to Ms. Srang, who was the Behavior Education Program (BEP) team leader. Ms. Srang conferred with the BEP team, and they decided on a multicomponent intervention. First, they identified the students being bullied and taught them social skills on how to react to bullying by Idwal (assertiveness training, specific phrases to use when they saw him to prevent the bullying behavior), as well as establishing a peer buddy system when they were in areas that Idwal had often engaged in his bullying behavior. Second, Ms. Srang contacted Idwal's parents to notify them about the situation and also provided information on how they might talk with Idwal about his behavior. Third, the SWPBS team put into place a school-wide policy regarding bullying. As part of the policy, they included students in developing and implementing classroom rules regarding bullying. Classroom instruction also occurred to make bystanders aware of their supportive role in bullying and to discourage them from observing and remaining present when bullying occurs. Fourth, staff increased their supervision in places where Idwal had been bullying (the locker room and in bathrooms). Fifth, Ms. Srang met with Idwal's teachers, and they all expressed concern about his reading ability as this part of the curriculum was becoming more and more difficult for him. Ms. Srang then arranged for a reading specialist to meet with high school peer tutors (who were meeting their community service requirements) to teach them various instructional strategies to use with Idwal to help his reading, especially around comprehension of technical words. In addition to this help with his reading, the tutors provided Idwal with older students who were positive role models. Finally, Ms. Srang helped Idwal to join a student homework support group, which met once a week to provide assistance on assignments. She also provided homework support through phone calls and social networking sites. Together these interventions had a positive impact on Idwal's bullying behavior, which was quickly eliminated due to his decreased need to bully, and the positive interventions increased his academic performance.

WINDOW OF THE WORLD CASE STUDY 2

Ariel was only ten years old but already having multiple crises in her life. Her family had lost their home and was moving from one living situation (with relatives, homeless shelters, and their car) to another. Ariel was having migraine headaches with related vision problems; however, her family had no health care (her father only worked part-time with no health benefits). Ariel was falling behind academically due to her missing a lot of school. When at school, she was unable to focus, and thus was developing behavioral problems as the academic work became harder for her. In addition, her mother was having mental health substance abuse issues, and Ariel was often responsible for caring for her younger sister.

Ms. Montero, Ariel's teacher, was in touch with Ariel's parents and aware of the difficulties facing Ariel. She knew that she could help Ariel academically and with her behavior problems; however, she knew the family needed comprehensive help (known as wraparound services). Ms. Montero, with the help of the school counselor, Mr. Kasparov, brought together Ariel's parents, a nurse from a community health program, a peer counselor from a program for recovered addicts, a career counselor from the local community college, and, since Ariel's father was a veteran, a staff member from Veterans Administration Supported Housing (VASH) who was responsible for Section 8 housing (which authorizes the payment of rental housing assistance to private landlords).

This team came up with objectives to help Ariel and her family work together on a plan of appropriate interventions. Each team member was assigned a specific intervention. Ms. Montero developed a self-management strategy and relaxation technique for Ariel when she was faced with difficult academic tasks. In addition, she had Ariel sign up for lunch time and after school tutoring from older peers at the school. A reading specialist was also brought in to work with Ariel one hour a week. The nurse and Ariel's father took Ariel to a local community health clinic, which provided services for children without medical insurance and Ariel received medication for her migraines, underwent an assessment of her vision, and was provided with glasses. The peer counselor worked individually with Ariel's mother, who then joined a peer support group for the addiction issues. The VASH staff member obtained an affordable two-bedroom apartment for the family with the Section 8 housing support. Finally, the career counselor from the community college helped Ariel's father obtain a job at a solar energy company that was partnering with the community college to provide jobs for veterans. Together these interventions provided a comprehensive package that turned around the family's circumstances. Now, Ariel and her family live in a manner that would not have been accomplished by any one of the interventions by itself.

Key Point Question 1: Why Is Family Involvement Important?

Parents[1] can be important allies and supports for teachers. In many ways, parents play the critical role in the education of their children, as they provide important information and insight about the student. Furthermore, generalization of skills and interventions, from school and home and from home to school, can be enhanced with a productive relationship between the teacher and the parents (such as the student being reinforced both at school and at home for completing homework assignments). Table 12.1 provides an overview of benefits to teachers, parents, and students for successful school and family collaboration.

It is important that teachers establish professional and positive contact with parents early in the school year, which can help keep undesirable student behaviors from occurring. Table 12.2 provides a list of methods that teachers can use for communicating with parents. A variety of methods should be used throughout the school year with a focus on the communication preferences of the parents (providing parents with a list of options can be helpful). In these communications, teachers can provide information about the class (rules, expectations, how to best communicate with the teacher, upcoming events, etc.) as well as academic information (assignments, homework, grading criteria, how to reinforce classroom learning at home, etc.). Communication with parents can also be about a specific student. In these particular communications, teachers should be informing parents of what their children are doing well (a positive statement such as Denise is doing a very good job of turning in all of her homework on time) more than what they are doing wrong (sometimes Denise's homework is a bit

---

1 We use the term "parents" in this chapter, although we are including parents, siblings, grandparents, foster parents, and other adult care providers under this term.

Table 12.1
Benefits of Teacher/Parent Collaboration

Benefits to Teachers of a Productive Parent–Teacher Relationship
1. Greater understanding of the student's strengths and needs.
2. Access to more meaningful reinforcers (tangible and activity).
3. Increased opportunities for reinforcement (transenvironmental programming).
4. More cooperation from parents.
5. Easier to face hard decisions together rather than alone.
6. Avoiding potential problems such as implementing an intervention that has been unsuccessfully tried before.
7. Better behavior from students if they know parents and teachers are working together.

Benefits to parents of a productive parent–professional relationship
1. Takes away sense of helplessness in dealing with the school system.
2. Have an advocate (teacher) within the system.
3. Inside view of what is going on in the school.
4. Greater access to resources and services.
5. Better understanding of what the child can do in school.

Benefits to Students of a Productive Parent–Teacher Relationship
1. Greater consistency in his or her two most important environments.
2. More opportunities for learning and growth.
3. Better supports in both environments.
4. Better advocacy from both teacher and parents.
5. Better access to resources and services.

Table 12.2
Effective Strategies for Communicating with Parents

1. Phone calls.
2. Emails.
3. Texts.
4. Notes home in student's backpack.
5. Journal back and forth between teacher and parents.
6. Teacher blog, social network site, or website that posts classroom rules, syllabus, course assignment, how students and parents can best ask for assistance from the teacher, etc.
7. Teacher–parent meetings.
8. Introductory letter to parents at beginning of year.
9. Introductory video to parents at beginning of year.
10. Home visits.
11. Back to school nights.
12. Regular progress reports.
13. Class newsletters.

sloppy in terms of quality). Teachers should always end the communication on a positive note (with more careful editing of her homework, Denise will get a very good grade in the class). In communications and collaborations, teachers need to be aware of linguistic, cultural, ethnic, and socioeconomic differences between themselves and also among the different parents of their students (Aguilar, 2010; Araujo, 2009; Sung & Clark, 2005).

The relationship between the teacher and parents should not be adversarial, though, unfortunately, it can sometimes become so. In these situations, it is important that the teacher have documentation of the contact and content covered with the parents. Teachers need to analyze what they can do to improve the relationship with the parents rather than laying blame on the parents for the situation.

Robinson and Fine (1994) suggest a six-step solution-oriented approach for teacher and parent collaboration. These steps can keep the focus on the tasks to accomplish and offer greater assurance of the participants reaching resolution. These six steps are:

1. First, clearly state the purpose for collaborating together. This creates an atmosphere where the participants openly and nondefensively express an interest in discussing concerns and in working together to resolve those concerns.
2. Second, use accurate listening skills to explore the parents' view of the situation. The teacher's observations and inquiries should not be judgmental but are intended to further clarify the parents' views.
3. Third, both parents and teacher reach a common understanding of both the problem and the solution. The term "solution" refers to what the participants want to happen, for both the process and the outcome.
4. The fourth step is a review of options of appropriate interventions and outcomes.
5. The fifth step is the agreement on the specific intervention and outcome. The intervention should include specification of each person's role in carrying out the intervention, as well as a timetable. This helps to create a sense of accountability for all parties.
6. Finally, an evaluation of the success of the intervention and outcomes is important.

Key Point Question 2: What Mental Health Resources Are Available?

One in ten children and adolescents have a mental health disorder that causes some level of impairment, yet only one in five of such children receives specialty mental health services (Burns et al., 1995). Depression, suicide, anxiety disorders, child abuse, and substance abuse are all threats to students doing well in school. Even students who do not have serious mental health issues will face stressful or traumatic events that will affect their well-being and school performance (Cornell, 2006). A person's mental health condition is best viewed as being on a continuum or spectrum, as a student is not necessarily either totally mentally healthy or unhealthy; thus, one's mental health condition can move around on the continuum depending on life circumstances (Weare, 2000).

Mental health programs should be integrated into schools as much as possible with providing services where they are needed (push in model). This allows collaboration among school teachers and staff, counselors, psychologists, social workers, nurses, and police officers, rather than each providing their services in an isolated context. The logic is that the more complex the problem, the more there is a need for a comprehensive cohesive system approach that involves a variety of supports from a team of professionals and others, such as family friends (Adelman & Taylor, 1998). The focus is on prevention and promoting wellness for specific students as well as across the student body as a whole. It can be that mental, emotional, and social health is the "missing piece" of positive behavior supports for many students (Weare, 2000).

Mental health services should focus on:

Personal competencies: Social skills, problem-solving skills.
Emotional well-being: Happiness or joy as well as understanding and being able to express one's emotions.
Thinking clearly: Having the ability to process information, make good decisions, and set goals.
Ability to grow: Having the ability to change positively, learn from experiences, and build skills.
Resilience: Having the ability to bounce back from stress and difficulties and move on.

Emotional intelligence and Emotional literacy: Having the ability to identify, assess, and control the emotions of oneself, as well as the ability to express emotions productively.

Key Point Question 3: What Are Wraparound Services?

Wraparound services are a team-based planning process (not a specific intervention or service) to providing community-based care for students with complex mental health and related issues. The team includes the student, family members, service providers, and members of the family's social support network. Team members work together to create, implement, and monitor a plan to meet student and family needs.

Wraparound services are based on:

1. Engaging youth, caregivers, and families in a strengths-based process,
2. Identifying priority needs,
3. Assembling an integrated team that provides the basis for collaboration,
4. Managing the work of the team so that cross-system, solution-based problem solving occurs,
5. Building the youth and family's self-efficacy and social support, and
6. Setting goals and monitoring success over time (Bruns, et al., 2011).

The purpose of the wraparound process is to bring together the student and the family with needed supports, such as medical coordinators, family and youth peer-to-peer support partners, mental health workers, social workers, and so on to develop comprehensive interventions (rather than piecemeal approaches from each individual or agency) to meet the needs of the student, the family, and others. Wraparound is not based on any single theory of intervention; wraparound is best understood as a planning process and a philosophy of care (Eber, Hyde, & Suter, 2011). Wraparound is operationalized as a process with activities that occur across four distinct phases in which a team is formed that develops, monitors, and continuously revises a plan that is focused on achieving success as defined by the student and family (Eber et al., 2009; Walker 2008).

Phase I: Engagement and Team Development

This phase provides the foundation for success by building positive relationships and support networks among the student, the family, and the team members. During this phase, a wraparound facilitator meets with the student and family to engage them in the process, address concerns, explain how this process is different from traditional interventions, and help the family decide who they want on their wraparound team. Baseline measurements are established during Phase I for continued updating and evaluation of the success of the intervention.

Phase II: Initial Plan Development

In this phase, the facilitator helps the family and team reach consensus and buy in on the desired outcomes. Both the needs and strengths are used to identify specific interventions as well as to clarify roles for all team members.

Phase III: Plan Implementation

This phase starts the intervention process to effectively meet the needs of the students by combining supports such as child care, mentoring, social networking with specific interventions such as counseling, specialized academic instruction (such as for reading), and addressing medical issues. Wraparound teams can also arrange supports for the adults or other family members who care for the student, such as assisting family members in accessing stable housing, recreation opportunities, and social supports. Supports can also come from or be provided to teachers as well for meeting the unique needs of the student.

Phase IV: Plan Completion and Transition

In this final phase, the student and family are transitioned from the ongoing wraparound team to progress monitoring through less intensive structures, such as parent–teacher conference or agency contacts. Movement to Phase IV is determined by the ability of the student and family to continue successful functioning with supports and skills that have been developed, and to continue interventions as necessary, such as a self-management system at school and home, counseling services, or access to appropriate medical services.

Key Point Question 4: How Can School Violence be Prevented?

Violence is an unfortunate possibility in schools. Having police officers on campus, installing video cameras and closed circuit television systems, utilizing weapon-detection systems (e.g., metal detectors), and blocking/restricting access to school facilities with entry-control devices (e.g., electronic key cards) are some preventative strategies that have been employed (see Table 12.3 for roles that police school liaison officers can play in school settings).

Table 12.3
Role of Police School Liaison Officers

1. Counsel, advise, and talk informally with students.
2. Teach classes on alcohol and drug use prevention.
3. Advise school personnel on security precautions.
4. Offer safety and crime prevention education for students, families, and school personnel.
5. De-escalate volatile situations.
6. Investigate, document, and record important incidents in the school.
7. Serve as a liaison between the school and the juvenile justice system.

Adapted from James, Logan, and Davis (2011) and Lawrence (1998).

Positive Behavior Support strategies can also play a key role in preventing violence and keeping schools safe. Well-developed antisocial behavior patterns and high levels of aggression evidenced early in a child's life are among the best predictors of delinquent and violent behavior years later. Thus, by implementing Positive Behavior Supports, it is possible to diminish the likelihood of these behavior occurring. Research indicates that some interventions for violent behavior are ineffective. These are Correctional Boot Camps, Drug Abuse Resistance Education (DARE), Scared Straight programs, and school uniforms (Cornell, 2006).

School violence by students is not a spontaneous event. Students build up to the act and display signs and show preponderance toward the violent behavior (Jones, 2001). Examples of early warning signs are presented in Table 12.4. It is important to note that these signs do not necessarily mean that a student is prone to violence, but they do provide an impetus to address these concerns and the support needs of the student (Jones, 2001). Examples of imminent warning signs of violent behavior are provided in Table 12.5. These signs cannot be ignored and require an immediate intervention, which usually requires mental health provider assistance (Jones, 2001). If violent, homicidal, and suicidal statements and behavior do occur, they must be taken seriously. The teacher should remain with the student at all times until assistance arrives. All potentially hazardous objects should be removed from the student or vicinity. If the student is unmanageable or poses an immediate risk, then police and emergency services should be notified immediately (Shafii & Shafii, 2001). Teachers and others should respond to the threat of violent behavior by remaining calm, keeping the interaction with the student brief, avoiding becoming involved in a power struggle, and removing other students from the setting (Jones, Dohrn, & Dunn, 2004).

Table 12.4
Early Warning Signs of Violent Behavior

1. History of violence.
2. Close family member has committed a violent act.
3. Access to a weapon or other means to commit violence.
4. Lack of coping skills to handle personal crisis.
5. Lack of inhibition in displaying anger.
6. Acts of cruelty to animals.
7. Abusive behavior toward adults.
8. Being a loner with no social network.
9. History of mental health treatment.
10. Expression of violence in writings or drawings.
11. Signs of depression or mood swings.
12. Poor social skills.
13. Gang involvement.

Adapted from Jones (2001).

Table 12.5
Imminent Warning Signs of Violent Behavior

1. Serious physical fighting with peers or family members.
2. Severe destruction of property.
3. Severe rage for seemingly minor reasons.
4. Detailed threats of lethal violence.
5. Possession of firearms or other weapons.
6. Self-injurious behavior or threats of suicide.

Adapted from Jones (2001).

Sprague and Walker (2000) provide a number of useful suggestions for preventing violent behaviors in schools:

Intervene as Early as Possible: It is very important to intervene as early as possible (the younger the student, the more likely the intervention will be successful) with positive behavior supports to break the pattern of antisocial behavior.

Address Both Behavioral Risks and Strengths: The undesirable behavior that students display has a negative impact on their social environment (e.g., teacher and peer rejection, school failure), as well as academic performance, and these undesirable behaviors need to be directly addressed. At the same time, these same students have strengths (sometimes referred to as personal assets), both socially and academically, and these positive behaviors need to be strengthened or increased. Thus, interventions need to be comprehensive and focus on the simultaneous reduction of undesirable behavior and development of personal strengths and assets, as well as academic competence (which is often overlooked although it is a critical component to analyze).

Involve Families as Partners in the Intervention: Families of students can face a variety of issues (poverty, drug use, poor parenting skills, violence in the community) that can negatively impact students' social and academic behavior (Patterson, 1982). Many parents of students with violent behaviors do not have a positive history with schooling in their own lives and may resist participating in joint school–home intervention approaches. Nevertheless, it is important that the family be involved as partners as much as possible in the behavior support intervention so the student has a consistent pattern of expectations, rules, and reinforcement at school and home.

Match the Strength of the Intervention to the Antisocial Behavior:
Interventions for students with the potential for violence may be ineffective because: (a) they are poorly matched to the severity and complexity of the problems they are designed to ameliorate, (b) they do
not address the function of the behavior, (c) they are not focused on
building positive desirable behaviors, and (d) they are not comprehensive enough (Kazdin, 2005; Reid, Patterson, & Snyder, 2002;
Sprague & Walker, 2005). Thus, the intervention must look broadly at
a variety of strategies to develop skills and supports for the student and
to make sure that they are being implemented in an effective manner.

Key Point Question 5: How Can Bullying be Prevented?

While there is no one legal definition of bullying (also known as
peer harassment), it can be conceptualized as repeated inappropriate
behavior that may be direct or indirect, verbal or physical, or some
form of negative interaction between one or more persons against
another or others (see Table 12.6 for examples of bullying behavior).
Bullying can be more than student to student behavior, it can also
involve group dynamics such as a group of individuals bullying one
student or a group watching the bullying. Bullying may harm, intimidate, threaten, victimize, undermine, offend, degrade, or humiliate
another student. Bullying can occur at school, in the community, at
home, and/or online. Supports can thus occur outside of school in
addition to interventions within the school. There tend to be two types
of victims: those who are passive and submissive (insecure, fearful, or
withdrawn) and those who are provocative (aggressive responses to
bullying). In addition, bullies are also at risk for later criminality: thus,
it is very important that these students receive support as soon as possible (Olweus, 2011).

Table 12.6
Examples of Bullying

1. Saying mean or hurtful things.
2. Using derogatory names.
3. Hitting, kicking, shoving, or physically intimidating a peer.
4. Telling lies or spreading false rumors.

Bullying often goes unnoticed by adults as it often occurs where adults are not present (especially in cyberspace) and is often unreported (there can be a fine line discriminating between positive teasing among peers and bullying behavior, especially among adolescents). School is often a prime location for bullying and can extend into other settings as well. Unfortunately, the effects of bullying can last a lifetime for the victim.

Bullying can be:

Physical: Where the bully uses force and body strength to overpower the victim.

Verbal: Where the bully use words to intimidate and hurt the victim.

Relational: Where the bully damages a victim's social status and relationship with others.

Cyberbullying: Where the bully uses social networking, email, blogs, and other sites to harass the victim; it is often done with anonymity.

Bullying calls for intervention on an individual level (for both the bully and the victim, as well as for bystanders) and also a school-wide level as a preventative strategy (Pearce, Cross, Monks, Waters, & Falconer, 2011). For example, Wong, Cheng, Ngan, and Ma (2011) found that a Restorative Whole School Approach was effective in reducing bullying and involved the setting up of restorative justice goals, clear instructions, team building, and good relationships among students, parents, and teachers. For cyberbulling, a variety of intervention programs are available, and these have been reviewed by Mishna, Cook, Saini, Meng Jia, and MacFadden (2011) and Snakenborg, Van Acker, and Gable (2011). Table 12.7 provides examples of strategies for addressing bullying behavior.

Ross and Horner (2009) analyzed that the function of bullying behavior is to gain attention and praise from others. Combining both a school-wide and an individual intervention system, Ross and Horner taught students respectful behavior skills (avoiding the use of the term bullying) and how to handle situations in which a peer is not respectful. Teaching these skills reduced the reinforcement to the bully and included:

Table 12.7
Strategies for Addressing Bullying

---

1. Discourage the bully from attacking peers.
2. Teach the victim strategies for avoiding and escaping from bullying.
3. Make bystanders aware of their supportive role in bullying and discourage them from observing and remaining present when bullying occurs.
4. Teach nonparticipants to discourage bullying among their peers and how not to approve in any form if it does occur.
5. Have a school-wide policy in place regarding bullying with a clear definition, reinforcement for the absence of bullying behaviors, and negative consequences for bullying behaviors. Include students in developing SWPBS and classroom rules regarding bullying.
6. Closely supervise places where bullying is likely to occur (recess, locker rooms, bathrooms, hallways, etc.).
7. Communicate with parents regarding bullying prevention programs and provide anti-bullying and cyberbullying information.
8. Take immediate action when bullying occurs and document the incident. Have a meeting among teachers and other staff, parents, and students (both the bully and victim) if bullying does occur.
9. Teach positive skills for reacting to bullying to students, especially those at risk for bullying. These skills may include assertiveness training and/or social skills instruction.
10. Provide classroom activities and discussions related to bullying.
11. Confront the bully in private, as doing so in public may enhance the status of the bully and reinforce the bullying behavior.
12. Refer both bully and victim to counseling, if appropriate.
13. Provide protection to victim, such as peer buddy system or additional adult supervision.
14. Avoid attempts to mediate the bullying situation.

Adapted from Olweus (1991); Savage and Savage (2010); U.S. Department of Education (1998); and Walker, Ramsy, and Gresham (2004).

1. understand what behaviors are respectful and not respectful.
2. if someone is not respectful to you (victim), say "stop" and use the stop gesture (hand held up);
3. if you see someone being treated disrespectfully (bystander), say "stop" and take the victim away;
4. if, after you say "stop," disrespectful behavior continues, walk away;
5. if, after you walk away, disrespectful behavior continues, tell an adult;
6. if someone says "stop" to you, stop what you are doing, take a breath, and go about your day.

When bullying occurs, a teacher or staff person should:

1. Defuse the situation.
2. Report the situation to an administrator/supervisor.
3. Seek advice from administrators, counselors, and other qualified individuals.
4. Keep a record of what occurred.

Using Restorative Justice with bullying

Focus is on education of the bully.

1. Educate the bully on how his or her actions were hurtful.
2. Create a learning assignment based on the incident.
3. Have the bully commit to service hours related to the incident.

Key Point Question 6: What Is the Juvenile Justice System and How Does It Interface With Positive Behavior Supports?

Students in legal trouble are considered to be in juvenile status if they are under the age of 18. These juveniles have different court proceedings from adult offenders (see Table 12.8). In addition, consequences for juveniles are different than for adults: they are more focused on rehabilitating the student and keeping them out of future trouble than with punishment, although this can of course occur as well (see Table 12.9). Although these students may be in restricted environments outside of the school setting, they are still entitled to receive educational services.

Table 12.8
Features That Distinguish Juvenile Court Proceedings from
Adult Criminal Court Proceedings

---

1. Absence of legal guilt because the child is less mature and often unaware of consequences of actions; not held legally responsible to the same extent as adults.
2. Focus is on treatment rather than punishment.
3. There is an evaluation of the juvenile's background and social history. The need and amenability for treatment are of equal importance with the offense when making a decision.
4. Shorter terms of supervision and/or incarceration.

Adapted from Lawrence (1998).

Table 12.9
Potential Outcomes for Students in the Juvenile Justice System

1. *Volunteers in Probation:* Court-sponsored program where trained volunteers meet regularly with the student and engage in activities such as tutoring, attending a sporting event, etc. This is an opportunity for the student to develop a positive relationship with a supportive adult.
2. *Probation:* The student is not incarcerated following certain conditions set forth by the court, often under the supervision of a probation officer. The student may be required to refrain from firearms, and to a curfew, etc. in order to minimize the potential for future trouble.
3. *Intensive Probation Supervision:* The Probation Office makes regular (often daily) contact with the student to closely monitor his or her activities.
4. *Electronic Monitoring/House Arrest:* The student is to be at home except for school, employment, or medical reasons.
5. *Restitution Programs:* Monetary or service; with service, the student is to provide service to the victim or community.
6. *Residential Programs:* Group homes, wilderness programs, foster care, or day treatment programs.
7. *Detention Centers (Juvenile Halls):* Temporary holding facility for juveniles who need to be held for their own safety or for that of the community.
8. *Correctional Institutions:* Prison settings for juveniles.

Adapted from Lawrence (1998).

Although the juvenile justice system is often focused on punitive interventions, a variety of more positive intervention programs are available for students in the juvenile justice system, such as Reclaiming Futures, Functional Family Therapy, and Multisystemic Therapy strategies (Greenwood, 2008). Many of these programs have elements in common with Positive Behavior Support strategies including such elements as:

1. a focus on prevention and the involvement of community agencies as part of the interventions,
2. a focus on assisting students to build skills, and
3. developing positive and enduring connections with others so that they have a strong recovery network for ongoing support (Nissen 2011).

BEST PRACTICE RECOMMENDATIONS

1. Interventions need to be comprehensive in order to be effective and may involve parents and agencies from outside of the school, students, teachers, and staff.
2. Community agencies can be housed on school grounds to provide easy access to students as well as coordination across agencies and the school.
3. Bullying behavior needs to be addressed with supports to the bully, as well as to the students being bullied, and the bystanders.
4. Potentially violent behaviors cannot be ignored and must be directly addressed.

DISCUSSION QUESTIONS

1. Is it the role of the school to get involved in bullying that occurs outside of the school or in cyberspace?
2. How often and under what circumstances should parents and teachers communicate?
3. How do you build a successful relationship with adversarial parents?

CLASSROOM AND SCHOOL ACTIVITY SUGGESTIONS

1. Interview a teacher or teachers about a student with complex support needs and analyze supports in terms of medical, mental, social, academic, and other needs. Analyze what a comprehensive intervention package might need to entail.
2. Follow up this interview with the student and the family with analyzing the supports in terms of medical, mental, social, academic, and other needs. How are the viewpoints of the teachers, the student, and the family similar and/or different? Analyze what a comprehensive intervention package might need to entail.

REFERENCES

Adelman, H. S., & Taylor, L. (1998). Reforming mental health in schools and expanding school reform. *Educational Psychologist, 33,* 135–152.

Aguilar, E. (2010). Teaching secrets: When the kids don't share your culture. *Education Digest, 76,* 52–54.

Araujo, B. E. (2009). Best practices in working with linguistically diverse families. *Intervention in School and Clinic, 45,* 116–123.

Bruns, E., Sather, A., Pullmann, M., & Stambaugh, L. (2011). National trends in implementing wraparound: Results from the state wraparound survey. *Journal of Child and Family Studies, 20,* 726–735.

Burns, B. J., Costello, E. J., Angold, A., Tweed, D., Stangl, D., Farmer, E. M., & Erkanli, A. (1995). Children's mental health service use across service sectors. *Health Affairs, 14,* 147–159.

Cornell, D. G. (2006). *School violence: Fears versus facts.* Mahwah, NJ: Lawrence Erlbaum Associates.

Eber, L., Hyde, K., Rose, J., Breen, K., McDonald, D., & Lewandowski, H. (2009). Completing the continuum of schoolwide positive behavior support: Wraparound as a tertiary-level intervention. In W. Sailor, G. Dunlap, & G. Sugai (Eds.), *Handbook of positive behavior support* (pp. 671–703). New York: Springer.

Eber, L., Hyde, K., & Suter, J. (2011). Integrating wraparound into a schoolwide system of positive behavior supports. *Journal of Child and Family Studies, 20,* 782–790.

Greenwood, P. (2008). Prevention and intervention programs for juvenile offenders. *Future of Children, 18,* 185–210.

James, R. K., Logan, J., & Davis, S. (2011). Including school resource officers in school-based crisis intervention: Strengthening student support. *School Psychology International, 32,* 210–224.

Jones, T. L. (2001). *Effective response to school violence: A guide for educators and law enforcement personnel.* Springfield, IL: Charles C Thomas.

Jones, V., Dohrn, E., & Dunn, C. (2004). *Creating effective programs for students with emotional and behavior disorders: Interdisciplinary approaches for adding meaning and hope to behavior change interventions.* Boston, MA: Pearson/Allyn & Bacon.

Kazdin, A. E. (2005). *Parent management training: Treatment for oppositional, aggressive, and antisocial behavior in children and adolescents.* New York: Oxford University Press.

Lawrence, R. (1998). *School crime and juvenile justice.* New York: Oxford University Press.

Mishna, F., Cook, C., Saini, M., Wu, M. J., & MacFadden, R. (2011). Interventions to prevent and reduce cyber abuse of youth: A systematic review. *Research on Social Work Practice, 21,* 5–14.

Nissen, L. B. (2011). Community-directed engagement and positive youth development: Developing positive and progressive pathways between youth and their communities in reclaiming futures. *Children and Youth Services Review, Supplement 1, 33,* S23–S28.

Olweus, D. (1991). Bully/victim problems among school children: Basic facts and effects of a school-based intervention program. In D. J. Pepler & K. H. Rubin

(Eds.), *The development of childhood aggression* (pp. 411–446). Mahwah, NJ: Lawrence Erlbaum Associates.

Olweus, D. (2011). Bullying at school and later criminality: Findings from three Swedish community samples of males. *Criminal Behaviour and Mental Health, 21,* 151–156.

Patterson, G. R. (1982). *Coercive family process.* Eugene, OR: Castalia Publishing.

Pearce, N., Cross, D., Monks, H., Waters, S., & Falconer, S. (2011). Current evidence of best practice in whole school bullying intervention and its potential to inform cyberbullying interventions. *Australian Journal of Guidance and Counseling, 21,* 1–21.

Reid, J. B., Patterson, G. R., & Snyder, J. (2002). *Antisocial behavior in children and adolescents: A developmental analysis and model for intervention.* Washington, DC: American Psychological Association.

Robinson, E. L., & Fine, M. J. (1994). Developing collaborative home-school relationships. *Preventing School Failure, 39,* 9–15.

Ross, S. W., & Horner, R. H. (2009). Bully prevention in positive behavior support. *Journal of Applied Behavior Analysis, 42,* 747–759.

Savage, T. V., & Savage, M. K. (2010). *Successful classroom management and discipline: Teaching self control and responsibility* (3rd ed.). Los Angeles, CA: Sage.

Shafii, M., & Shafii, S. L. (2001). Diagnostic assessment, management, and treatment of children and adolescents with potential for school violence. In M. Shafii & S. L. Shafii (Eds.), *School violence: Assessment, management, and prevention* (pp. 87–116). Washington, DC: American Psychiatric Publications.

Snakenborg, J., Van Acker, R., & Gable, R. (2011). Cyberbullying: Prevention and intervention to protect our children and youth. *Preventing School Failure, 55,* 88–95.

Sprague, J., & Walker, H. (2000). Early identification and intervention for youth with antisocial and violent behavior. *Exceptional Children, 66,* 367–379.

Sprague, J. R., & Walker, H. M. (2005). *Safe and healthy schools: Practical prevention strategies.* New York: Guilford Press.

Sung, J. B., & Clark, G. M. (2005). Incorporate diversity awareness in the classroom: What teachers can do. *Intervention in School & Clinic, 41,* 49–51.

U.S. Department of Education. (1998). *Preventing bullying: A manual for schools and communities.* Washington, DC: Author.

Walker, H. M., Ramsey, E., & Gresham, F. M. (2004). *Antisocial behavior in school: Evidence-based practices* (2nd ed.). Belmont, CA: Thomson/Wadsworth.

Walker, J. S. (2008). *How, and why, does wraparound work: A theory of change.* Portland, OR: National Wraparound Initiative, Portland State University.

Weare, K. (2000). *Promoting mental, emotional, and social health: A whole school approach.* New York: Routledge.

Wong, D. S., Cheng, C. H., Ngan, R. M., & Ma, S. (2011). Program effectiveness of a restorative whole school approach for tackling school bullying in Hong Kong. *International Journal of Offender Therapy and Comparative Criminology, 55,* 846–862.

Appendix

RESOURCES FOR POSITIVE BEHAVIOR SUPPORTS

It is important to join professional organizations, read professional journals, and visit web sites. Here is a list of suggestions. Joining an organization will help you in your professional development and assist you in staying current in the field.

Journals

American Educational Research Journal
Behavior Analysis in Practice
Behavior Modification
Behavior Therapy
Behavioral Disorders
Child and Family Behavior Therapy
Education and Treatment of Children
International Journal of Positive Behavioural Support
Intervention in School and Clinic
Journal of Applied Behavior Analysis
Journal of Behavioral Education
Journal of Cooperative Education
Journal of Emotional and Behavioral Disorders
Journal of Positive Behavior Interventions
Journal of School Psychology
Preventing School Failure
School Psychology Review

Resources

All Kinds of Minds
2800 Meridian Parkway, Suite 100
Durham, NC 27713
www.allkindsofminds.org

The Association for Behavior Analysis
550 West Centre Avenue, Suite 1
Portage, MI 49024
269/492-9310
www.abainternational.org
mail@abainternational.org

Association for Direct Instruction
P.O. Box 10252
Eugene, OR 97440
541/485-1293
www.adihome.org
info@adihome.org

The Association of Positive Behavior Support
P.O. Box 328
Bloomsburg, PA 17815
570/389-4081
www.apbs.org
tknoster@bloomu.edu

B. F. Skinner Foundation
18 Brattle Street, Suite 451
Cambridge, MA 02138
www.bfskinner.org
info@bfskinner.org

Cambridge Center for Behavioral Studies
P.O. Box 7067
Cummings Center, Suite 340F
Beverly, MA 01915
www.behavior.org

Council for Exceptional Children
2900 Crystal Drive, Suite 1000
Arlington, VA 22202-3557
888-232-7733
www.cec.sped.org

National Alliance for the Mentally Ill
3803 N. Fairfax Dr., Suite 100
Arlington, VA 22203
800/950-6264
www.nami.org

National Center for Learning Disabilities
318 Park Avenue, South, Suite 1401
New York, NY 10016
888/575-7373
www.ncld.org

Parent Advocacy Coalition for Education Rights
8161 Normandale Blvd.
Minneapolis, MN 55437
952/838-9000
www.pacer.org
pacer@pacer.org

Relevant Websites

A Place for Us...Oppositional Defiant Disorders Support Group
www.conductdisorders.com

Behavior Homepage
www.state.ky.us/agencies/behave/homepage.html

Center on Juvenile and Criminal Justice
www.cjcj.org

Center for the Prevention of School Violence
www.ncdjjdp.org/cpsv/

Intervention Central
www.interventioncentral.org

Positive Behavioral Supports and Interventions
www.pbis.org

Positive Discipline
www.positivediscipline.com

The Preventive Ounce
www.preventiveoz.org

Research and Training Center on Family Support and
Children's Mental Health
www.rtc.pdx.edu

AUTHOR INDEX

SUBJECT INDEX